Why Read?

Portrait of Kenneth Baker by Eileen Hogan, 2025

Why Read?

The Battle Between Book and Screen

Kenneth Baker

UNICORN

To my father, for he introduced me to reading novels and planted in me a love of Dickens.

And to my two teachers at St Paul's – P.D. Whiting for History and C.P. Longland for English Literature, both of whom infected me with a love for these two subjects which has lasted all my life.

Contents

Foreword

BOOKS HAVE BEEN AN IMPORTANT PART OF MY LIFE. As I have spent more time reading books than any other activity, I want to share the joy and pleasure I have had with those who may not be natural readers. In 2024, the National Literacy Trust reported that 56 per cent of children no longer consider reading as a pleasurable pastime – the highest level since tracking began in 2005. In primary schools, half of pupils between the ages of eight and twelve read poetry, but when on attending secondary school the number fell to 17 per cent – only one in six children. Sir Jonathan Bate, Professor of Literature at Oxford and Arizona Universities, in 2024 deplored the amount of reading by his American and British students. Far fewer long novels were being read, and he had also discovered that students from private schools read far more than those from state schools – a cultural divide is opening up. The National Literacy Trust also reported that many young men between the ages of eighteen and thirty-five do not read novels. This means that today is much less of a reading age than the one I experienced in the 1940s and 1950s when there were no distractions like televisions, computers, video games, smartphones and social media – one had to fill the long winter evenings, meaning there was always time for reading. Today, instead of reading a hard copy of a book, many young people are increasingly dependent upon visual media like films, documentaries and videos streamed online, and aural media like radio and podcasts.

I remain convinced that reading is the one essential skill that all children should master and come to enjoy. What memories do you have of reading? Probably not the books you had to read for an exam, but the ones given to you by your parents, recommended by friends or which you had chosen yourself. Opening up a book spells the end of ignorance. It also opens the world of the imagination, capturing your interest in adventures, romances, thrills, fantasies, exciting new experiences, new ideas, new places and new countries. Reading frames our imaginative life forever, and it taps into our inner lives. That is why it is so important to persuade children to find time to open a book.

So, I want to reveal the magic of reading to those who are not natural readers. Stephen King, the American writer of over seventy thrillers, described books as 'uniquely portable magic'. Thomas Carlyle in the 1840s also recognised the magic in books, explaining, 'All that mankind has done, thought, gained, or been, is lying as in magic preservation in the pages of books.' How right both have been.

Emily Dickinson said it so succinctly:

> There is no frigate like a book,
> To take us lands away.
> Nor any coursers like a page
> Of prancing poetry.

Charles Dickens will walk you through the streets of London; Robert Louis Stevenson will take you to a desert island; F. Scott Fitzgerald to parties on Long Island; Seamus Heaney to the Dark Ages of Beowulf; Jane Austen to eighteenth-century country house life; Joseph Conrad to the seas of Southeast Asia; Ted Hughes to the windswept moors of Yorkshire; H.G. Wells to the planets; George Orwell to Big Brother and *Animal Farm*; Hilary Mantel to the court of Henry VIII; Ernest Hemingway to Spain and bullfights; Ian Fleming to glamorous espionage; Graham Greene to Cuba, Mexico, Vietnam and Africa; Agatha Christie, the most widely read author of all time, to the murderous worlds of Hercule Poirot and Miss Marple; Kazuo Ishiguro, who came from Japan to Britain as a five-year-old, takes you to Nagasaki and to 1930s Britain; Jez Butterworth to his Jerusalem in a caravan in a Wiltshire wood; J.K. Rowling to the School of Witchcraft and Wizardy; Benjamin Zephaniah to the poetry of Jamaica; and Maya Angelou to civil rights struggles.

Many books have been written about the art of writing, principally by authors themselves, but very few have been written about reading. I did come across an accurate description of the act of reading in Dickens' *Oliver Twist*, when an elderly man picks up a book from a stall and is so engrossed in reading it that he does not notice that the Artful Dodger has stolen his pocket handkerchief.

> He had taken up a book from the stall, and there he stood, reading away as hard as if he were in his elbow-chair in his own study. It was very possible that he fancied himself there, indeed; for it was plain, from his utter abstraction, that he saw not the book-stall, nor the street, nor the boys, nor, in short,

George Cruikshank's 1838 sketch of the pickpocketing Artful Dodger in *Oliver Twist*

> anything but the book itself, which he was reading straight through, turning over the leaves when he got to the bottom of the page, beginning at the top line of the next one, and going regularly on with the greatest interest and eagerness.

I did not come from a bookish family. My two grandfathers left school in the 1890s at the age of twelve to become dock labourers in Newport and Barry Docks, which were busy exporting Welsh coal from the valleys. One became the secretary of the Dockworkers Trade Union, as he could write. Keir Hardie asked him to become an MP and move to Westminster but he could not afford to do so, as he had a young family and MPs were not paid back then. He ended his career by being part of the management of the docks during the Second

World War. One of the things he gave me, and of which I am most proud, is a beautifully painted and decorated testimonial, paid for by the dockers in 1919, to thank him for his work in collecting money for the wives they had left behind.

He married an Irish girl, Margaret Desmond, who went to a teachers' school in Wandsworth in the 1890s, and I still have a few of her books, including a copy of *Hamlet* heavily annotated in her beautiful copperplate writing. Her son, my father, stayed on at school until the age of sixteen when the school leaving age was still twelve. This was the first time in our family that anyone had stayed so long in education. He certainly used those four extra years to read widely, for he received a prize in 1913 of a leatherbound copy of Sir Walter Scott's *Kenilworth*.

My father came to love Dickens and he would read aloud to me and my sister the description of some of the characters – Miss Havisham, the Artful Dodger, Uriah Heep, Micawber, Mrs Gamp, Little Nell, Scrooge, Pecksniff and Podsnap. We got to know them so well that we almost expected them to walk through the door. I was lucky to inherit his bookishness.

During the Second World War, I went to a Church of England Primary School in Southport, as we had been evacuated there from the Blitz in London. It was a large, red-brick building with a walled yard for the playground, and I got a good old-fashioned education – copying the copperplate handwriting of teachers, chanting the times tables aloud in class, reading books and learning poetry.

One book that I especially remember is a book of poems that I won as a prize, which included William Blake's poem *The Tyger*. I had never seen a tiger but his poem made one come alive. This poem triggered my love of poetry and I learnt the poem by heart. I can still recall the first and fifth verses:

> Tyger Tyger, burning bright,
> In the forests of the night;
> What immortal hand or eye,
> Could frame thy fearful symmetry?
>
> When the stars threw down their spears
> And water'd heaven with their tears:
> Did he smile his work to see?
> Did he who made the Lamb make thee?

During the war years the radio was an easily available alternative to books. On Wednesday afternoons I hurried home by 4:30pm to listen to the BBC for half an hour before *Children's Hour* with Uncle Mac, when there were short plays

William Blake, *The Tyger* from *Songs of Innocence and Experience* (copy Y), plate 42, [1794] printed *c.* 1825

of the *Father Brown* and *Sherlock Holmes* stories, which led me to discover the books of G.K. Chesterton and Arthur Conan Doyle.

The first time I came across Shakespeare was in the 1940s when our whole class was taken to see Laurence Olivier as Henry V in the glorious technicolour film which Churchill had approved for its patriotism. I was very impressed by hearing, for the first time, poetry about exciting historic events – how Henry's soldiers prepared for war by letting 'silken dalliance in the wardrobe lie' and Henry rallying his men on the eve of Agincourt by 'a little touch of Harry in the night'.

The first play I was taken to was *The Scarlet Pimpernel* at the Crane Theatre in Liverpool. Baroness Orczy's Scarlet Pimpernel helped French aristocrats escape the guillotine but he was never uncovered as the foppish Sir Percy Blakeney:

> They seek him here, they seek him there
> Those Frenchies seek him everywhere
> Is he in heaven or is he in hell?
> That damned elusive pimpernel.

As the curtain rose, we saw an inn near Calais in which a waiter, with a long apron, was setting plates on a table. If he came across a dirty plate, he wiped it on his trousers rather than his apron, leading to a gust of laughter. This incident is lodged in mind even though I have no recollection of the rest of the play!

After seeing this film and the play I wanted to read the books. I also found that illustrations helped their reading and so I decided to include in this book many pictures and illustrations to catch your eye for, as Alice in Wonderland observed, 'What is the use of a book without pictures and conversations?' Illustrations are a bridge to reading.

I grew up in the 1940s and 1950s when there was plenty of time for reading. My mother used to take me to the library in Southport on a Saturday to borrow books – most of which are no longer widely read, like *Beau Geste* by P.C. Wren, *Fire Over England* by A.E.W. Mason, *Prester John* by John Buchan, *The Four Just Men* by Edgar Wallace, many detectives like Sexton Blake and Sapper's Bulldog Drummond, and the green Penguin books that recorded criminal trials, including the devastating cross-examinations by Edward Marshall Hall.

I am not suggesting that these books should be read today. Although I enjoyed them, they are of another time. We are lucky today to be experiencing a golden age of children's novels which started with J.K. Rowling's seven *Harry Potter* novels which have been translated into forty-seven languages, and are probably the most widely read books in the history of children's literature even though they are a demanding read with hundreds of pages without illustrations. There are many talented authors of children's books, including my favourite Katherine Rundell, and since 2022 the following children's authors have won prizes: Katrina Charman, Phil Earle, S.F. Said, Alex George, Louie Stowell, A.F.F Steadman, Katya Balen, Nadia Mikail, Danielle Jawando and Malorie Blackman. *The Times* often devotes a full page for the reviews of children's books, covering those that appeal to three- to six-year-olds, and others to the ages of nine plus and fourteen plus. It is these books that should be in primary and secondary school libraries, but in some disadvantaged areas one in four primary schools do not have a library.

Reading should not be taught just in English lessons but should be extended across all other subjects as well. Children who struggle with reading could benefit from a course in functional literacy and be relieved of the pressure of taking an English GCSE, which they might fail. They should be encouraged to read more widely than the books set for exams. Non-exam books should be made available in schools and given to the students to take home.

Reading a book at home on a sofa or in bed is much better than reading at a school desk with its many distractions. Michael Morpurgo, the celebrated children's writer and famous for *War Horse*, and the former Children's Laureate and author of *The Gruffalo*, Julia Donaldson, asked the then Education Secretary to legislate to ensure that each school had a library, particularly as many schools have changed their libraries into computer-dominated information centres. There was little enthusiasm from the Conservative Government – 'Leave it to each school.' Let us hope the Labour Government has better ideas.

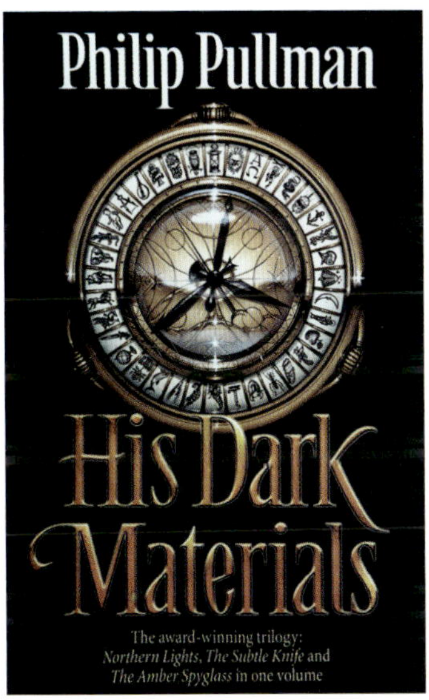

This campaign was supported by Philip Pullman, the author of the much-read trilogy *His Dark Materials*, the third volume of which, *The Amber Spyglass*, reached the Booker Prize longlist when I was the chair of judges in 2001. It was the first children's book listed for this prize. Pullman's' comment was:

> The school library is the most important room in the entire school, because it contains – or used to contain, or should contain – books that are not required for examination purposes ... But the library should be the heart, the soul,

the mind, the source, the gold-bearing seam, the engine-room, the treasure chamber, the priceless inheritance, the joy and the pride of the school. Every school.

Book Lovers Should Help Weaker Readers

One of the purposes of this book is to try to encourage people, particularly young men and also school children, to read novels and poetry. Grandparents and parents can help by giving books as presents.

My two years of National Service was as an artillery instructor in the Canal Zone in Egypt, where I found that several of the soldiers in my battery were poor readers. After being appointed the education officer, I introduced reading and writing lessons in the hope of persuading the soldiers to read more than just the sports pages of the *Daily Mirror*. I managed to get hold of paperbacks of thrillers and westerns so the soldiers could enjoy them during the long evenings, as we were not permitted to leave the barracks at night. I managed to get some Agatha Christies from Collins, but the soldiers preferred the sexier thrillers by Peter Cheyney. The lessons were very popular because when they passed simple tests, their pay went up.

This was the first time that I realised those of us who find reading easy should do what we can to help those who find it more difficult. In 1986 I was given the opportunity by Margaret Thatcher to do just that. As Education Secretary I introduced a National Curriculum to improve basic standards with a broad and balanced curriculum. I even managed to include reading and learning poetry by heart in primary schools.

The first poetry which we all hear and remember are nursery rhymes – *Hickory Dickory Dock*, *Three Blind Mice*, *Jack and Jill* and *Mary, Mary, Quite Contrary* – such rhymes helped us to learn to speak. There is a large mass of English poetry that rhymes, and poems often have four beats per line and an easy rhyme, like Blake's 'Tyger, Tyger burning bright', and Robert Herrick's:

> Gather ye rosebuds while ye may,
> Old Time is still a-flying;
> And this same flower that smiles today
> Tomorrow will be dying.

The pattern of four beats to a line and the rhymes help me to remember lines of poetry easily and they become lodged in my memory until a glimmering shaft of life brings them back.

In trying to spread the habit of reading more widely, I am not a lone crusader. I recall how Virginia Woolf, one of our most gifted writers, made a brilliant answer to 'Why read?':

> We get pleasure from reading. It is a complex pleasure and a difficult pleasure; it varies from age-to-age and from book-to-book. But that pleasure is enough. Indeed that pleasure is so great, that one cannot doubt that without it the world would be a far different and inferior place from what it is. Reading has changed the world and will continue to change it. When the Day of Judgment comes therefore and all secrets are laid bare, we shall not be surprised to learn that the reason why we have grown from apes to men, and left our caves and dropped our bows and arrows, and sat round the fire and talked, and given to the poor and helped the sick – the reason why we have made shelter and society out of the wastes of the desert and the tangle of the jungle is simply this – we have loved reading.
>
> Virginia Woolf

In July 2024 Pope Francis wrote a Papal Letter, originally urging student priests to embrace literature, but on further reflection he decided it should apply to all Christians:

> What I would like to address here is the value of reading novels and poems as part of one's path to personal maturity ... Likewise, in moments of weariness, anger, disappointment or failure, when prayer itself does not help us find inner serenity, a good book can help us weather the storm until we find peace of mind.

The Pope mentioned only a few authors, including C.S. Lewis and T.S. Eliot, but he did recall how, as a young teacher at a Jesuit School in Argentina, he had tried to encourage his students to read *El Cid*, a Spanish epic of the eleventh century. The students told him they preferred to read García Lorca, the popular contemporary poet:

> So I decided that they could read *El Cid* at home, and during the lessons I would discuss the authors the students liked best. Of course, they wanted to read contemporary literary works. Yet, as they read those works that interested them at that moment, they developed a more general taste for literature and poetry, and thus they moved on to other authors.

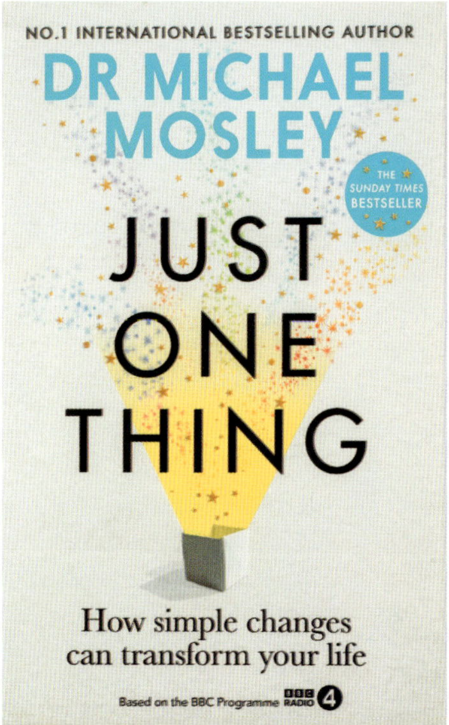

When I tried to find out whether reading poetry and novels improve mental health and wellbeing, I came across the BBC podcasts, *Deep Calm* and *Just One Thing* recorded by Michael Mosley, the TV and radio doctor who so tragically died of heat exhaustion while on a Greek island in June 2024. The episode *Read A Poem* explored reading poetry aloud and *Five ways to unwind and find Deep Calm* encouraged adults to read novels. These fascinating podcasts are available from BBC Sounds and BBC iPlayer.

He answered my question by stating, 'reading poetry aloud builds vocabulary, memory and empathy because it engages the ear as well as the eye which are stimulated in different parts of the brain. The rhythmic stress of poetry brings a sense of positivity and peace.' He asked Colin in Manchester, who had only read poetry in school, to read a poem for 5 minutes a day and he chose some by Seamus Heaney. Colin was going through a rough patch at that time, but reading the poems helped him to relax and he had the best sleep for months.

Mosley argued that reading for just 30 minutes before going to sleep each night could improve mental wellbeing and protect against cognitive decline and dementia by stimulating brain activity. Reading novels forces attention away from oneself, towards the characters in the book, and that can reduce anxiety and stress. He asked a woman from South Wales who did not read novels to read one for half an hour every day and she chose *Alice's Adventures in Wonderland*, which she enjoyed greatly: 'It taught me how to switch off, and left me much more restful, more calm.' She intends to continue reading novels. Mosley quoted research from Yale and Toronto Universities which found that 'reading a novel for just 30 minutes a day can extend your life by 23 months'. I found that astonishing but rather welcome! I do know that reading novels does make me more relaxed and that must be good for me.

Alexei Navalny (1976–2024)

When I read *Patriot*, the book that Navalny had written while he was imprisoned by Putin, and where he suffered bullying, starvation, deprivation of sleep and psychological torture, he found comfort in reading books as it reduced his stress and helped to keep him sane. On his admission to prison in 2021, he asked his jailers, 'Give me a book, please.' Later he recorded, 'In the last month I have read six books in English. A good score ... ', and mentions Shakespeare (whom he took to task for sexism in *The Taming of the Shrew*), *Harry Potter*, *Oliver Twist*, *Vanity Fair*, *Grapes of Wrath* and Hemingway. Reading helped him to bear the brutality of his imprisonment and books nourished his mental acuity. At one time he was trying to unravel the complexity of the Wars of the Roses by the *Henry VI* plays, and knowing that Putin's FSB would seize his papers he wrote, 'I do hope my research at least prompts the officers of FSB to compile an analytical report for the Kremlin, warning that I am conspiring to engage active government activities in Lancaster, Percy, York and others ... outlining the roles in my criminal organisation.' Putin was not even able to destroy Navalny's sense of humour.

This book is very much the record of my personal reading which has enriched my life. The novels and poetry which I include create different worlds – contemporary, historical or fantastical. Each book has to capture your eye and colourful dust jackets, which first appeared in the twentieth century, help. Then the skill and the imagination of the author must hold your attention for days or weeks. I was lucky to find out that as politician I was not entirely alone in enjoying books. The Emperor Julian in a letter to Ecdicius, the Prefect of Egypt , spoke of his love of books:

> Some men have horses, others birds, and some wild beasts,
> but from when I was a child a terrible longing the ownership
> of books has been deep within me.

Poetry has the advantage of being shorter than a novel. In just a few seconds or minutes it must attract you through the beauty of its words, its cadences and its rhymes. For me, poetry is articulate music. Its emotional appeal is immediate: it promotes reflection and can be soul-searching. Some of the poems I have included are famous and will be familiar, but others will be less well known, and I hope that they may lead you to read more of them. Great poetry has a way of surviving and being re-quoted over centuries. Above all, do not be dismayed if you cannot cope with the length of Dickens or the poetry of Shakespeare, and if the set examination books are boring, try and find a writer who brings you joy and pleasure. That will be instinctive to you and not imposed by others.

I have a personal experience of the decline in reading by teenagers. Over the last fifteen years I have established a network of forty-five University Technical Colleges which provide high quality technical education for students aged fourteen to eighteen. We now have over 21,000 students and instead of the national curriculum they will be taught English, Maths, three Sciences as well as technical subject like computing, AI, advanced manufacturing, product design, the skills required by hospitals and the burgeoning industries of streaming and TV. As we recruit at fourteen we found that several students join us with a reading age of only six or eight. So we provide intensive periods to improve their reading. Several colleges start the day by their teachers irrespective of the subject which they teach, reading to their class from 8:50 – 9:20 am. They also encourage the students to read aloud themselves. These lessons are popular as they increase the student's vocabulary and improve their self-confidence. We also encourage students to take books home, since a few come from families that have very few books or, in some cases, none.

I have read all the books, poems and plays in this book and, indeed, many more. Parts of them stick in my memory, and I hope that you will find your own way through this great garden of literature. Some of the paths are well trodden, others do not bear many footprints, and you may well find a path of your own. So do set out on your journey by choosing a book and follow the advice of the Venerable Bede writing in the seventh century: *Lege feliciter* (Read happily).

Kenneth Baker talking to teenagers at the Baker Awards, January 2026

Chapter 1

History of the Book

History is so eagerly sought after.
The men in the streets aspire to know it.
Kings and leaders vie for it.

Ibn Khaldūn,
fourteenth-century historian

Our ancestors would have first communicated with each other by ape-like grunts. These developed over 400 million years into languages, which allowed humans to protect their families, develop patterns of survival, exchange ideas, express grief and joy, and to pass on to their children not only their skills, but also the songs of poets, folktales told over fires on long winter evenings and the wisdom of their elders. It was the oral tradition that shaped words that led humans to need a written record of activities covering trading transactions, the births and deaths of their kings, their fables and their songs. This eventually led to a series of technical revolutions – clay tablets, papyrus, parchment, paper, ink, and writing utensils starting with birds' quills leading to writing separate metal characters to form words and alphabets, and eventually to typewriters, keyboards, computers and artificial intelligence.

This clay tablet used in Mesopotamia between 3100 and 2900 BCE, is an administrative account of a trading record

Egypt

This illustration comes from *The Book of the Dead of Hunefer*, *c.* 1275 BCE (Hunefer was a scribe who owned a copy of the Egyptian *Book of the Dead*). It shows Hunefer himself, accompanied by the jackal-headed Anubis, being led into the afterlife. His heart must be weighed in the scales of judgement before he can be presented by a falcon-headed creature to Osiris, the god of the afterlife. The words are prayers and advice as to how Hunefer should address the god. It was printed on a papyrus scroll approximately 3m in length. It is extraordinary that the ink and the colours have retained their vividness over the last 1,000 years.

Papyrus was a plant found in the Nile and after its bark had beewn ripped off, the pith was cut into long strips and soaked in water for three days. The strips were then laid side-by-side, then other strips were placed across them to hold them together, and the water was forced out of them by wooden boards. Then they were polished with a stone to remove ridges and cut into single sheets for the scribe to write upon them. Papyrus had many advantages: it was thin and could contain a lot of writing in a small space. The pages were then rolled into a scroll which, for a play, could amount to a metre but for a more substantial document by Plato possibly to 3–4m. This involved a great deal of rolling and unrolling and was usually read on a table from left to right.

The dry climate of Egypt meant that the pages were always white, but European humidity made them darker and, as they dried, they tended to disintegrate. A papyrus scroll had other disadvantages in that it could only be written upon one side and had to be stored in wooden boxes or clay vessels to protect its fragility. Derived from a plant, papyrus was perishable and could be attacked by insects. Nonetheless, the culture of Greece was preserved on papyrus rolls, and Roman writers like Tacitus, Cicero, Ovid, Horace and Virgil had their works first recorded on such rolls. When the Egyptian King Ptolemy stopped the export of papyrus to Ephesus in Turkey, because he resented the way they had built up a library at his expense, they decided to develop a new way of printing on animal skins. The library of Pergamum gave these skins the Latin name of *pergamenata*, which in English became 'parchment'.

The Dead Sea Scrolls

The remnants we still have of the Dead Sea Scrolls are thanks to the dry heat of the Egyptian climate.

One of the most astonishing survivals of a written record was the discovery of the Dead Sea Scrolls, which were found by a Bedouin boy in 1947 while searching for a goat. In seven caves he found tall pots in which the scrolls were stuffed. Only a few were complete but there were over 25,000 fragments, most in Hebrew and the rest in Aramaic and Greek. One of the scrolls had most of the Book of Isaiah dating from the second century BCE and others had fragments from Exodus and Deuteronomy. These were clearly read by rabbis and even possibly by some secular people, and may have been hidden during the Roman occupation of Jerusalem in the first century CE.

The Middle East

The spread of Islam following Mohammed's death in 632 CE led to a considerable expansion in printing. Baghdad was founded in 762 as a cultural centre bringing together the Persian and Arabic worlds. At that time, most of the Prophet's teachings were handed down by word-of-mouth, and some dwindled to old men's tales, dimly remembered over winter fires and waning every year. Scholars wanted more reliable records, and a printing mill was established in 794. This led to many early Korans being printed on paper which was made from rags which had to be cut up and then beaten flat. It was Islamic technicians who improved the effectiveness of scissors and the use of waterpower to drive the machines to beat the rags. Their scholarship extended beyond religious texts to cover science, philosophy, maths and geometry, the mechanics of good government, astronomy, calligraphy and poetry – all of these were made possible by printed records and books which were usually protected from constant use by vellum and leather bindings.

The Diamond Sutra, 868 CE

The oldest book in the world, *The Diamond Sutra,* dating from 11 May 868, is held by the British Library. It was only discovered in 1900 by a Chinese Taoist monk in Dunhuang, a town in northwest China on the edge of the Gobi Desert. Buddhists had managed to establish a major shrine in this remote place on the Silk Road by digging hundreds of small caves into a cliff. When I visited Dunhuang, the front of the cliff was covered with a network of wooden paths which led to the entrances of some caves. These were necessary, as the caves had become a major tourist attraction, even for the Chinese themselves. In each cave the ceiling was completely covered with images of the Buddha's face, but many had been disfigured by the Muslims when they reached Dunhuang.

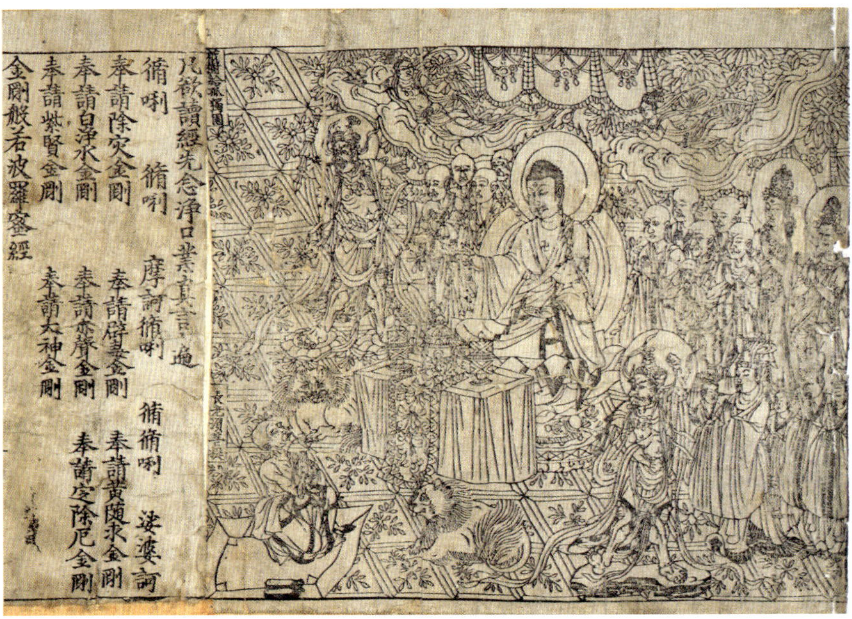

The book was written in Chinese characters in columns, so that it read from top to bottom. Wood blocks were used, and the paper was dyed by a substance from the Amur cork tree, possibly to stop the ink sinking too far into the paper. The seven sections of the book containing the manuscript were pasted together to form a scroll with a wooden pole so that it was read from left to right. It contains only one illustration, depicting the Buddha surrounded by his disciples, imparting his wisdom and possibly telling a kneeling Chinese figure that by reading the *Sutra*, it would help him find happiness in his rebirth. This is a major missionary document to spread Buddhism from its birthplace in India to a country more than 1,000 miles away. The foot of the scroll carries an inscription, 'reverently made for universal free distribution by Wang Jie on behalf of his two parents, 11 May 868'.

China, 960–1279

China invented papermaking during the second century BCE and its actual making changed very little until the early nineteenth century.

The first part of the process started with rag-pickers who collected old clothes and sheets, and separated the white linen rags for white paper and coarser cloths for brown paper. In the paper mills the rags were soaked in water for six weeks and then pulped in a stamping trough in which nails macerated the fabrics. This pulp was then washed again, warmed over a charcoal stove, and a vat-man would dip into it a rectangular wooden frame with stretched metal wires to collect each sheet from the pulp. Another worker, called the coucher, drained away the water and deposited each sheet on to damp woollen felt. A pile of 144 sheets, interleaved with felt, was pressed to squeeze out the dampness and then hung up to dry. Finally, the sheets were washed with an emulsion to fill pores and improve quality, then rubbed with a stone to polish and smooth it. Much of the work was done by women and children, paid by the day.

Paper was also made from the bark of the mulberry tree and later the sandalwood tree. The finest paper produced was rice paper, but it had nothing to do with the rice plant, being, in fact, thinly peeled from the white spongy pith of a small tree, the *Tetrapanax papyrifera*. So a more appropriate name would be 'pith paper'. The stems were harvested, some 5cm in diameter, cut into sections, the pith forced out and then dried. Next, the cylindrical pith was rested between two thin metal strips on a slab. The pith was rolled against the sharp blade of a broad knife held on top of the strips to produce a long, continuous sheet. As one writer observed, the process was like unwinding a roll of ribbon. This plant was grown in Formosa (Taiwan) and in southwestern China.

The prosperity of China during the Song Dynasty (960–1279) saw the expansion of the elite class beyond the hereditary nobility, and this led to the establishment of a standard curriculum for the Imperial examinations based on Confucian learning that increased readership significantly. In the early Ming Dynasty (1368–1646) there was an outburst of printing. A larger pool of labour, capable of carving wood blocks, reduced the cost of a book. Private libraries were formed, and China's most famous library, Tianyi Ge, was founded in 1561, almost half a century before the Bodleian in Oxford in 1602.

By 793 CE, paper mills were set up in Baghdad and spread throughout the known world, and papyrus production stopped in the eleventh century. This change spread to Europe in the thirteenth century and paper mills bloomed in Fabriano in northern Italy. England's first paper mill was only established in the 1490s in Hertfordshire. William Caxton had to import his paper when he established his printing press in 1476. Fine white paper was first produced in 1690s by French Huguenots immigrants.

Reading Before Gutenberg's Invention of the Printing Press

Dr Christopher de Hamel, Life Fellow at Corpus Christi College, Cambridge, has written two brilliant and beautiful books about manuscript books from the sixth century to the fifteenth century – *Meeting with Remarkable Manuscripts* (2016) and *The Posthumous Papers of the Manuscripts Club* (2022). De Hamel is exceptionally qualified, as his college in 1547 was given the collection of early books made by Matthew Parker, the Archbishop of Canterbury, amounting to 600 books with the earliest being *The Gospels of St Augustine* from the late sixth century. Christopher de Hamel invites his readers to join his visits to twelve libraries, museums and churches to view a particularly fine example of a manuscript book and he creates the best tour of medieval European culture covering Cambridge, Aberystwyth, Copenhagen, Florence, Dublin, Leiden, Oxford, Munich, St Petersburg, New York and Los Angeles. He is very engaging and informs his readers of the trains, buses and roads they will have to take to reach each destination, and sometimes offers the tip of a shortcut and a comfortable hotel.

The high point of culture in the medieval period pre-1455, apart from architecture, were the manuscript books which contained thousands of small, beautifully painted miniature illustrations. They were dedicated to devotional matters, but some recorded the history of regal and noble families. Their creation involved a huge industry calling upon many talents across Western Europe. In Florence, Paris and Venice there were a network of booksellers who were the key practitioners in this cultural explosion. They were the managers of the production of books which was a complicated and slow process undertaken by monks, by scriveners whom the monks trained and by illustrators.

The first task was to prepare the parchment which was made from the skins of sheep and cows that were soaked in lime, scraped clean and stretched over a frame, then rubbed down with a stone to reduce ridges and to make it consistently smooth. The production of parchment and vellum had to take place outside a city as it involved the slaughter of calves and sheep, and then the malodorous task of turning the skins into leather and vellum. The parchment was then taken into the cities to be sold in specialist shops, and in Paris the street name has survived to this day: La rue de la Parcheminerie.

Hugo Pictor (Hugh the Painter), Late Eleventh Century

Christopher de Hamel visited the Bodleian Library in Oxford to re-examine an eleventh-century text – a commentary in Latin on the Book of Isaiah by Jerome – and as he turned to the last page he saw a picture of a scribe, Hugo Pictor, who had drawn himself, so making this the very first self-portrait in the world. The words beside Hugo's head are his name and those above his head declare, 'Picture of the Painter and Illuminator of this Work'. In his right hand, Hugo holds a knife to correct any mistakes; his left hand holds a feathered quill as it advances into the ink held in an inkhorn. The ink is probably oak gall made from crushed apples mixed with ferrous sulphate. The desk is angled to make it easier for him to inscribe and illustrate.

Sometimes the monks and lay scriveners formed themselves into a *scriptorium*. The scribe would prepare his own quill using a feather from a goose – a right-handed scribe would choose a feather from the left-wing of the bird and vice-versa for a left-handed scribe. The tip of the quill was placed into hot sand to help harden it.

Each monastery and *scriptorium* had to make its own ink from linseed oil kept for a year to allow the mucilage to settle; rosin may have been added. The black colour was made by collecting the soot from burning pitch and roasting it several times to rid it of tarry oils. This was an exacting and not a particularly popular process, for the risk of fire was ever present. The first book about printing ink was published in Venice in 1619.

Artists and miniaturists were also needed to decorate the manuscript books. Some of these miniaturists have been identified and became well-known artists, such as the three Dutch de Limbourg brothers. The artists had to create their own pigments and paints using plants and minerals like lapis lazuli to create a very deep blue. It took months to create verdigris when various liquids like vinegar, honey, lime or egg white were added. The paints were often kept in oyster shells, as they had the smoothest interiors.

Simon Bening (*c.* 1483–1561), The Illuminator of Bruges

In the fifteenth and sixteenth centuries the Netherlands had become an important centre of the book trade. The book-buyers expected their manuscript books to be illustrated with small, brightly coloured and exquisite miniature paintings. Wealthy patrons did not just want Bibles; they also wanted personal prayer books, Books of Hours, breviaries, psalters and bestiaries. Such books did not lie unread in libraries, as they were often given as gifts to important people to help show to others their sophisticated culture. A group of illuminators wanted their craft to be professionally recognised and formed themselves into the Guild of St Luke. Such was the demand for illustrated manuscripts that it became a highly paid profession.

Simon Bening followed his father as an illuminator. He not only had patrons in Belgium, but also in France, Germany and Italy. He was the only illustrator to include his self-portrait in a book for a patron – it shows him sitting at a sloping desk, with the brush in his right hand and possibly a knife in his left. The house is clearly that of a prosperous man – a peacock in the garden, a spaniel at his feet and a horse awaiting him.

These books were made page-by-page and then glued or bound together, protected by leather boards to ensure that the first and last pages did not become dog-eared and unreadable, and some had a metal clasp and corner. The process was laborious. The number of readers was limited not only by their ability to read but also by the booksellers' ability to produce sufficient numbers of copies.

Simon Bening's self-portrait in Jacques de Lalaing's manuscript, *c.* 1510–20

Christine de Pisan presenting her book to Charles VI
(an illustration from the beginning of *Le Livre du chemin de long estude*)

When a book was printed, a patron could decide to keep it for the family or present it as a gift to a king or an important noble. The ever-resourceful Christine de Pisan is depicted in a miniature which she must have commissioned, presenting a copy of one of her books to the future Charles VI in the hope that he would recommend it to his friends. Already, two of the courtiers are looking at the book rather than the King.

The Gutenberg Bible, 1455

When Johannes Gutenberg, the father of printing, published a Bible in 1455 which had been printed using moveable metal type, he changed the history of the world. Earlier Bibles had been written on manuscript, page-by-page, by expert scriveners using a quill pen and ink with which they would write every word on to vellum. Their output was limited, as was their readership. Gutenberg replaced that by creating an individual movable metal shape for each letter of the alphabet which needed a different type of ink to adhere to the metal, and he used one that had been invented by the printers of Mainz that left a clear impression upon the paper.

The Library of Congress's copy of The Gutenberg Bible

Thomas Carlyle recognised the political significance of Gutenberg:

> He who first shortened the labour of copyists by putting on record the device of moveable types was creating the whole, new democratic world.

Gutenberg had started printing it three years earlier and produced about 180 copies, of which forty-eight survive. He had rejected the use of parchment or vellum as pages because his Bible of 1,282 pages in two volumes would have required 320 sheepskins. Instead, he imported paper from Italy, which had been making rag paper for over 150 years.

Paper had been expensive and had hitherto been used principally for letters such as those written by the Paston family in England, whose head, Sir John, referred to paper as 'dainty'. Over the decades and centuries that followed, the Gutenberg revolution involving moveable metal type, new ink and the use of paper allowed the Bible to become the most widely read and most published book in the world. Although it was printed in Latin, it conversely led to Latin disappearing as the universal common language across Europe. In 1522 Martin Luther (1483–1546) translated the New Testament into German and had it printed as a book. That was followed by William Tyndale's translation into English in 1526. For those who could not read, the Bible was read to them by a priest, but for those who could read, it launched the age of reason, lessening the grip of the church, and allowing individuals to create their own relationship to God.

Before Gutenberg, a scrivener would have handwritten each letter with a quill and ink on to parchment. The illustration below shows how a printer selects an individual letter, each made from lead, and places it into the word in a line on a page that is held together by a wooden frame called a *visorum*. A smaller box stores additional lead characters, including capitals and punctuation. It is not surprising that Aldus Manutius, the great Venetian printer, described the whole process as 'a Metallic Hand'. Typesetting replaced handwritten documents, meaning hundreds of thousands of copies, even millions, could be rapidly printed.

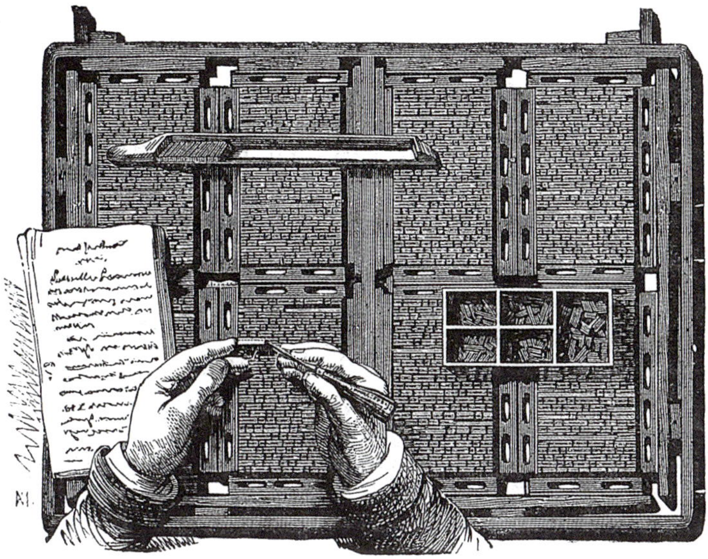

The Role of the Publisher

Throughout history, the spread of reading did not depend just upon teachers and students, but also the enterprise of publishers. Indeed, Shakespeare's First Folio would not have been published without the support of Edward Blount. Publishers seized the opportunity to print books more cheaply and easily at prices which many people could afford. Books created an industry that involved many skilled workers making and preparing paper, typography, illustrations, design, book binding, bookselling and critical reviewing. The publishers held the keys that brought all these together.

Publishers bring to the public all the advantages of reading, such as curiosity, empathy, imagination, creativity, innovation, surprise and enjoyment. It is to the credit of publishers that today more books are being produced in Britain than ever before and the price remains as affordable as it ever was. In 2023 Nigel

Newton, Chief Executive and founder of Bloomsbury Publishing, reported on their latest results:

> Book sales had risen by 5% and sales of children's books were up by 17%.

Shakespeare's First Folio of 1623 would not have been published if its publisher, Edward Blount, had not financed the young Isaac Jaggard to print it. The reading explosion of 1790–1820 was mainly due to the relaxation of copyright which allowed publishers to produce a wide range of books more quickly and cheaply. Victorian England benefitted from not being involved in any major European war between 1815 and 1914 (other than the brief Crimean campaign in the 1850s), and this enjoyment of peace allowed a huge outburst of reading for pleasure. Publishers responded by creating new genres of emerging writing: travel, exploration, science, astronomy, architecture and the history of painting.

Book publishing is something of a gamble. There are four big publishing companies that supply 50 per cent of the book trade and the largest, Random House, employs 10,000 people. Smaller publishing houses are currently doing well, winning important literature competitions which always help to increase book sales substantially. In 2023 the Booker Prize was awarded to *Prophet Song* by Paul Lynch and published by Oneworld, which employs twenty-five people led by a husband-and-wife team. The 2022 Booker Prize went to Shehan Karunatilaka's *The Seven Moons of Maali Almeida*, also published by the small independent publisher, Sort of Books. The 2023 Nobel Prize for Literature winner was Jon Fosse, who is published by the non-profit Transit House which actually operates from a house in San Francisco, and in the UK by Fitzcarraldo Editions founded in 2014 with a team of seven people. Small publishers can take greater risk with smaller margins than larger ones.

These publishing successes are very good news for all booklovers because it means more and more books are being bought today.

MR. WILLIAM
SHAKESPEARES
COMEDIES,
HISTORIES, &
TRAGEDIES.

Publiſhed according to the True Originall Copies.

Martin Droeshout sculpsit London.

LONDON
Printed by Iſaac Iaggard, and Ed. Blount. 1623.

Chapter 2

Books that Shaped the English Language

> ... bold, licentious, full of gall,
> Wormwood and sulphur,
> Sharp and toothed withal.
>
> BEN JONSON

The Anglo-Saxon Chronicle, c. 890

The Anglo-Saxon Chronicle was written in the late ninth century in Wessex. Many copies were made, with some still surviving today, and most were written in Old English, though some had additions in Middle English. This is the main source of our English history from the fall of the Roman Empire in 476 CE.

The Domesday Book, 1085–6

This is England's first public record of the landownership of 13,148 places. Each county, which was accompanied by a map, records the land owned by the king, then the abbots, and finally the lords and laymen. Each of their lands are divided into hundreds (areas) and then into the manors. It is quite a remarkable administrative achievement. The reason for writing it has never really emerged – some believe it might have been to provide a tax base, others that it was a recognition and a confirmation of the changes of ownership of land following the Norman Conquest in 1066.

This was clearly designed for the secular market which needed many other separate documents like charters, wills, court verdicts, ceremonial records and agreements on events of 'perpetual memory'. The powers of the king or nobles were often justified in print. Some of these documents carried signatures and were clearly important. The financial records of the court of Henry VII were personally signed by him. After the Reformation, both Catholics and Protestants recorded births, marriages and deaths, which meant that parish records would become a significant source of information for future historians.

The Philobiblon, 1345

The Bishop of Durham, Richard de Bury, wrote this collection of essays in Latin in 1345 and, being an ardent book collector, it was all about his love of the book. Very few copies have survived but there is one in the British Library. The book was reprinted in Oxford in 1599 and it contains twenty chapters, the first of which is, 'The Whole Treasury of Wisdom in Books'. It has some wonderful quotations which are still relevant today, such as:

> In books I meet the dead as if they were alive; in books I see what is to come.
>
> In books warlike affairs are set forth; from books come forth the laws of peace.
>
> In books we climb the mountains; and scan the deepest gulfs of the abyss.

In the fifteenth century, after Gutenberg, printing presses spread rapidly across Europe, with the first in Germany in 1466, in Italy in 1471 and in England in 1476 by Caxton in Westminster. They published not only religious texts but also the great classical authors and philosophers from Greece and Rome who had been discovered in the Renaissance. By the end of the fifteenth century there were over one hundred printing towns in England. In Chapter 8, on religious reading, I show how important printed books were in the reformation in England under Henry VIII. Here are five books which have helped shape the English language.

The Canterbury Tales, c. 1387–1400

Geoffrey Chaucer (*c.* 1340s–1400) enjoyed the patronage of John of Gaunt, Edward III's third son, and travelled as a diplomat to Flanders, France and Italy where he became aware of the works of Dante and Boccaccio. Among Chaucer's works was an elegy on the death of John of Gaunt's wife, and a long love poem *Troilus and Cressida*. He started to write *The Canterbury Tales* during the 1380s, which was the first work printed by William Caxton in 1476 at his press near Westminster Abbey. Wynkyn de Worde, another printer who was known to have worked with Caxton, also published many copies in 1498.

The Canterbury Tales is written in rhyming couplets, which makes it easy to read, but it is an immense book and the Penguin Classic edition runs to over 500 pages. It is a magnificent masterpiece that helped to shape the English language. In the seventeenth century John Dryden dubbed Chaucer 'The Father of English poetry' and his comment on the *Tales* was, 'Here is God's plenty.' It is also the best contemporary social history of late medieval England, as it tells of thirty pilgrims setting out from the Tabard Inn in Southwark, London, for a five-day journey to visit the shrine of Thomas à Becket in Canterbury, and on the way, twenty-four pilgrims tell a story. The Prologue describes the lives of the pilgrims, who include a miller, a merchant, a knight, a shipman, a doctor, a ploughman and a wife of Bath, and not surprisingly many who served the Church – a prioress, a monk, a nun's priest, a pardoner, a parson and a summoner. The most memorable figure is the wife of Bath, a sexually voracious woman who had been married five times, the first at the age of twelve. She tells how she mastered each of her husbands, taking over their money and their houses. This is the first vivid description of an Englishwoman's life in our literature and Chaucer clearly had a soft spot for her – Chaucer is almost winking at her. She would be at home in *Coronation Street*.

At school we read *The Canterbury Tales*, first in Old English, but in 1951 Nevill Coghill, of Exeter College, Oxford, translated the book into modern English, making it much easier to read.

I have a copy of the second folio which was printed in 1542, and below is the woodcut of the wife of Bath.

The Wife of Bath's Prologue

If there were no authority on earth
Except experience, mine, for what it's worth,
And that's enough for me, all goes to show
That marriage is a misery and a woe;
For let me say, if I may make so bold,
My lords, since when I was but twelve years old,
Thanks be to God Eternal evermore,
Five husbands have I had at the church door;
Yes, it's a fact that I have had so many,
All worthy in their way, as good as any ...

I'll speak no evil of virginity,
Let them be pure wheat loves of maidenhead
And let us wives be known for barley-bread;
Yet Mark can tell that barley-bread sufficed
To freshen many at the hand of Christ.
In that estate to which God summoned me
I'll persevere; I'm not pernickety.
In wifehood I will use my instrument
As freely as my Maker me it sent.
If I turn difficult, God give me sorrow!
My husband, he shall have it eve and morrow
Whenever he lies to come and pay his debt,
I won't prevent him! I'll have a husband yet
Who shall be both my debtor and my slave
And bear his tribulation to the grave ...

But bed-time above all was their misfortune;
That was the place to scold them and importune
And baulk their fun. I never would abide
In bed with them if hands began to slide
Till they had promised ransom, paid a fee;
And then I let them do their nicety.
And so I tell this tale to every man,
'It's all for sale and let him win who can.'

Wynkyn de Worde (died *c.* 1534)

In 2024 I learnt about the importance of Wynkyn de Worde as a publisher when I read *The Book-Makers* by Adam Smyth, Professor of English Literature and History of the Book at Balliol. He cites eighteen people who have been largely left unknown by history but who helped to increase the reading of books. It is a fascinating work of high scholarship, very readable and anyone interested in English Literature should read it. One of Smyth's heroes is Wynkyn de Worde who had first worked under Caxton, but then set-up his own printing press in Fleet Street from where he published hundreds of books. The works were not only religious books, for his staple was Latin grammars, but he also published books on history, *The Book of Margery Kempe*, *The Ship of Fools*, *The Canterbury Tales* and single-page ballads. To make his publications more appealing to readers, he included many woodcut illustrations. He was one of the founders of the book trade when ordinary people could buy books for a few shillings for the first time.

William Camden, *Britannia or a Chorographical Description*, 1586

This is the Baedeker of Elizabethan England. It is an amazing book of over 1,000 pages on the history of all the peoples in Britain, including the Picts, Scots, Anglo-Saxons and Britons, and the places where they lived. There is a map for every county, carrying the names of towns, villages, rivers and hamlets, and those names have for the most part all survived to this day. William Camden was a scholar who for four years was the Headmaster at Westminster School, but he must have spent the rest of his life walking across the whole of Britain. Quite frequently he gives advice on how to reach a particular place by taking a shortcut or how to avoid a steep hill. It was the first topographical book and also pointed the way to a new type of history which was not just about kings and battles. I have a folio of 1695 with 1,116 pages and one of the previous owners has interleaved prints of the cathedrals, churches, castles and large houses which Camden had not included. This is an early example of an *extra-illustrated* book which have been given the name *Grangerised* – after the Devon vicar James Granger who started one in 1769. They became a fad and then fashionable until the 1840s. The later invention of photography would make illustrated books easier and cheaper.

The Holy Bible, newly translated out of the original tongue, 1611

In 1603 when James VI of Scotland became James I of England, five English versions of the Bible existed, but only two had been authorised by the Anglican Church. The first was the Great Bible of 1539 which had been authorised by King Henry VIII, and the second was the Bishop's Bible of 1568, translated

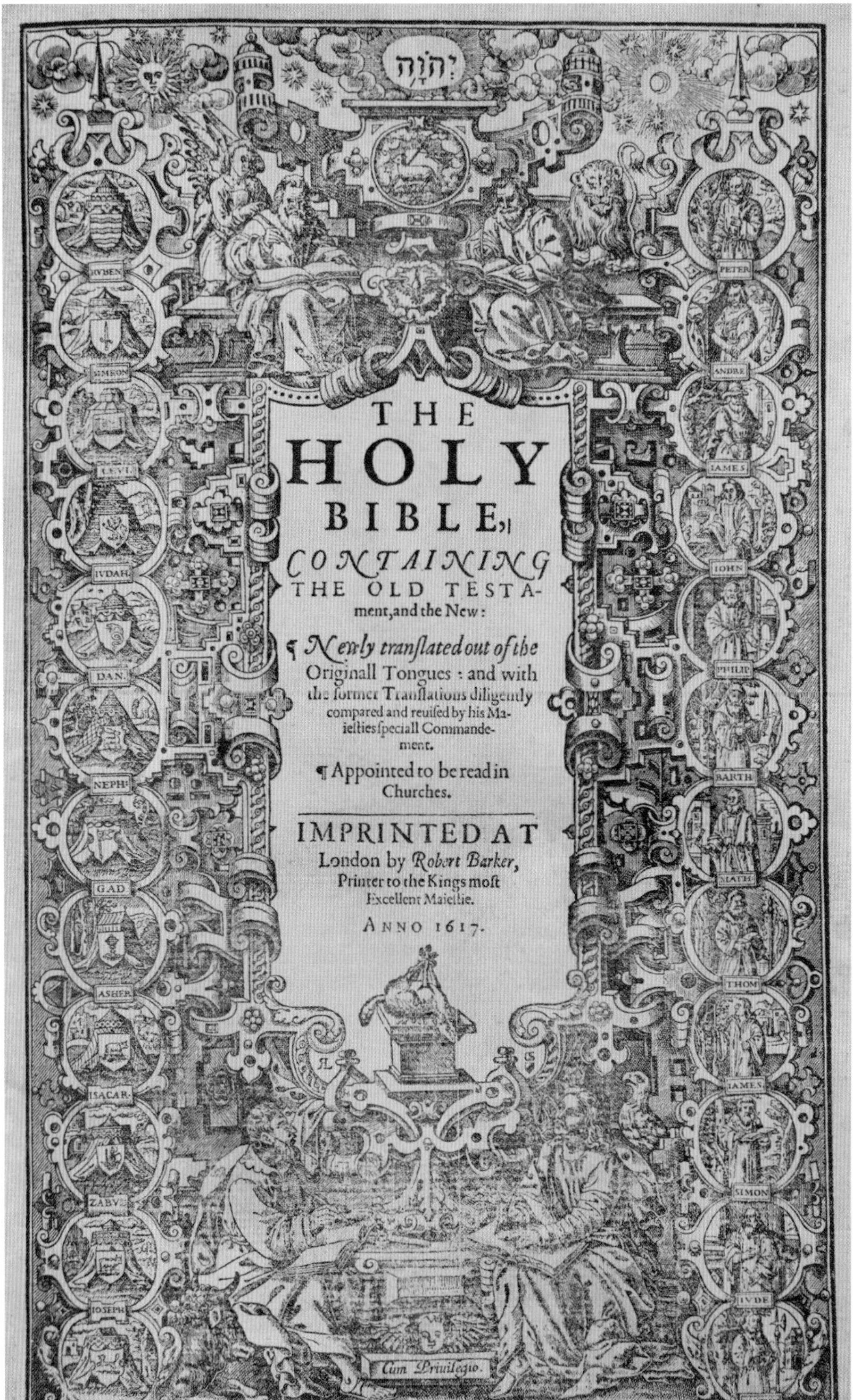

THE
HOLY
BIBLE,
CONTAINING
THE OLD TESTA-
ment, and the New:

¶ *Newly translated out of the*
Originall Tongues: and with
the former Translations diligently
compared and reuised by his Ma-
iesties speciall Commande-
ment.

¶ Appointed to be read in
Churches.

IMPRINTED AT
London by *Robert Barker*,
Printer to the Kings most
Excellent Maiestie.

ANNO 1617.

during Elizabeth I's reign but little read as it was rather obscurely written. The Geneva Bible of 1560 was more popular but it was unauthorised and full of anti-royalist notes. In 1604, the Puritan party petitioned the King to improve upon the two Bibles. Six committees in Oxford, Cambridge and Westminster were appointed and worked for six years to complete their translation from Hebrew, Latin and Greek. Apart from the original text in those three languages, they also drew upon earlier translations, particularly by Tyndale that contributed nearly 85 per cent of the final version. They read out the passages aloud and the best were then forwarded to an overseeing committee of six sitting daily for several months in the Stationers' Hall in London. It was published in 1611 and it has become known as The King James Bible.

It is extraordinary that a book of such beautiful language should have been decided by committees. Its words have been read out in churches for hundreds of years and it is engraved into our language. Lord Macaulay, the Victorian historian, said of it, 'A book which if everything else in our language should perish would alone suffice to show the whole extent of its beauty and power.'

The Bibles were sold for 10 shillings unbound and 12 shillings bound. It is one of the most read books in the world, for it has been estimated that over six billion copies have been published, making it one of the world's most influential religious texts.

William Shakespeare (1564–1616)

I first came across Shakespeare when my whole class was taken to see Laurence Olivier play *Henry V* in the glorious technicolour film which Churchill had approved, for it showed 'English courage at its best.' Later, *Henry V* was the play we read at the age of sixteen for the School Certificate. It made me aware of Shakespeare's beautiful poetry, especially the inspiring speech before Agincourt:

> He that shall live this day, and see old age,
> Will yearly on the vigil feast his neighbours,
> And say 'To-morrow is Saint Crispin Day':
> Then will he strip his sleeve and show his scars.
> And say 'These wounds I had on Crispin's day.
> Old men forget: yet all shall be forgot,
> But he'll remember with advantages
> What feats he did that day ...
> We few, we happy few, we band of brothers;
> For he to-day that sheds his blood with me
> Shall be my brother ...

We also read *Henry IV Part I*, *Romeo & Juliet*, *The Merchant of Venice* and, at A-level, *King Lear* – which I consider to be the greatest plays ever written. I have seen many famous actors play Lear but the one I remember most – after taking half a day off school to go to a matinee at a theatre in Hammersmith, now closed – was Donald Wolfit. He was an actor-manager with his own touring company of actors, and I still have a recording of him declaiming the famous speeches of Lear as he goes mad.

As Education Secretary (1986–9) I visited schools in America and the one I remember vividly was in the most disadvantaged part of the Bronx. I was amazed to watch a class of twelve- and thirteen-year-olds acting the first scenes from *Macbeth*. I was sure they had never heard of him or Scotland, but they loved shouting out the words of the witches. The teacher told me that when they turned over the pages and reached Macbeth contemplating the assassination of the King of Scotland, which included for the first time the phrase 'a poisoned chalice', it reminded them of scenes from the TV show *Dallas*.

This is how the poet Wendy Cope saw her first Shakespeare:

Young Love

School outing, 1960: *Romeo*
And Juliet. First time I had seen a play
By Shakespeare on the stage. We had to go
By bus to the Old Vic. A matinee.
Don't know what I expected, probably
To find it rather boring. It was not.
Enchanted, I went back four times to see
The play again. I was in love. With what?
The characters (Mercutio!)? The actors –
Judi Dench and several dishy males?
The language? Maybe all of them were factors
Compelling me to boost the ticket sales
For Shakespeare plays as often as I could.
That teenage crush: I think it did me good.

In 2026, in a strikingly modern production of *Romeo and Juliet* in London, Juliet was played by Broadway star, Sadie Sink. At just twenty-four, she wore a skimpy dress, not a long medieval one. And Romeo, played by twenty-one-year-old TV star Noah Jupe, didn't wear a Tudor doublet, in fact sometimes he was half naked. This production captured the overwhelming passion of two young lovers and in some scenes there was a much-used double bed.

JULIET: I shall forget, to have thee still stand there,
Rememb'ring how I love thy company.

ROMEO: And I'll still stay, to have thee still forget,
Forgetting any other home but this.

JULIET: 'Tis almost morning. I would have thee gone,
And yet no farther than a wanton's bird,
That lets it hop a little from his hand,
Like a poor prisoner in his twisted gyves,
And with a silken thread plucks it back again,
So loving-jealous of his liberty.

ROMEO: I would I were thy bird.

JULIET: Sweet, so would I.
Yet I should kill thee with much cherishing.
Good night, good night. Parting is such sweet sorrow
That I shall say 'Good night' till it be morrow.

Sadie Sink, Noah Jupe and Clare Perkins in *Romeo and Juliet*, 2026

First Folio, 1623, William Shakespeare's comedies, histories, and tragedies

> Not of an age, but for all time.
>
> Ben Jonson

Two friends of Shakespeare, John Heminge and Henrie Condell, both of whom had been left mourning rings in Shakespeare's will, and who had acted in some of his plays, decided to collect all his plays and to publish them. They knew the plays were masterpieces and without this publication many would have disappeared altogether, for at the time of Shakespeare's death only fourteen of his thirty-six plays had been printed, either in a small quarto or in a folio, and these copies often differed from each other. Heminge and Condell had been able to find copies of the missing twenty-two plays, often from the acting copies of the actors or from prompt copies.

They found a young printer, Isaac Jaggard, to undertake the printing in his family's printing press and bookshop, and he established a partnership with Edward Blount as the publisher. The support of a publisher was critical because Blount provided the capital for the metal of the printing fonts, the paper and the ink, as well as employing workers to make the metal fonts. Their reward would be to sell the books and in 1622 they advertised in a catalogue for the Book Fair

An English printing press, 1619. This is the type of press on which the two most important books in the English language, the King James Bible and Shakespeare's First Folio, were printed.

in Frankfurt: 'Jaggard a collection of "*Playes written by Mr William Shakespeare all in one volume*".' In September 1623, the first copies of the book were delivered to Blount's bookshop, The Black Bear, in Paul's Cross Churchyard.

In the First Folio, Heminge and Condell in a letter urged people to buy it:

> TO THE GREAT VARIETY OF READERS
>
> FROM the most able, to him that can but spell: There you are number'd. We had rather you were weighd. Especially, when the fate of all Bookes depends vpon your capacities: and not of your heads alone, but of your purses. Well! it is now publique, & you wil stand for your priuiledges wee know: to read, and censure. Do so, but buy it first. That doth best commend a Booke, the Stationer saies. Then, how odde soeuer your braines be, or your wisedomes, make your licence the same, and spare not. Iudge your sixe-pen'orth, your shillings worth, your fiue shillings worth at a time, or higher, so you rise to the iust rates, and welcome. But, what euer you do, Buy. Censure will not driue a Trade, or make the Iacke go. And though you be a Magistrate of wit, and sit on the Stage at Black-Friers, or the Cock-pit, to arraigne Playes dailie, know, these Playes haue had their triall alreadie, and stood out all Appeals; and do now come forth quitted rather by a Decree of Court, then any purchas'd Letters of commendation ...
>
> But it is not our prouince, who onely gather his works, and giue them you, to praise him. It is yours that reade him. and there we hope, to your diuers capacities, you will finde enough, both to draw, and hold you: for his wit can no more lie hid, then it could be lost. Reade him, therefore; and againe, and againe: and if then you doe not like him, surely you are in some manifest danger, not to understand him. And so we leaue you to other of his Friends, whom if you need, can bee your guides: if you neede them not, you can leade your selues, and others, and such Readers we wish him.
>
> IOHN HEMINGE
> HENRIE CONDELL

The book was offered for sale in 1623 at 20 shillings for a bound copy and 15 shillings for an unbound copy, and in the following nine years 750 copies were sold. Then a second edition, which was an exact copy of the first, was published in 1632, and a third in 1663, and the last, the fourth, in 1685. These editions were so popular that readers tended to discard the first folio, particularly as through constant reading many had become quite frayed with pages missing from the first and last plays, *The Tempest* and *Cymbeline*, respectively. In the eighteenth and nineteenth centuries, these imperfect copies were often broken up so that a perfect copy from the first folio of a separate play could be removed and inserted in another which had a missing page, or indeed sold separately. I have been lucky to have collected seventeen of these individual printings.

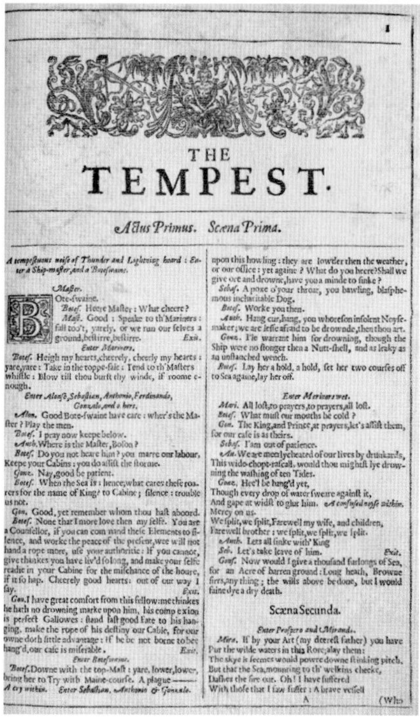
THE TEMPEST.

Actus Primus. Scena Prima.

The first page of Shakespeare's First Folio plays

Today only 235 copies of the First Folio still exist – three are in Stratford upon Avon in Shakespeare's house – but seventy-nine are in the Folger Shakespeare Library in Washington. Henry Folger, a prosperous businessman, tried to corner the folio market, not to a make profit by selling them but by providing a remarkable academic base where scholars could compare the individual printing from copy to copy, and to appreciate that at times the printing of a copy was stopped when the metal letters were needed for another book for which the publishers had an immediate sale.

The First Folio has now become the most valuable English book – a copy was sold in 2023 for £7.2 million. I am indebted to the scholarly and fascinating book, *Readers in a Revolution: Bibliographical Change in the Nineteenth Century* by David McKitterick, who has researched the prices that Victorians paid for the First Folio. The cheapest sold for £2.50 but the 2nd Earl of Charlemont's First Folio reached £455, and the highest was £716.2 p in 1864. Poor copies missing a play or with well-worn battered leaves sold for £100 and some of these were broken up for the plays to be sold separately.

Adam Smyth's *The Book-Makers* is a brilliant work of scholarship, a paean of praise for the book, completely fascinating, and all booklovers should read it. In the chapter on binding, he identified William Wildgoose as the binder who was asked to bind a copy of the First Folio in 1623, together with nine other religions books. Wildgoose had a habit of using pages from discarded books, particularly ones by Cicero, and pasting them on to the covers of the books he bound, which were either parchment or vellum. In 1663, the Bodleian Library sold its First Folio which had shown signs of wear, particularly through the considerable re-reading of *Romeo and Juliet*, and replaced it with the Third Folio. In 1909 a Derbyshire bibliophile in need of some cash offered a First Folio to the Bodleian who bought it for £3,000 after a fundraising appeal. When later examining the work, Professor Smyth discovered this Folio contained all the distinguished marks of Wildgoose with pasted pages from Cicero showed that the Bodleian had bought back its own copy.

Poetry before Shakespeare was very limited in its portrayal of human emotion, but his genius covers the whole range of human life, describing the frailty of power, the destruction of quarrelling families, the fun of confused identities, the darkness of despair, the compulsion of lust and the resignation of the old. Shakespeare has had a profound effect upon the English language, introducing for the first time over 1,700 new words like 'assassination'. Bernard Levin paid tribute to him by reminding the readers of the *Spectator* of all the phrases that have moved into common use which Shakespeare invented:

> If you cannot understand my argument, and declare 'It's Greek to me', you are quoting Shakespeare; if you claim to be more sinned against than sinning, quoting Shakespeare; if you recall your salad days, you are quoting Shakespeare; if you act more in sorrow than in anger; if your wish is father to the thought; if your lost property has vanished into thin air, you are quoting Shakespeare; if you have ever refused to budge an inch or suffered from green-eyed jealousy, if you have played fast and loose, if you have been tongue-tied, a tower of strength, hoodwinked or in a pickle, if you have knitted your brows, made a virtue of necessity, insisted on fair play, slept not one wink, stood on ceremony, danced attendance (on your lord and master), laughed yourself into stitches, had short shrift, cold comfort or too much of a good thing, if you have seen better days or lived in a fool's paradise – why, be that as it may, the more fool you , for it is a foregone conclusion that you are (as good luck would have it) quoting Shakespeare; if you think it is early days and clear out bag and baggage, if you think it is high time and that that is the long and short of it, if you believe that the game is up and that truth will out even if it involves your own flesh and blood, if you lie low till the crack of doom

because you suspect foul play, if you have your teeth set on edge (at one fell swoop) without rhyme or reason, then – to give the devil his due – if the truth were known (for surely you have a tongue in your head) you are quoting Shakespeare; even if you bid me good riddance and send me packing, if you wish I was dead as a door-nail, if you think I am an eyesore, a laughing stock, the devil incarnate, a stony-hearted villain, bloody-minded or a blinking idiot, then – by Jove! O Lord! Tut tut! For goodness' sake! What the dickens! But me no buts! – it is all one to me, for you are quoting Shakespeare.

John Milton, *Areopagitica*, 1644

I only discovered this book because it was set to be read for my Higher School Certificate (A-level). I do not think I would have come across it otherwise, for I did not know that Areopagus is a hill in Athens, the home of the highest court in the land. Printed as a pamphlet, *Areopagitica* is a passionate plea to the Highest Court in Britain, then the House of Commons, to defend the freedom of the press.

John Milton and the Presbyterians had earlier worked together to abolish the Court of Star Chamber, which Charles I had used to censor books and to approve only those he liked with an imprimatur. In 1643, during the Civil War, the Presbyterians had won control of Parliament and they decided to censor pamphlets from independent protestants and those who supported Charles I. Milton, however, remained consistent to his beliefs and put pen to paper to write the greatest defence of the freedom of the press:

> Give me the liberty to know, to utter, and to argue freely according to consciences, above all liberties.

Areopagitica has been much quoted, and its philosophy was keenly followed by Locke in the seventeenth century, by John Stuart Mill in the nineteenth century, and adopted by America as the basis of its constitution. For me, it is one of the reasons why I went into politics.

John Bunyan, *The Pilgrim's Progress*, 1678

The Pilgrim's Progress is one of the most widely read books around the world. It has never been out of print and has been translated into over 200 languages. I was attracted to read it by the way that Bunyan described the various people whom Christian met on his journey from the City of Destruction to the Celestial City.

Frontispiece to John Bunyan's *The Pilgrim's Progress*, *c.* 1682

These included people who tried to stop and hinder him, as well as those who helped him. His first companion was Obstinate, who tried to stop him, and then Pliable, who abandoned him after he had sunk into the Slough of Despond:

> Now I saw in my Dream, that just as they had ended this Talk, they drew nigh to a very *Miry Slough* that was in the Midst of the Plain, and they being heedless, did both fall suddenly into the Bog. The Name of the Slough was *Despond*. Here therefore they wallowed for a Time, being grievously bedaubed with Dirt; and *Christian,* because of the Burden that was on his back, began to sink in the Mire.
>
> Pli. *Then said* Pliable, *Ah Neighbour* Christian, *where are you now?*

Chr. Truly, said *Christian*, I do not know.

Pli. At this *Pliable* began to be offended, and angrily said to his Fellow, Is this the Happiness you have told me all this while of? If we have such ill Speed at our first setting out, what may we expect betwixt this and our Journey's End? May I get out again with my Life, you shall possess the brave Country alone for me. And with that he gave a desperated Struggle or two, and got out of the Mire on that Side of the Slough which was next his own House; so away he went, and *Christian* saw him no more.

Christian's other companions were Mr Worldly Wiseman who came from the Carnal City, Hypocrisy, Mistrust and Timorous, The Flatterer, Talkative who lived on Prating Row and was the son of Say-Well and Mrs-Talk-About-The-Right-Things, Mr Valiant-for-Truth, and Giant Despair. Then there were the places which Christian had to cross or pass through – the Valley of the Shadow of Death, Doubting Castle, Hill Lucre where Money-Love and Save-All lived, and of course Vanity Fair. The readers of this great saga would recognise through these people their own weaknesses, temptations and perils, but perhaps inspired by Christian's determination, courage and resilience they could follow his path to the Celestial City. This was so popular that in the eighteenth century a shortened version sold for 4 pence. The copy that I have is the thirty-first edition, published in 1766.

My father bought us a pack of playing cards where each of the 52 cards had characters and pictures from *The Pilgrim's Progress* instead of the usual four suits. The rules involved dealing each player a number of cards and then a card numbered 7 was placed in the middle of the table. Each player in turn had to put

down the next numbered card – 5 or 6 – or if this was not possible to pick up another card. The four lines of each suit slowly built up on the table, reflecting the journey of Christian.

Towards the end of the journey, as Christian approaches the promised land, he reflects on how a pilgrim has to be valiant to overcome all his weaknesses and temptations from such women as Mrs Lechery, Mrs Inconsiderate and men like Helpless, Little Faith, Toe-end and Obstinate. Bunyan's verses have been turned into the popular hymn, 'He who would valiant be':

> Who would true Valour see,
> Let him come hither;
> One here will constant be,
> Come Wind, come weather;
> There's no discouragement
> Shall make him once relent
> His first avowed intent
> To be a pilgrim.
>
> Who so beset him round
> With dismal Stories,
> Do but themselves confound -
> His Strength the more is.
> No lion can him fright;
> He'll with a giant fight,
> But he will have a right
> To be a pilgrim.
>
> Hobgoblin nor foul Fiend
> Can daunt his Spirit.
> He knows he at the End
> Shall life inherit.
> Then, Fancies flies away
> He'll fear not what Men say;
> He'll labour Night and Day
> To be a pilgrim.

Chapter 3

Helping Children to Read

What is the use of a book without pictures!

LEWIS CARROLL, *ALICE'S ADVENTURES IN WONDERLAND*

THE HISTORIAN NICOLAS ORME has written several books of profound scholarship on early schools. In *Medieval Schools: From Roman Britain to Renaissance England* he charts the development of schooling over ten centuries and includes brilliant illustrations.

Most children in the early centuries learnt from their parents and grandparents, but slowly schools emerged in cities, towns and villages. These rarely exceeded seventy students who came from the nobility, the gentry, the rural yeomen, merchants and leading figures of their communities. In the feudal world, the children of bondmen, known as villeins (serfs), had to obtain consent to study from their Lord of the Manor, for which he charged a fee. Some Lords of the Manor were reluctant to approve study, since they believed that they would lose their working vassals once they had learnt to read and write. Some managed to break through this feudal ceiling. It was said of Cardinal Wolsey, 'Begot by butchers, but by bishops bred.'

Piers The Plowman's Creed, 1390, made much the same comment:

> Now may each cobbler his son set to school,
> And each beggar's brat on the book learn,
> And rank as a writer and with the Lord dwell,
> Or falsely a friar, the fiend more to serve!
> So of that beggar's brat a bishop shall come,
> Pressing to sit among peers of the land,
> And Lords' sons lowly to those wastrels bow down
> Knights bend them and crouch full low.

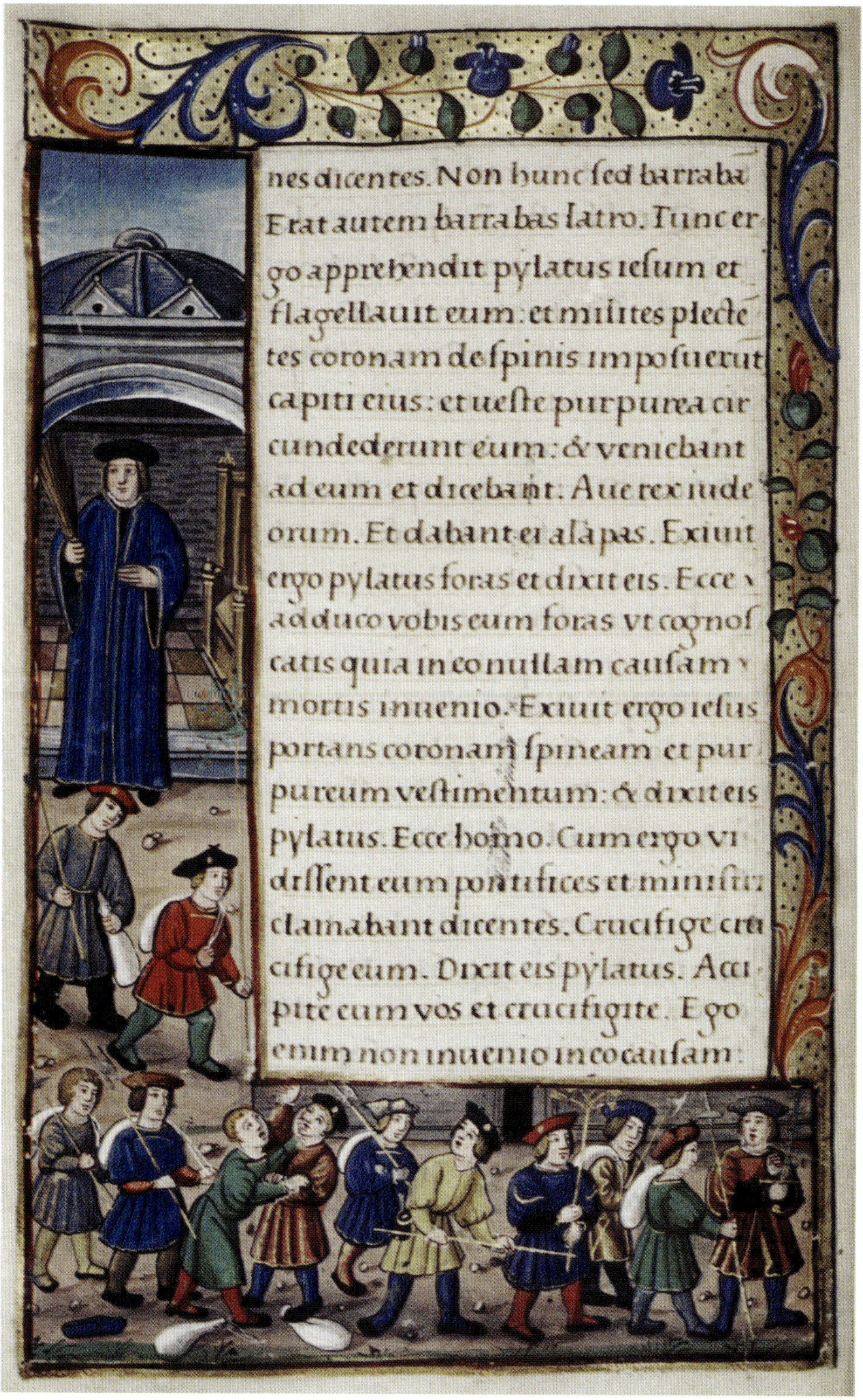

A fifteenth-century print of a master watching his students leave school

The Church also needed to have priests who could read, and in 1314 the prior of St Germans in Cornwall freed two boys to be tonsured and allowed to study for three years.

In the prints of thirteenth, fourteenth and fifteenth centuries, schoolmasters are always depicted as carrying a birch made from twigs. It became a badge of office. Clearly, beatings were frequent, for in 1500 a teenage boy wrote to his Master, 'Master Molesworth, I would pray and beseech that you would be my good master for such stuff as I learn. That you would show it to me by fair means and punish me reasonably. I did learn more by your fair means than I do now.'

In 1573, Thomas Tusser published a book, *Five Hundred Points of Good Husbandry*, in which he recorded his punishment at Eton in the 1530s under the headmaster Nicholas Udall:

> 53-stripes given to me
> At once I had;
> For faults but small or none at all.

Udall had a great reputation for ferocity, but that was not all as he was sacked from Eton for sexually abusing a young boy. The teachers did not always have their own way, for an Oxford teacher, John Newsham, in 1301 was cutting rods from a tree to control his students near Magdalen Bridge when he fell into the river and drowned. John Clare, the poet, commented in 1820 that, 'a dull boy never turns with pleasure to his schooldays, when he was often beaten four times for reading in five verses of scripture',

Nicholas Orme has identified that there were 114 places in the fifteenth century that had schools and some may have had two schools, so it would be reasonable to say there were nearly 200 schools. The print on the next page is from the fifteenth century and shows a teacher instructing his wealthy students to read; two are already tonsured, heading towards a bishopric in their later lives.

Lessons started early at 7:00am and went on to 5:00pm in order to make the best use of daylight. Students would begin in a Song School where they learnt prayers, scriptures and their catechisms. At the age of eight some went to a Grammar to study Latin as well as English – fortunately Latin and English alphabets were similar. They would also learn to write, but students had to bring their own pen, ink and paper, and pay 1 shilling a week. There were a small number of Chantry Schools for the poor, but this depended upon philanthropic support, which was not constant. but this depended upon philanthropic support which was not constant. These schools preceded the foundation of Winchester College by William of Wykeham in 1382, Eton by Henry VI in 1440, Magdalen College

School by William Waynflete in in 1480, and St Paul's by John Colet in 1509. They did not have large school rolls and St Paul's set a high target of 153 students, which was the number of the miraculous draught of fishes. After the dissolution of the monasteries in 1536, Henry VIII and Edward VI had to provide new schools to replace the monastic schools.

Much education during these ten centuries took place at home, where children learnt a great deal by listening to, rather than reading, ballads, songs, riddles, fables and stories from their parents and grandparents as they gathered around the fire at home during the long winter evenings. They also learnt nursery rhymes and some have survived – for example, *Three Blind Mice* – and they enjoyed riddles, some of which were quite puzzling:

> He went to the wood and caught it.
> He sat him down and sought it.
> Because he could not find it.
> Home with it he brought it.
> (= A thorn in his foot)

Tudor children had a wide range of books to choose from. Caxton had published *Aesop's Fables* in 1484 with illustrations, and five editions were printed between 1485 and 1582. One of the most popular was *A Mery Geste of Robyn Hoode*. This was a fifteenth-century poem whose hero lived in a forest with Little John as outlaws, helping the poor against the rich. The 'goodies' in the story were the yeomen of England and the 'baddies' the Sheriff of Nottingham and the Abbots of the Church. There was no Maid Marian, and Robyn was eventually killed by a treacherous prioress while he was being bled. A copy of *Mery Geste* was offered by an Oxford bookseller for tuppence in 1520.

Puritans repeatedly attacked popular literature and in 1528 William Tyndale, the biblical scholar and linguist (*c.* 1490–1536), criticised the clergy for not discouraging the young from reading Robyn Hoode, and 'a thousand histories and fables of love and wantons and ribaldry so filthy as the heart can think to corrupt the minds of youth withal'. Tyndale commented that he had translated the Bible into English in order to allow poor boys to read it, 'To cause a boy that driveth the plough to know more of the Scriptures than thou dost.'

As the Renaissance blossomed, children at school were able to read Virgil, Cicero, Plato and Horace for the first time. However, as the century wore on, the English language came to replace the Latin language. Acts of Parliament were printed in English. Before the Reformation in 1527, John Colet, the Dean of St Paul's and the founder of St Paul's School, translated the catechism into English and from then the boys would have learnt it in English. From 1536 they were able to read the Bible in William Tyndale's or Myles Coverdale's translations. The Book of Common Prayer was published in 1549, which helped to establish Protestantism in the country by being read in Church every Sunday. In 1563, John Foxe published his famous *Book of Martyrs* with its horrifying illustrations, which became one of the bestsellers over the next two centuries.

Roger Ascham, *The Scholemaster*, 1570

A teacher of Greek and Mathematics, Ascham was appointed a tutor to the Princess Elizabeth. Following a dispute over dinner with William Cecil on the pros and cons of flogging in schools, he was asked to write a book on 'the right order of teaching', which resulted in *The Scholemaster*. It was mainly concerned with 'the bringing up of youth in Jentlemen and Noble mens houſes'. The key to its success was that it was written in English, which persuaded students to learn, and that was better than being flogged.

Latin continued to be a staple of university education in the sixteenth, seventeenth and eighteenth centuries, and when English Literature was introduced as a subject in Oxford in 1894 one of its proponents said, 'It would obviously ease matters if English could be made to look like a dead language.' University College London, founded in 1826, had included English Literature as early as 1828.

Shakespeare, who was said to have little Latin and less Greek, could not resist taking a dig at a Latin teacher in the Scene I of the fourth Act of *The Merry Wives of Windsor*. Mistress Page tells the teacher, 'My husband says my son profits nothing in the world at his book.' The teacher questions the boy William about Latin articles, and he replies:

> Articles are borrowed of the pronoun, and be thus
> declined, Singulariter, nominativo, hic, hæc, hoc.

The teacher responds, 'Nominativo hig, hag, hog', but Mistress Quickly retorts:

> You do ill to teach the child such words: he
> teaches him to hick and to hack, which they'll do
> fast enough of themselves, and to call 'horum:' fie upon you!

The Sluggish Developments of the Eighteenth Century

In the eighteenth century, Charles Hutton, the son of a colliery manager started as a pit boy but became a mathematics teacher. As teaching in schools was fragmentary, in 1764 he published *A Schoolmaster's Guide* which included *A Complete System of Practical Arithmetic* and adapted single and double entry bookkeeping to be taught to schoolchildren. In 1773 he became a professor, and published *The Ladies Diary* in which he provided puzzles for its readers. He also supported a female teacher, Margaret Bryan, who set up schools in London and Margate to teach mathematics and astronomy to young ladies.

1783

In the late eighteenth century, Mary Ann Kilner (1753–1831) wrote several children's books, the most well-known being *The Adventures of a Pin Cushion – Designed Chiefly for the Use of Young Ladies*, but after attending a book reading by a friend to his children, she noticed that some were not paying attention and in response, in 1783 she wrote *A Course of Lectures for Sunday Evenings – Containing Religious Advice to Young Persons*. The frontispiece depicts how on a Sunday evening upper class children would listen to their father reading by candlelight from the Bible or other religious tracts.

The title of her first lecture was *On a Habit of Attention* which warned children that there was 'a God who observes all your actions'.

The Infant Library

John Marshall (1756–1824), a London publisher of broadside ballads, prints, songs and maps, moved into children's publishing in 1781. He created The Infant Library and dubbed himself the 'Children's Printer'. He commissioned authors to write light, easy-to-read books and his catalogue had 113 titles in 1793, selling at sixpence which was affordable for many middle-class children, and several went into extra editions, selling well into the nineteenth century. Marshall believed in illustrations and his pamphlets of familiar fairy tales were 'Embellished with Coloured Engravings'.

Cinderella is a good example of a good story surviving several centuries.

Reading in Schools

The Sunday School Movement

The first Sunday School started in St Mary's Church Nottingham in 1751 and others were slowly established over the country. Robert Raikes, the editor of the *Gloucester Journal*, wrote an article on 3 November 1781 about the schools in Gloucestershire seeking to teach youngsters reading, writing, cyphering (Maths) and a knowledge of the Bible. He wanted to help children who lived in the slums from being tempted to take up a life of crime. Charles Wesley, a co-founder of the Methodist movement, recognised the success of the Sunday Schools and by 1786 there were over 200,000 pupils attending them. They were principally for the children of factory workers and farm labourers who received no formal education, but they could attend a school on the only day they were not working. By 1831 there were 1,250,000 children at Sunday Schools. By 1835 the Society for the Promotion of Sunday Schools had distributed 91,915 spelling books, 24,232 New Testaments, and 5,360 Bibles.

Ragged Schools

This movement started in Portsmouth in 1818 when John Pounds, a disabled shoemaker, started to teach poor children without charging fees.

These schools depended upon philanthropic and charitable gifts, and many spread across the industrial heartlands of Victorian England. Sometimes they had only one or two – or, exceptionally, three – rooms for children of the same age to be taught together. Many opened in the evening after the children had finished working. Records are few but it has been estimated that over 300,000 children attended Ragged Schools between 1842 and 1870. In 1842 the great social reformer, the Earl of Shaftesbury, became the Chairman of the London Ragged School Union.

Charles Dickens in 1852 visited a Ragged School in Field Lane (now replaced by Farringdon Road) an area of great poverty where he was to set Fagin's den, and wrote an article about it:

> Attempts are being made in certain of the most obscure and squalid parts of the Metropolis where rooms are opened at night for the gratuitous instruction of all comers, children or adults, under the title of Ragged Schools. The name implies

> the purpose. They are too ragged, wretched, filthy and forlorn to enter any other place; who could gain no admission into no charity school and would be driven from any church door, are invited to come in here and find some people not depraved, willing to teach them something and to show them some sympathy, and stretch a hand out which is not the iron hand of law for their corrections.
>
> The close, low chamber at the back in which the boys were crowded were so foul and stifling as to be, at first almost insupportable. But its moral aspect was so far worse than its physical, that this was soon forgotten. Huddled together on a bench about the room, and shown out by some flaring candles, stuck against the walls, were a crowd of boys, varying from mere infants to young men, sellers of fruit, herbs, Lucifer matches, flints; sleepers under the dry arches of bridges; young thieves and beggars – with nothing natural to youth about them. With nothing frank, ingenuous, or pleasant in their faces; low-browed, vicious, cunning, wicked; abandoned of all help but this; speeding downward to destruction and unutterably IGNORANT.

Dickens also parodied the substance of education in his novel, *Hard Times* with the Headmaster Gradgrind stating:

> Now, what I want is, Facts. Teach these boys and girls nothing but Facts. Facts alone are wanted in life. Plant nothing else, and root out everything else. ... Facts: nothing else will ever be of any service to them. ... Stick to Facts, sir!

In the early nineteenth century illiteracy was the norm. In the artisan part of my earlier parliamentary constituency, St Marylebone, it was recorded in the 1820s that there were 740 children who could spell, but 823 who could not. This was a major reason for the founding of the Religious Tract Society in 1799 to distribute millions of Bibles and popular religious tracts to those unable to afford them. In 1844, 3,014 copies were distributed, and by 1861 its annual output was over two million, but this did not significantly reduce the illiteracy of their readers. In his 1861 book, *London Labour and the London Poor*, Henry Mayhew reported that of the forty costermongers (fruit and vegetable sellers) who received tracts from the hands of benefactors, scarcely one could read. In Dickins' 1853 *Bleak House*, Mrs Pardiggle, a loud voiced and determined benefactor decides to take her five sons, all of whom have to donate their pocket money to her missionary causes, to visit a wretched hovel of a bricklayer and read the Bible to him. The bricklayer greets her with:

> An't my place dirty? Yes, it is dirty – it's nat'rally dirty, and it's nat'rally onwholesome; and we've had five dirty and onwholesome children, as is all dead infants, and so much the better for them, and for us besides. Have I read the little book wot you left? No, I an't read the little book wot you left. There an't nobody here as knows how to read it; and if there wos, it wouldn't be suitable to me. It's a book fit for a babby, and I'm not a babby.

Mrs Pardiggle's visit to the bricklayer

Poor families living in these conditions could rarely afford a light to allow them to read, as two dozen candles, each of which could only last for two to three hours, would cost 7 pence, so they had to resort to smoky tallow dips (rushlights) until paraffin lamps were introduced into wealthier households in the 1850s and then gas lamps. Illiteracy was still extensive. A report on prisons in 1851 recorded that of 700 persons put on trial in four counties, 260 of them could not read a single word.

The range of books available to the poor was limited and various religious bodies attacked the circulating libraries for providing fiction and 'the Romances of Byron and Scott' as they were 'dangerous'. John Ruskin's mother each year read through the entire Bible with her son and apart from that he was only allowed to read Bunyan's *The Pilgrim's Progress* and *Foxe's Book of Martyrs*.

1833 was the first year in which public money amounting to £20,000 was provided for the building of schools, but nearly thirty years later under the Prime Minister, Lord Palmerston, it had only reached £800,000 when in the same year he spent £26 million on the army and navy. The other problem affecting school education was that it did not attract good quality teachers. In 1847 Lord Macaulay told the House of Commons that teachers were 'the refuse of other callings – discarded servants or ruined tradesmen who cannot do a sum of three, who could not be able to write a common letter, and who do not know whether the earth is a cube or a sphere, and cannot tell whether Jerusalem is in Asia or America'.

Fundamental reform was needed, and this came in the Great Education Act of 1870.

The Forster Education Act, 1870

The 1861 census revealed that of the 4.3 million children of school age, one million were at voluntary church schools and 1.3 million in state-aided schools, with two million not recorded as going to school at all. In 1870 the Liberal minister of education, William Forster, introduced the Elementary Education Act, which established in England and Wales compulsory education up to the age of twelve, and locally elected school boards which were to provide them.

A *Punch* cartoon about the Elementary Education Act 1870, 26 March 1870

The immensely important 1870 Act, more widely known as Forster's Education Act, was recognised in that Forster is the only education minister who has been remembered by two statues. The first was prompted by business leaders in the new industrial towns who paid through public subscriptions. These industrial leaders had complained that the school system reflected the needs of an agricultural economy and neglected the skills required for their large manufacturing companies. The second statue is in the Embankment Gardens, London.

As the school leaving age was twelve, my grandfather left school at that age to work in a bakery and later became a dock labourer. In 1871 English Literature was included for the first time as a subject. It focused on poetry and drama, as the long novels of Charles Dickens, George Eliot and Thomas Hardy were a bit too much.

In the fifty years following the 1870 Act, there was a very determined campaign to increase reading for, by that time, Britain had universal male suffrage and it was necessary for the new electors to know what the political parties were promising and achieving. Robert Lowe, a former and future Liberal Cabinet member, was resolutely opposed to Disraeli's Bill in 1867 to extend the franchise, saying during the debate, 'I believe it will be absolutely necessary that you should prevail on our future masters to learn their letters.' This was summarised as 'We must educate our masters.'

This picture was painted in 1874 by Edwin Hughes (1842–1922) of a grocer's delivery boy stopping at a bookshop and picking out a book to read before delivering his basket of flowers. He is a teenager who would have left school aged eleven or twelve, but at least he had picked up the ability to read and made the most of it, as he probably had no books of his own.

A Rural Primary School in the North – The Lucky Ones

Louisa Anne Beresford, Marchioness of Waterford, (1818–91), was a wealthy widow with properties in Dorset and Northumbria. She was also a gifted watercolourist, tutored by Dante Gabriel Rossetti and had attended art lessons given by John Ruskin. To improve her tenants welfare, she designed and built a school in the village of Ford in Northumbria, decorating it with large frescos of biblical scenes using some of the village children and adults as models. The parents of Ford were fortunate as Louisa Anne was a generous philanthropist and landlord, but the parents would have been charged a small fee. It remained a school until 1951 and today it is a cultural centre, Lady Waterford Hall. To commemorate the school, on Heritage Day, modern young girls wear late Victorian dresses and read from contemporary books.

Louisa Anne Beresford, *The Writing Lesson*, 1880

The Development of Children's Literature

After the copyright change of 1774, some publishers produced books specifically for children. These tended to replace the old tales about Guy of Warwick and Robin Hood. There were five major books written which substantially increased children's reading: *Alice's Adventures in Wonderland* by Lewis Carroll (1865), *Black Beauty* by Anna Sewell (1877), *Treasure Island* by R.L. Stevenson (1883), *Peter Pan* by J.M. Barrie (1902), and *The Railway Children* by Edith Nesbit (1905). In 1922 Enid Blyton published her first book and by the 1930s she had become the favourite children's writer with *Noddy*, *The Famous Five*, *The Naughtiest Girl* and *The Faraway Tree* series. She sold hundreds of millions of copies and they were translated into ninety languages. In 1950, C.S. Lewis published *The Lion, the Witch and the Wardrobe* (the first of seven in his *Chronicles of Narnia*). Millions of copies have been sold.

Children's books have now become established as a separate popular genre of literature, with an annual market of over £500 million. The most outstanding success has been the *Harry Potter* novels by J.K. Rowling, first published in 1997, with seven sequels over the following ten years. More than 700 million copies have been sold and they have been translated into over eighty languages. Eight *Harry Potter* films have been made and these are regularly shown on television. The *Harry Potter* series has been the greatest success of any children's books in our literary history and its author the wealthiest of all English writers.

Today, children's books are reviewed in a separate section of magazines and papers that carry book reviews. There are over fourteen literary prizes for children's authors, including the Carnegie Medal, the Blue Peter Book Prize, and Nestlé, Guardian and Costa prizes.

Ted Hughes, a former Poet Laureate, promoted a poetry competition in the *Observer*, which is how I came to meet him. Quentin Blake was the first Children's Laureate, and he has been followed by Michael Rosen the poet, Chris Riddell the cartoonist, and the children's authors Jacqueline Wilson, Lauren Child, Cressida Cowell, Joseph Coelho and Frank Cottrell-Boyce. Today, the Waterstones Children's Laureate receives a bursary of £30,000 and a silver medal to promote reading, storytelling and the appreciation of illustrated books.

THE DEN

It was ferociously hot, and he was still alive. Those were the first thoughts that came to Fred as he opened his eyes and found himself staring straight up at the Brazilian sun. Instinctively he looked down at his wristwatch, but the face was cracked and the minute hand had fallen off.

The two girls were asleep next to him. Both of them were covered in blood and scabs, but they were breathing easily. Con had her thumb in her mouth. There was a host of dragonflies in luminous blues and reds dancing around them. He thought they might be attracted to the blood.

But there was no sign of the little boy. Max was missing.

'Max!' Fred whispered, jumping to his feet. There was no answer, no movement except the burr of dragonfly wings.

Fred's heart started to pound. 'Max?' he called louder. Lila stirred in her sleep.

He ran to the edge of the trees. There was no trace of the boy.

'Max!' he roared, staring wildly around.

'What?' Max looked up; he was lying on his stomach behind some fernlike plants next to the vile-smelling puddle, plashing his fingers in the water.

'Max!' Fred ran over to him, wincing as one of his ribs protested sharply. 'You haven't been drinking that water, have you?'

Max stared up at Fred

The popularity of children's books has also attracted writers of adult fiction. Katherine Rundell, a Fellow of Literature at All Souls College, Oxford, won the 2022 Baillie Gifford Prize for Non-Fiction for her biography of John Donne, *Super-Infinite*, but she has also won four children's book awards. I have read her 2017 Costa Children's prize book, *The Explorer*, which tells of four children aged five to fifteen who crash-land in the Amazon jungle. I simply did not believe that you could hold the interest of children for 400 pages, but it is superbly written, an absolute page-turner that is greatly enhanced by the opening page of each chapter being beautifully illustrated. The quality of Rundell's writing is so good I would encourage adults to read her children's books as well. Listening to the BBC Radio 4 *Today* programme one morning, I heard a mother say that *The Explorer* was one of the best books she had ever read.

Rundell's latest work is *The Impossible Creatures* (2023) for readers from the age of nine, and one review called her the next Tolkien. It tells of the adventures of two young people who discover an archipelago inhabited by impossible creatures, some friendly and some viciously hostile, and all illustrated. In 2023,

Waterstones made this book its choice of the year, which I believe is the first time that any major bookseller has selected a children's book. She recognises that:

> Children's fiction necessitates distillation, at its best it renders in their purest, most archetypal forms – hope, hunger, joy and fear – think of children's books as literary vodka.

The most popular children's books are adventure stories, with heroes and heroines, joy and fear, and defeats as well as triumphs. C.S. Lewis recognises how good stories feature all of these and encourage resilience:

> Since it is so likely that they will meet cruel enemies, let them at least have heard of brave knights and heroic courage. Otherwise you are making their destiny not brighter, but darker.

I have established forty-four University Technical Colleges with 21,000 students specialising in high-quality technical education for fourteen- to eighteen-year-olds, alongside English, maths and science. Some of the students joining at fourteen have low reading ages and so we gave fifty of them *The Explorer* to read, and I was delighted that some read the book right through.

Teaching Shakespeare

Teaching Shakespeare in schools is always challenging. The Royal Shakespeare Company (RSC) offers five days' training for primary school teachers. All the schools chosen were in areas where above-average numbers of pupils were eligible for free school meals. The RSC trained the teachers to deliver twenty hours of Shakespeare lessons to nine and ten year olds. The results showed significant improvement in the language development of the children. Shriti Vadera, the RSC chair, commented in the *Financial Times*:

> The pupils wrote and spoke more. Their writing was longer. They used more detailed and complex language. They employed richer, broader and more sophisticated vocabulary and were better at expressing emotions. The improvement after using the RSC methods was up by 24%. The research found other significant differences: the children were more confident with language and saw themselves as good learners and problem solvers. If you can crack Shakespeare, you can do algebra.

The RSC has raised funds to introduce this programme in 350 schools by 2025–6 and some have already started, for example, in Skegness, Corby, Hartlepool, Coventry and Peterborough. This is such a success that the Department of Education should provide more funds to help all primary schools.

In schools, most books are read at a desk to prepare for an exam rather than for enjoyment. To achieve the latter, you need to unchain literature from desks, move to an easy chair or lie on a bed and treat it as a pastime.

In October 2024, the BBC broadcast five essays on reading by Katherine Rundell, making her the modern champion for reading children's books. She explained why reading great books was so good for children because books have 'the strangeness, the freedom, the intellectual and ethical power – how liberating they can be. Saluting human difference, and insisting over and over again on the value of human joy.'

Book Tokens

Book tokens made it easier for young people to read books, as they could be cashed in at any bookshop in the British Isles.

They were invented in 1932 by Harold Raymond, a director at Chatto & Windus publishers, who realised that the problem of what books to give to children or friends could be solved by sending a token with a monetary value that could be exchanged for a book, and thus allowing the recipient to choose the book they wanted to read. In the 1930s a book token was also a much cheaper and easier way of mailing a present, as the postage stamp cost just 4 pence. I remember receiving tokens for £5 and £10. Book tokens flourished for over fifty years and were so popular that artists were commissioned to design them, and some included a book lying beside an open window or upon a table close to a cosy fire. They are still available online.

BOOK
Token
EXCHANGEABLE AT ANY BOOK TOKEN BOOKSHOP IN GT. BRITAIN & IRELAND
SEE INSTRUCTIONS ON BACK PAGE

Chapter 4

Why Reading Spread Through Society

He ate and drank the precious words,
His spirit grew robust;
He knew no more that he was poor,
Nor that his frame was dust.
He danced along the dingy days,
And this bequest of wings
Was but a book. What liberty
A loosened spirit brings!

EMILY DICKINSON

WILLIAM ST CLAIR (1937–2021) was a senior civil servant who resigned to become a literary scholar and in 2004 he published a book, *The Reading Nation in the Romantic Period*, in which he approached the popularity of reading in an entirely novel way by scrupulously recording the number of books that were published, either in prose or poetry, and the prices they sold at from 1750 to 1830. His scholarship is extensive and profound, and he has identified the readership of books across the classes of society and it was the price of books that determined their readership. I am indebted to him for discovering how Britain became a reading nation by helping the disadvantaged to read.

It all started in 1695 when Parliament decided not to renew the Licensing of the Press Act of 1662, which had given the Stationers' Company the right to licence printing presses, to set the price of books, to approve apprenticeships and to extend state censorship. One of the greatest advocates for this freedom of expression was John Locke (1632–1704), 'The Father of Liberalism'. The consequences of the new freedom built up slowly, as many publishers still asserted that they owned the intellectual copyright of new books. However, it did lead to the publishing of what was Britain's first novel, *Robinson Crusoe* by Daniel Defoe in 1719, with a print-run of 1,000 copies at a sale price of 5 shillings and a further 2,000 copies in a second edition later that same year. Following that, it was not reprinted until 1754. One of the most interesting things about *Robinson Crusoe* is that unusually its hero did not come from the nobility or the upper classes, but from 'the upper station of low life' – later known as the lower middle class.

The book was available mainly to wealthy people, but the readership did expand by it being lent to relatives and friends. Thomas Dolby, a thatcher in Lincolnshire, recalled in his memoirs that he found his uncle had a copy of *Robinson Crusoe*:

'I made repeated journeys to his house, more than three miles distances, to beg the loan of it, but it was always lent to somebody or another. I was very near to having it once, for it had been lent to somebody the evening before I got there.'

Thomas Turner (1729–93) was a shopkeeper, an undertaker, a schoolmaster and overseer for the poor in the village of East Hoathly in East Sussex, where we lived for a time. From 1754 he kept a diary for eleven years and confided in it, 'Oh what an unspeakable pleasure it is to be busied in one's trade, and at a leisure hour to unbend one's mind by reading.' He records that he read Shakespeare, John Locke, Joseph Addison, Samuel Richardson, and newspapers. He enjoyed reading aloud to his family and neighbours, which was common, and had become a source of information for many people who could not read in the eighteenth century.

A book in the eighteenth century could cost as much 40 shillings, which included a tax of 3 shillings, and that sum represented a third of a working man's weekly wage. It was not surprising that William Wordsworth, in a letter to a friend in 1802, remarked that the readers of quarto or octavo books were 'gentlemen, persons of fortune, professional men, ladies, persons who can afford to buy or can easily procure books of half a guinea (10/5 shillings), hot-pressed and printed on super-fine paper'.

Poems cost much less and the most popular poem was *The Seasons* by James Thomson (1726) with 6,000 copies sold at 6 shillings. The enterprising son of a shepherd from Essex, Tom Kelly, recognised the large demand for affordable reading matter and in the early 1800s bought the remainder of works out of copyright, split them into parts, copied them on to cheaper paper, and sold them door-to-door for just a few coppers.

Less expensive reading material was helped by a surge in the printing of Chapbooks mainly directed at children and young students. They ran to about twelve to twenty-four pages and had illustrations, comments on social and personal matters, ballads and songs. It was not a London trade, but printers in seventy-four towns, using the latest printing machinery, published them in considerable quantities at a low price. In 1790 the weekly wage of a labourer was 10 shillings, meaning books were unaffordable, but he may be able to afford a Chapbook, or a ballad costing one penny. In 1820 the poet John Clare observed that ordinary people had only heard of Shakespeare by seeing a playbill.

William St Clair shows that the real breakthrough occurred in 1771 when the Court of Session in Edinburgh decided by votes of 11:1 that an author's copyright, rather than that of a publisher, was lawful in Scotland. This went to the Supreme Court in the House of Lords and eventually the whole House had to vote upon the matter in 1774, when it upheld the decision reached in Scotland, despite members of the House of Lords being lobbied by a very well-financed campaign of publishers to keep their copyright.

This new freedom did not just cover books; it also covered almanacs, maps, text books, law books, medical books, and school and university books. It also led to more publishers setting up and many considerable fortunes were made. The book-binding industry doubled in size as the works of Shakespeare, John Milton, Oliver Goldsmith, Alexander Pope, Jonathan Swift and John Gay were no longer controlled by private owners. From 1780 the price of books out of copyright fell by half and then to a quarter of their previous levels and John Bew, a Scottish publisher, made his name and fortune by opening up a shop in Paternoster Row as the first cheap reprint publisher by offering 109 volumes of fifty British poets for just 1 shilling and sixpence.

However, this expansion of reading was not welcomed by everyone. Soame Jenyns (1704–87) was a writer and also the Member of Parliament for Cambridgeshire, and one of his books had been described by Samuel Johnson as 'slight and shallow'. Undeterred, Jenyns wrote in 1759:

> To encourage the poor man to read and think, and thus to become more conscious of his misery, would be to fly in the face of divine intervention.

Henry Fielding's *History of Tom Jones, a Foundling*, published in 1746, was in six volumes, meaning that again it was only available to the wealthier, but in 1790 Cooke's Select Novels offered eighteenth-century novels for 1 shilling. William Hazlitt noted that '*Tom Jones* came down in numbers once a fortnight in Cooke's pocket editions – I had hitherto only read school books and tiresome ecclesiastical history. But the world I found was to me a dance through life, a perpetual gala day.' Little wonder that a German, Karl Philipp Moritz, in his 1782 book, *Travelling in Several Parts of England*, commented, 'The moderate price of this book deserves also to be noticed as by such means books in England, more came within the reach of the people and are of course more generally distributed among them.'

In 1791 Thomas Paine published *The Rights of Man*, originally priced at 3 shillings and sixpence, but a second edition was offered at sixpence. There is no record of the print run, but an estimate has been made that in the following decade over 200,000 copies were sold. I was lucky enough to acquire a first edition in which Michael Foot, a former Leader of the Labour Party, has pencilled his name. Paine was charged with seditious libel and had to flee the country, and some booksellers went to jail for selling the pamphlet.

Britain had its glorious revolution in 1689, and through gradual reforms in the eighteenth and nineteenth centuries it had successfully embedded Paine's rights in our constitution – human rights, democracy, a commitment to equality and the rule of law – but we did not follow his revolutionary proposals to abolish monarchs, noblemen and the established church. The French Revolution, on the other hand, was a disaster which led to the undemocratic supremacy of Napoleon. When Paine went to France, they soon became tired of him and threw him out. He was not welcomed in America either.

This print of 1792 by Isaac Cruikshank captures many of Paine's revolutionary ideas. He poses the question, 'Who wants me?' and the answer at the particular time was 'No One'.

After the French Revolution, Conservative MPs came to believe that revolutionary books might lead to revolutionary England, and so they welcomed their high cost. Prime Minister William Pitt commented, 'A three guinea book could never do so much harm among those who had not three shillings to spare.' But that was only a stopgap, as the price of books began to fall. In the early nineteenth century, the average cost for three volumes of Jane Austen was 12 shillings, and Walter Scott for his last novel *Kenilworth* got 31 shillings. These were too expensive for the majority of the population where family incomes fell between 10 and 20 shillings a week.

The Reading Explosion

The period from 1817 to 1824 saw a large increase in the number of very cheap books which poorer people could afford to buy. In 1817 an enterprising publisher, Sherwood, discovered a play written in 1794 but never published entitled *Wat Tyler*, about the Peasants' Revolt of 1381 which lauded rebels and attacked the King and several nobles. It had been written by Robert Southey in his early radical days, but by 1817 he had become the leading conservative poet and was so furious that he tried to have the book withdrawn. The Lord Chancellor decided that it could only be achieved if he, as the author, prosecuted the publisher. Southey refused, as it was too costly. This meant that as Southey did not own the intellectual copyright of the book, other publishers could print it. The price of *Wat Tyler*, if published with the support of the author, would have been 10 shillings, but the pirate editions were offered first at 1 shilling each, and some fell to thruppence, helping it to become widely bought and read.

Percy Bysshe Shelley (1792–1822)

A book that sold widely amongst the poor was the poem *Queen Mab* by Shelley, an avowed atheist, and this attacked kings, statesmen, priests, marriage and religion. He expressed his support for free love, 'the flame of consentaneous love inspires all life'. Shelley had published the poem privately in 1813, but in 1817 he was prosecuted for blasphemous libel and the court decreed that he should not continue as a father responsible for his two children who were removed from him and passed to foster parents: he never saw them again. After his death in 1822, all his most famous poems were out of print, but several publishers printed cheap pirated editions on poor paper of *Queen Mab* that were offered for sale at sixpence. When George Bernard Shaw was shown a collection of surviving copies, he commented that the books were, 'Blackened with the finger-marks of many heavy-handed trades.'

Ozymandias is my favourite Shelley poem. It is still popular in school text books for its simplicity and clear message that all temporal power is a fleeting passage of history. I like to think that Shelley might have had Napoleon in mind for, in 1817 when the poem was written, his empire had disappeared and he was exiled to the lonely and distant island of St Helena which corresponded to the most famous line, 'Look on my Works, ye Mighty, and despair!'

Ozymandias

I met a traveller from an antique land,
Who said—'Two vast and trunkless legs of stone
Stand in the desert. ... Near them, on the sand,
Half sunk a shattered visage lies, whose frown,
And wrinkled lip, and sneer of cold command,
Tell that its sculptor well those passions read
Which yet survive, stamped on these lifeless things,
The hand that mocked them, and the heart that fed;
And on the pedestal, these words appear:
My name is Ozymandias, King of Kings;
Look on my Works, ye Mighty, and despair!'
Nothing beside remains. Round the decay
Of that colossal Wreck, boundless and bare
The lone and level sands stretch far away.

Lord Byron, *Don Juan*, 1819–24

Between 1819 and 1824 Byron published sixteen cantos of the life of Don Juan which was completely different from the romantic poetry that had made him famous and very rich. *Don Juan* was an epic satire questioning the conventions and institutions that held society together – marriage, the church, the monarchy – and the chastity of women, for they were described in the poem as being 'sexually voracious'. It also derided and scoffed at the local heroes of the day – politicians, generals and even the great Duke of Wellington. It was full of ribald wit and blasphemy, and Robert Southey described these volumes as 'the preparatory schools for the brothel and the gallows'. However, a Lincolnshire weaver Ben Brierly revealed that his soul 'was not much lifted by poetry books until I joined the companionship of Burns and Byron (in the 1830s) that I felt the god within me'.

George Gordon Byron, Lord Byron, engraved by H. Meyer, from an original drawing by George H. Harlow

Many booksellers refused to sell *Don Juan*, and some literary clubs which had ordered it had to withdraw it. The Church, in particular, condemned it: 'Young people should understand that to touch his volumes is like embracing a beautiful woman infected by the plague.'

Victorian parents did not want their daughters to read such explicit scenes:

> To view each other, panting, dying
> In a love's ecstatic posture lying.

Byron's regular publisher, John Murray, was so shocked he refused to handle the poem, so it was printed by an unnamed publisher and without mention of Byron's name. The quarto edition sold for 40 shillings, but a pirate publisher produced a copy for 4 shillings each. Dugdale, a bookseller who also sold pornography, went to court to prove that the work had no clear intellectual property protection and the court agreed. This opened the door to a mass of private editions which soon resulted in the price falling in 1823 to 1 shilling. In St Clair's judgment, '*Don Juan* was read by more people in its first twenty years than any other previous work of English literature.'

In the late eighteenth century, the population of England, Scotland and Wales amounted to 18.5 million, but there is no written record of the level of literacy. One estimate I have seen cited that two-thirds of men and half of women could read. What is more certain is that urban culture saw an explosive growth from the 1820s, and Frederick Engels in 1845 recalling his youth in Manchester wrote:

> It is the workers who are more familiar with the poetry of Shelley and Byron ... Shelley's prophetical genius has caught their imagination, while Byron attracts their sympathy by his sensuous fun and by the virulence of his satire against the existing social order. The middle class, on the other hand, have on their shelves only ruthlessly expurgated 'family' editions of these writers.

William St Clair called the period after 1774 'a reading explosion' and his research shows how young women were greatly attracted by novels and poetry. Charles Dickens, writing in 1836 about London Recreations in *Sketches by Boz*, also recognised the social changes that wider reading brought about:

> The wish of persons in the humbler classes of life to ape the manners and customs of those who fortune has placed above them ... does exist to a great extent in the small gentility of the middle classes. Tradesmen and clerks with fashionable novel-reading families and circulating-library-subscribing daughters.

In mid-Victorian England a shipping clerk could earn 27 shillings a week, while a millworker in Lancashire would earn 10 shillings; any one of them hoping to buy a book would think in pennies, not shillings. The working man could afford ballads and pamphlets reporting sensational crimes – murders, fires or executions – this was street literature for the poor. In 1827 James Catnach sold more than a million copies of a specially printed one sheet broadside, priced at a penny,

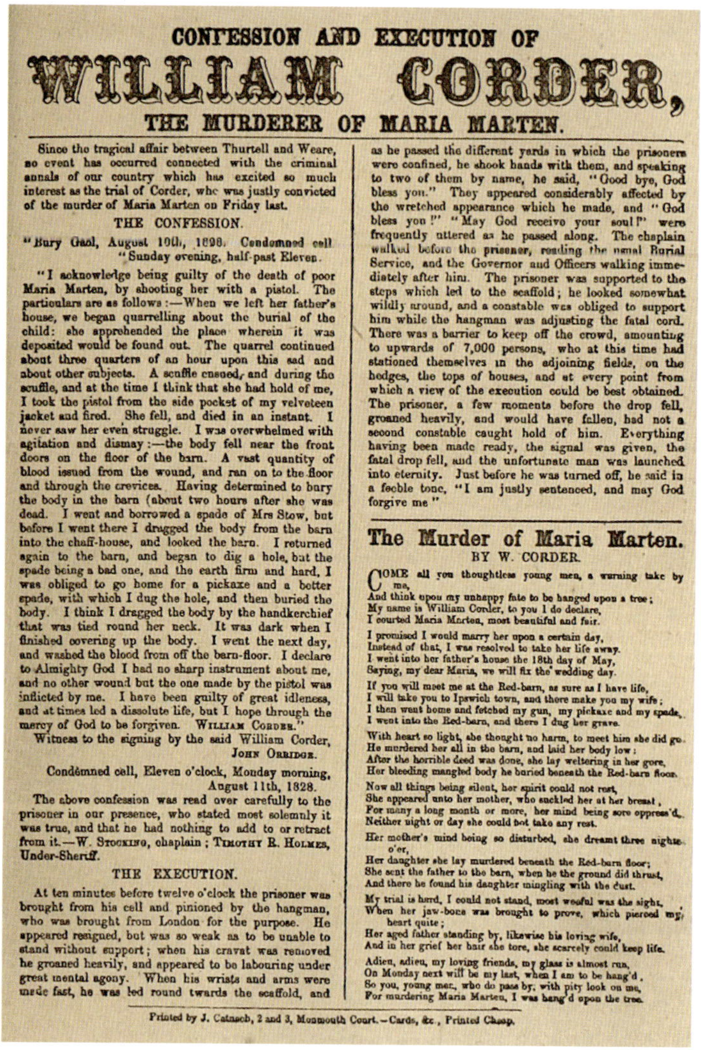

CONFESSION AND EXECUTION OF

WILLIAM CORDER,

THE MURDERER OF MARIA MARTEN.

Since the tragical affair between Thurtell and Weare, no event has occurred connected with the criminal annals of our country which has excited so much interest as the trial of Corder, who was justly convicted of the murder of Maria Marten on Friday last.

THE CONFESSION.

"Bury Gaol, August 10th, 1828. Condemned cell
"Sunday evening, half-past Eleven.

"I acknowledge being guilty of the death of poor Maria Marten, by shooting her with a pistol. The particulars are as follows:—When we left her father's house, we began quarrelling about the burial of the child: she apprehended the place wherein it was deposited would be found out. The quarrel continued about three quarters of an hour upon this sad and about other subjects. A scuffle ensued, and during the scuffle, and at the time I think that she had hold of me, I took the pistol from the side pocket of my velveteen jacket and fired. She fell, and died in an instant. I never saw her even struggle. I was overwhelmed with agitation and dismay:—the body fell near the front doors on the floor of the barn. A vast quantity of blood issued from the wound, and ran on to the floor and through the crevices. Having determined to bury the body in the barn (about two hours after she was dead. I went and borrowed a spade of Mrs Stow, but before I went there I dragged the body from the barn into the chaff-house, and locked the barn. I returned again to the barn, and began to dig a hole, but the spade being a bad one, and the earth firm and hard, I was obliged to go home for a pickaxe and a better spade, with which I dug the hole, and then buried the body. I think I dragged the body by the handkerchief that was tied round her neck. It was dark when I finished covering up the body. I went the next day, and washed the blood from off the barn-floor. I declare to Almighty God I had no sharp instrument about me, and no other wound but the one made by the pistol was inflicted by me. I have been guilty of great idleness, and at times led a dissolute life, but I hope through the mercy of God to be forgiven. WILLIAM CORDER."

Witness to the signing by the said William Corder,
JOHN ORRIDGE.

Condemned cell, Eleven o'clock, Monday morning,
August 11th, 1828.

The above confession was read over carefully to the prisoner in our presence, who stated most solemnly it was true, and that he had nothing to add to or retract from it.—W. STOCKING, chaplain; TIMOTHY R. HOLMES, Under-Sheriff.

THE EXECUTION.

At ten minutes before twelve o'clock the prisoner was brought from his cell and pinioned by the hangman, who was brought from London for the purpose. He appeared resigned, but was so weak as to be unable to stand without support; when his cravat was removed he groaned heavily, and appeared to be labouring under great mental agony. When his wrists and arms were made fast, he was led round twards the scaffold, and as he passed the different yards in which the prisoners were confined, he shook hands with them, and speaking to two of them by name, he said, "Good bye, God bless you." They appeared considerably affected by the wretched appearance which he made, and "God bless you!" "May God receive your soul!" were frequently uttered as he passed along. The chaplain walked before the prisoner, reading the usual Burial Service, and the Governor and Officers walking immediately after him. The prisoner was supported to the steps which led to the scaffold; he looked somewhat wildly around, and a constable was obliged to support him while the hangman was adjusting the fatal cord. There was a barrier to keep off the crowd, amounting to upwards of 7,000 persons, who at this time had stationed themselves in the adjoining fields, on the hedges, the tops of houses, and at every point from which a view of the execution could be best obtained. The prisoner, a few moments before the drop fell, groaned heavily, and would have fallen, had not a second constable caught hold of him. Everything having been made ready, the signal was given, the fatal drop fell, and the unfortunate man was launched into eternity. Just before he was turned off, he said in a feeble tone, "I am justly sentenced, and may God forgive me"

The Murder of Maria Marten.

BY W. CORDER.

COME all you thoughtless young men, a warning take by me,
And think upon my unhappy fate to be hanged upon a tree;
My name is William Corder, to you I do declare,
I courted Maria Marten, most beautiful and fair.

I promised I would marry her upon a certain day,
Instead of that, I was resolved to take her life away.
I went into her father's house the 18th day of May,
Saying, my dear Maria, we will fix the wedding day.

If you will meet me at the Red-barn, as sure as I have life,
I will take you to Ipswich town, and there make you my wife;
I then went home and fetched my gun, my pickaxe and my spade,
I went into the Red-barn, and there I dug her grave.

With heart so light, she thought no harm, to meet him she did go.
He murdered her all in the barn, and laid her body low:
After the horrible deed was done, she lay weltering in her gore,
Her bleeding mangled body he buried beneath the Red-barn floor.

Now all things being silent, her spirit could not rest,
She appeared unto her mother, who suckled her at her breast,
For many a long month or more, her mind being sore oppress'd,
Neither night or day she could not take any rest.

Her mother's mind being so disturbed, she dreamt three nights o'er,
Her daughter she lay murdered beneath the Red-barn floor;
She sent the father to the barn, when he the ground did thrust,
And there he found his daughter mingling with the dust.

My trial is hard, I could not stand, most woeful was the sight,
When her jaw-bone was brought to prove, which pierced my heart quite;
Her aged father standing by, likewise his loving wife,
And in her grief her hair she tore, she scarcely could keep life.

Adieu, adieu, my loving friends, my glass is almost run,
On Monday next will be my last, when I am to be hang'd.
So you, young men, who do pass by, with pity look on me,
For murdering Maria Marten, I was hang'd upon the tree.

Printed by J. Catnach, 2 and 3, Monmouth Court.—Cards, &c., Printed Cheap.

which contained 'the last dying words of William Corder, the murderer of Maria Marten in the famous Red Barn case, and a ballad supposedly written by him'.

William Cobbett (1763–1835)

Early in the nineteenth century, scholarly and critical reviews and pamphlets became popular. By 1809 the *Edinburgh Review* and the *Quarterly Review* in their heyday sold as many as 12,000 copies a week at 3 shillings each, but their actual readership probably exceeded well over 100,000 through the proliferation of reading clubs and lending libraries. In the troubled decade of the Regency from 1810 to 1820, there were many political pamphlets like *The Black Dwarf*, and the most widely read was William Cobbett's *The Political Register*, first published in 1802 and sold for 1 shilling. A shilling was expensive even for a respectable family whose weekly income was 48 shillings, when a shilling could buy 7 lbs of butter or 10 lbs of meat. So, in 1816 Cobbett published a condensed version costing two pennies which sold 50,000 copies, and earned it the nickname, 'Two Penny Trash'. Edition No.18, *Address to the Journeymen and Labourers* sold 200,000 copies and was aimed at the millworkers, miners, farm labourers and domestic servants who could join the reading public.

This is George Cruikshank's cartoon of Cobbett which appeared in *The Political House that Jack Built*.

The British government's network of spies followed Cobbett, and to avoid arrest he fled to America for two years, but he still managed to produce *The Political Register*. After the Peterloo Massacre in 1819, Lord Liverpool's government published Six Acts, which included laws to reduce free speech, to restrict the right to hold public meetings, to transport to Australia those who had engaged in blasphemous or seditious libels and increased the Stamp Duty on newspapers to 4 pence.

In this print by George Cruikshank, published in 1826, an elderly gentleman says he wants to read the latest Harriette Wilson, the memoir of a close friend and possible lover of the Duke of Wellington. The foppish gentleman is asking for the latest novel by Walter Scott. The maid servant, carrying a basket on her arm with a housekey in her hand, says, 'Have'n't you no Rum-ances in 5 Wollums?' The burly dustman, wearing a typical cap, heavy boots, leather apron and rolled up sleeves, says, 'I vants a Cobbett.'

The reading explosion of 1790 to 1820 was due to the many printing presses being set up which publishers used to produce greater numbers of cheap books. The other two factors that revolutionised literacy in Victorian England was, first, that from 1815 to 1914 Britain was not involved in any major European war, apart from the short-lived Crimean campaign in the 1850s – wars and invasions are bad for education. Secondly, the inventions from the Industrial Revolution starting in the 1760s, led to new industries, especially the inventions of James Watt, an apprentice, to harness the power of steam to allow machinery to draw up water from mines. Steam was used by other inventors to replace the traditional handwork carried out in small towns and villages. Machines drove the textile mills for cotton in Lancashire and for wool in Yorkshire, providing a career for many women who would have otherwise been domestic servants. Inventions create economic growth and soon steam power replaced horsepower for moving people around the country with trains and bicycles, and in ships steam replaced wind power.

All these industries needed a trained, skilled and literate workforce. The country's leading industrialist, Matthew Boulton (1728–1809) built the largest metal goods factory at Soho in Birmingham and 'Made in Brum' became a guarantee of quality recognised across the world. On recruiting employees for his factory, Boulton asked:

> Shall we find him among the unlettered Birmingham handicraft men or shall we find him amongst the speculative theorists whose knowledge has been drawn from Books? No neither will do: he is one that is both.

The need for a skilled and literate workforce was recognised by the Forster Education Act of 1870, which provided free education for children up to the age of eleven and the working class was the main beneficiary.

A dustman finding time to read the news

I bought this painting years ago during a visit to Manchester, as it is an interesting record of social history. Here is a late Victorian working man, wearing a dustman's cap, sitting in his humble home and reading a newspaper which might be *The Times*. By that time, daily newspapers were being widely published and through the spread of railways across the country, London editions could become national papers read in the most distant parts of England, Scotland and Wales. Newspapers cost just a few pence compared to books priced at several shillings. Reading a newspaper became a habit for all the classes in society.

Penguin Paperback Books

When in 1935 Allen Lane published the first Penguin Books, he started a revolution. They were paperbacks sold at sixpence each, when hard-backed books sold at 7 shillings. They were very affordable for working people and George Orwell remarked on 'their splendid value'. All the jacket covers included a black and white penguin, and their colours indicated different types of books – orange for novels, green for crime stories and purple for biographies. I first read two Penguin Books twelve years later: *The Mysterious Affair at Styles* by Agatha Christie (a friend of Allen Lane) and *Ariel* by André Maurois, which I later discovered was the first Penguin he published. Lane took an enormous risk by publishing in the first year 115 books over four areas of interest – novels, crime, adventures and biography. Eighty of these were novels and included a sprinkling of well-known novelists – Ernest Hemingway, Evelyn Waugh, H.G. Wells, E.M. Forster, and P.G. Wodehouse – but most were by lesser-known writers who were popular at that time and are now largely forgotten.

Allen Lane had wanted to produce a 'book to be bought as easily and casually as a packet of cigarettes'. He was able to persuade Woolworths to take 65,000 books which proved the breakthrough, and in the next twelve months over a million Penguins were sold.

Reading in the Armed Forces, 1940s

After the United States joined the Second World War following the invasion of Pearl Harbour on 7 December 1941, President F.D. Roosevelt declared that this was a war against tyranny and in defence of liberty. His speech included this passage on books that was made into a poster:

> Books cannot be killed by fire. People die, but books never die. No man and no force can put thought in a concentration camp forever. No man and no force can take from the world the

books that embody man's eternal fight against tyranny. In this war, we know, books are weapons.

To fulfil Roosevelt's pledge, the Council on Books in Wartime 1941–6, printed, published and delivered books to American servicemen and women. All the books were paperbacks which could be easily slipped into pockets. They were known as Armed Services Editions (ASE) and the number of copies sent out was massive – twelve million – with 1,300 titles and 494 reprints of older

books. Each of the soldiers who landed in Normandy on D-Day in June 1944 had all been given an ASE book as they embarked. For many servicemen this was probably the first time they had read a book since leaving school. It was an amazing operation, without precedent, and unfortunately without a successor. The American servicemen and women could be said to have been the best-read armed forces in history.

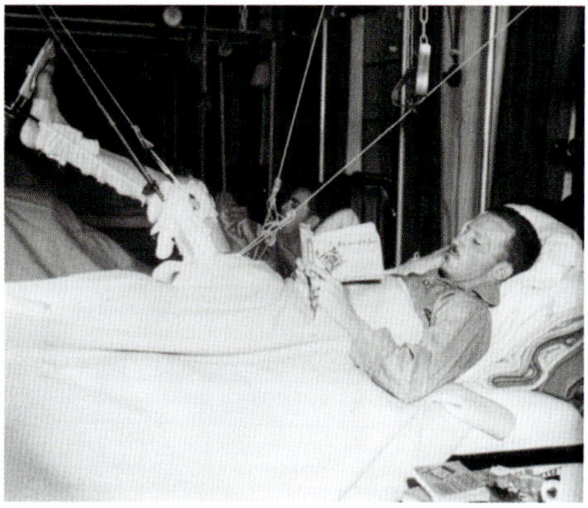

An injured American soldier recuperates with an Armed Services Edition

The British Army established the Armed Forces Book Club in 1942 to provide cheap reprints of a range of books, mainly novels. Each book had the words 'Services Edition' written on them, and Royal Mail delivered them without charge not only to the Armed Services but to hospitals and civilians like ARP wardens.

Penguin, not surprisingly, was the first publisher off the mark and they were given a special delivery of paper, which was rationed, to produce the first 120 paperbacks. However, their books were not popular, as they were too high-brow and serious. The publisher Collins was much more successful with their crime stories and westerns, which were very recognisable by the large white circle on their front covers.

In my National Service in the early 1950s, I served as an artillery instructor of large mortars based in the canal zone in Egypt where there were over 60,000 soldiers protecting the Suez Canal. After I was made the education officer for

my battery, I soon found out what a poor education many of my soldiers had and some were almost illiterate. I provided lessons in basic reading, writing and arithmetic. I encouraged them to read the news pages of the tabloids and not just the sports pages. I tried to ensure each had a paperback and I found some Agatha Christies with Poirot, but Peter Cheyne's thrillers with Slim Callaghan were more popular, as they were sexier. The lessons proved popular because if the soldiers passed tests their pay increased. In the past soldiers did not need to be highly literate, but as weaponry became more and more sophisticated, instructions on their use and maintenance were described in booklets which needed to be read and understood.

D.H. Lawrence, *Lady Chatterley's Lover*, 1965

Penguin was always an adventurous publisher – adding the works of Greek and Latin writers, and in 1965 boldly publishing D.H. Lawrence's *Lady Chatterley's Lover* which was to lead to the end of book censorship.

This book was printed privately in Italy in 1928, since the Obscene Publications Act of 1859 stopped copies being sold in England and any that were found could be seized by Customs or the Home Office. Censorship was extensive: between 1950 and 1953 four thousand books were deemed to be obscene and in 1955 a Soho bookseller was given two months in jail for selling a copy of *Lady Chatterley's Lover*. In 1959 a Labour Backbencher, Roy Jenkins, introduced a Bill to allow publishers the defence against prosecution if the book had 'literary merit'. Although it was a Private Members' Bill it passed through both Houses that year.

In 1960 Penguin Books decided to publish *Lady Chatterley's Lover* at 3 shillings and sixpence and sold 200,000 copies on the first day. The government decided to prosecute Penguin for obscenity and that led to a six-day trial during which leading writers E.M. Forster, Rebecca West and Richard Hoggart defended the publication. Reports of the trial were front-page news every day. The leading prosecutor for the government was Mervyn Griffiths-Jones, who astonished the jury and became a figure of ridicule when he asked them in his opening remarks whether this was a book which 'you will wish your wife or servants to read'. The jury found for Penguin and in the following year two million copies were sold.

Chapter 5

Why Women were Early Readers

> I declare after all there is no enjoyment like reading! How much sooner one tires of anything than of a book! – When I have a house of my own, I shall be miserable if I have not an excellent library.
>
> JANE AUSTEN, *PRIDE AND PREJUDICE*, 1813

HERE ARE TWO PIECES OF CONTRASTING ADVICE to women about reading literature. The first is from Lady Mary Montague (1689–1762), a poet and writer:

> Learning if she had a real taste for it will not only make her contented but happy. No entertainment is so cheap as reading, nor any pleasure so lasting. She will not want new fashions nor regret the loss of expensive diversions or variety of company if she be amused with an author in her closet.

The other is from the poet, Robert Southey writing to Charlotte Brontë in 1837:

> Literature cannot be the business of a woman's life and it ought not to be.

Fortunately, Charlotte Brontë did not listen to the advice, and ten years later in 1847 she published *Jane Eyre*, read by millions across the world. Nothing by Southey is read today.

In the Middle Ages boys were taught to read and write; very few girls were. The numbers increased in later centuries and when free education was provided in Britain from 1870 girls were taught equally with boys. GCSE results in 2022 confirm that girls are 9.6 months ahead of boys in reading. In this chapter I want to highlight exceptional women who have taken to reading and writing, particularly poetry.

Christine de Pisan (1364–1430)

Christine was born in Venice but at the age of four, as her father was appointed to be the astrologer to the French court in Paris, she was brought up in French court circles and introduced to the literature and scholastic culture of the late European Middle Ages. Her youth was surrounded by books because her father had to find books to fill the new library in the Louvre. She was well-read and in her books she referred to several authors – Aristotle, Boccaccio, Boethius, Livy, Ovid and Petrarch. At fifteen she married a royal secretary, Etienne du Castel, and they had three children, but after only eleven years he succumbed to the plague. Writing to support her family over four decades, she composed forty books, as well as poems, and also oversaw the printing of twenty-four manuscripts, fulfilling the roles of writer, printer, publisher and bookseller.

Christine de Pisan instructs her son, Jean de Castel, *Collected Works of Christine de Pisan*, attributed to the Bedford Master, *c.* 1410–11

Christine's first book was published in 1399 and her most famous book was a biography of Charles V, *Le Livre des fais et bonnes meurs du sage roy Charles V* (1404), which celebrated the support he gave to the literary culture of France. She also wrote about the nature of politics – extolling good governance and begging for an end to the Hundred Years' War between France and England.

A book of ballads, *Cent Ballades d'Amant et de Dame* (*c.* 1402) was one of her first books and the eleventh poem is probably her most famous verse:

Alone am I and alone I wish to be,
Alone my gentle love has left me;
Alone am I, without companion or master,
Alone am I, sorrowful and vexed;
Alone am I in anxious weariness.
Alone am I, more lost than any other;
Alone am I, left without a lover.

As war developed between Burgundy and Orleans, Christine had to be very astute to retain the support of noble patrons in a period of rapidly shifting power. An early supporter was Jean, Duc de Berry (1340–1416) who was at the centre of French politics, being the son of a king, a brother of a king and the father of a king. He became a great patron of the arts and commissioned the Limbourg Brothers to create what was to become the greatest pictorial document of the Middle Ages, *Les Très Riches Heures du Duc de Berry*. He was also a bibliophile who assembled a magnificent library, and became a personal friend of Christine de Pisan, a unique relationship at a time when most men did not have female friends. She spoke of him as 'a great lover of beautiful books, of moral philosophy, and of history on Roman conduct and exemplary behaviour'. He bought her book of ballads in 1402 and she presented him with her books in 1404 and 1409. Her recent biographer commented that, 'Nothing touched his heart so much as jewels and manuscripts.'

One of the most widely read books across Europe was a poem, 'Le Roman de la Rose', which related the progress of an affair from first sight to a touch, to a kiss and to the deflowering of the girl. The poem portrayed the woman as a shameless, lustful seducer and the narrator of the poem berates his wife and beats her:

All of you women are, will be and have been whores,
In fact or in desire, for, whoever could eliminate the
Deed, no man could constrain desire.
All women have
The advantage of being mistresses of their desires.
For no amount of beating or upbraiding can change
Your hearts, but the man who could change them
Would have lordship over your bodies.

The poem is aimed at male readers and is misogynistic. In her biography of Christine, Charlotte Cooper-Davis sets out in fascinating detail the dispute that rose between male defenders of the poem and letters from Christine refuting them. One male dismissed her interest as 'your own opinionated and impertinent presumptions', and many were enraged that a woman should be allowed to comment. Her replies were robust. When 'Le Roman' claimed that women deceived men and forced them to commit reprehensible actions, Christine asked, 'Do they come looking for you in your room?', 'Do they beg to take you by force?' These epistolatory exchanges took place in 1401 and Christine made a collection of them and sent them to the Queen.

In her book *Epistre* in 1401, Christine ridiculed the way that young gallants dressed, behaved, and gossiped about their success:

> Listen to how they make a game of it:
> Not satisfied with just betraying them,
> They've partners in their nasty liaison,
> ... the less they got
> The more they boast of having been shut in
> The chambers of ladies who've loved them.
> They swear on soul and body how events
> Turned out for them, and what the circumstance,
> And claim that naked, arm in arm, they lay.
> Their cohorts talk of it in every inn
> And nobles share the news in huddled groups
> In courts belonging to the dukes, our lords,
> Or yet before the king, or elsewhere spread.

Christine wanted to end the endless fountain of misogynistic literature. She published one book advocating the building of a 'City of Ladies' as a fortified place in which women would be protected against the diatribes against them, and she listed all the famous women from the past, claiming them to be the equal of men. She asserted that feminine modesty did not prevent them from being intelligent, have ideas of their own or to be ignored. She showed by her own career how a woman could be successful, respected and listened to.

Who's in charge? Miniature of Christine instructing a group of men. 'Proverbes moraulx', *The Book of the Queen*, *c.* 1410–14

Christine was not the only woman to contribute to the writings of the Church. In the fourteenth and fifteenth centuries there were two English mystics – Julian of Norwich and Margery Kempe. Dame Julian wrote of her visions in *Revelations of Divine Love*, which is the earliest surviving

Christine and the three virtuous ladies – Reason, Rectitude and Justice – and with Reason building the City of Ladies, 'Collected Works', *The Book of the Queen*, *c.* 1410–14

English language work by a woman. Margery Kempe wrote of her own life in *The Book of Margery Kempe*, which included her mystical 'conversations with God'. It is the first autobiography in the English language.

The Gift of a Book, 1530

Not many women would have bought their own books in the sixteenth century, and most would have been given to them by teachers, family or friends.

In 2023, the Bodleian Library's Curator, Nicholas Perkins, in his book *Gifts and Books*, summarised the story of *The Erle of Tolous* as 'a poem of love, loyalty and justice, in which the Earl falls in love with the Empress Beulybon and saves her from a false accusation of adultery. Fortunately for the Earl, the Emperor dies, so he is free to make her his wife.' The book is held in the Bodleian Library and its first illustration shows it is clearly a special gift, for books were sold unbound and it was the owner who paid for them to be bound, normally in vellum or calf's skin, at a cost of just 1 or 2 shillings, but this book has been elaborately bound, possibly in wood or metal, and certainly gilded. It may well be a gift from a prosperous young man who is saying, 'Take with pleasure,' in the hope of securing the same success as the Erle of Tolous.

One of the attractive features of a book is that it can be easily given as a gift to family and friends, as a reward for an achievement or possibly to influence a

The Earl of Toulouse, title-page, with fine drawing of book-presentation

person. Some inherent part of the giver remains in the book that is given, and that is what makes it rather special. Exchanges of gifts leave both sides better.

Lady Anne Clifford (1590–1676)

Lady Anne was the daughter of the Earl of Cumberland and on his death, as his two older sons had died, the estates passed to her younger brother. This breached an 'entail' from the fourteenth century that the estates should have passed to the eldest heir, whether male or female, namely Anne. She did inherit the ancient title of Baroness de Clifford, a barony created by writ in 1299. Her father had bequeathed her only £15,000, but she decided not to accept that and to press her claim for the estates through the courts, receiving encouragement from Queen

Anne of Denmark. She launched into a series of legal actions against her younger brother, but it was only when he died without heir in 1643 that she was able to reclaim the very extensive estates in the north of England, which included five castles, and she finally gained possession of them in 1649.

As a child Anne had been a favourite of Queen Elizabeth I and she played and danced in masques written by Ben Jonson for the Court of Queen Anne of Denmark. In 1646, a turning point in the Civil War, when Charles I surrendered to the Parliamentary Army, she decided to commemorate her own contribution to society by commissioning a Belgian artist, Jan van Belcamp, to paint *The Great Picture*. It is a very large triptych – 8 x 3 m. It depicts three stages during her life: the first on the left, she is fifteen years old; on the right she is the assured and experienced woman of fifty-six; and the middle shows her father and mother whose womb would carry Anne, and her mother is pointing to her two elder sons whose early deaths allowed Anne to inherit the barony.

Jan van Belcamp, *The Great Picture*, 1646

Anne wanted to show that she was not just a very wealthy woman responsible for vast estates in the north of England, but also a patron of literature and art. For her, books did not simply furnish a room and she wanted to show by making fifty book titles clearly identifiable in *The Great Picture* that she had not only collected but read them. The books in the painting include St Augustine's *City of God*, Ovid's *Metamorphoses*, Montaigne's *Essays*, Cervantes' *Don Quixote* and Chaucer – all books that she had read. She reserved a special place for Edmund Spenser's *Arcadia* (1611) with his collected poems, and in 1620 she commissioned a monument to Edmund Spenser in Westminster Abbey where he had been buried. Above the portrait of her as a young woman, she includes a portrait of one of her tutors, Samuel Daniel, the poet and playwright, and Ben Jonson's collected works can also be seen.

Anne kept a daily diary and recorded on 20 July 1617 that she had met John Donne, heard his sermons and a week later hosted a large banquet for him. His comment recognised the breadth of her interests: 'She could discourse on all things, from Predestination to Slea-silk,' which is a slender thread used in embroidery. On the top right of the *Great Painting* there is a copy of John Donne's *Sermons.*

Madame de Pompadour (1721–64)

As a child, Jeanne Antoinette Poisson suffered from poor health and was educated at home by her mother and guardian to promote a very well read, artistic young woman knowledgeable in the arts, drawing, engraving, painting, poetry and the theatre. This was deemed necessary, as a fortune teller had predicted that when she was grown up, 'She would reign over the heart of the king.' She married her guardian's nephew and told him that she would never leave him except for a king. She saw her chance in 1744, after Louis XV's official mistress had died, and she drew the attention of the King after a royal hunting party by driving her carriage right past him, first wearing a green dress in a red carriage, then in a red dress in a green carriage.

Madame de Pompadour became Louis's official mistress in 1745, as well as a close friend and confidante. She also wanted to be seen not just as a very attractive, sumptuously dressed courtesan, but a dedicated patron of the arts. She established her own salon, to which were invited writers like Voltaire and Diderot who were working on the *Encylopédie* which the Archbishop of Paris tried to stop. She made her own engravings and initiated book publishing. She adopted the Sèvres porcelain factory and made it the most famous in the world. She particularly patronised François Boucher, who produced several portraits of her, and in all of them she is wearing a sumptuous dress and holding a book, indicating that she was a well-read woman. This is a superb example of eighteenth-century spin.

François Boucher, *Madame de Pompadour*, 1756

Joseph Wright of Derby, *A Girl Reading a Letter with an Old Man Reading over her Shoulder* (c. 1767–70)

Joseph Wright painted this picture in *c.* 1767–70 but, as it has been in a private collection since that time, it was not seen in public until it was lent to the Derby Museum and Art Gallery in 2023 to sit alongside their own collection of Wright's paintings. In his painting Wright specialised in contrasting light and darkness. This painting is of interest since it shows how reading in the eighteenth century by the light of a single candle was insufficiently bright enough to allow more than one reader. The elderly man is making the most of the light by looking over the girl's shoulder and reading the letter through a lorgnette. As each candle lasted only a short time and was expensive, it meant many working-class readers could only do so in daylight. Middle-class women, on the other hand, were avid readers not only of letters but of novels.

Mary Wollstonecraft (1759–97)

An important book of rights, *A Vindication of the Rights of Woman*, was written by Mary Wollstonecraft as a pamphlet in 1792. It had a print run of 1,500 to 2,000 copies. It was not widely read. Copies had to be remaindered in 1794 and some lending libraries which had bought the pamphlet withdrew them at the end of the century as they were thought to be potentially revolutionary. The next edition appeared fifty years later and was distributed by the Chartists. The significant republication was in 1892 but it was not much mentioned by the Suffragettes, and its real impact upon women's rights had to wait for another one hundred years until the end of the twentieth century.

James Gillray, *Tales Of Wonder!*, 1 February 1802

Jane Collier, a satirist, wrote in 1753 that most men would 'rather have a woman could make a puddin, rather than one who could make a poem'. A treatise on female education in 1789 warned 'a passion for poetry is dangerous for a woman'. Nonetheless, many women could read, and young women frequently borrowed

James Gillray, *Tales Of Wonder!*, 1802

books from the local circulating library and would read them with their friends. This continues today with reading clubs where members choose a book for all to read and then discuss it in person or online.

In this reading group, the watch hanging from the waist of the reader shows that the time is 12:54am, so these friends have stayed up all night to read and hear about seduction, illicit romance and other scandals. The interest of this group is reflected in the picture on the wall showing an abduction, and also the figures on the mantelpiece. The title of the book lying on the table is *The Monk* written by Matthew Lewis, a Gothic novel containing demons, ghosts and witches. It is fairly clear that readers of the time did not want to hear about the bravery of British soldiers locked in a war to the death with the French.

The Early Nineteenth Century

A book that was designed to appeal to young women was the 'Keepsake', which was first published in 1828 and remained as a Christmas giftbook up to 1859, with all copies bound in scarlet leather. They featured prose, stories, essays, poetry, high-quality steel plate engravings, and some even had watercolours. Favourite poets included were Wordsworth and Coleridge, and very occasionally Shelley and Byron, though one of the collectors wrote about Byron, 'Love on his lips, and hatred in his heart.' The 'Keepsakes' proved so popular that some

William Chalon, *The Album*, 1836

women created their own albums in books published specifically with blank pages and which were, in effect, Commonplace books.

The albums conveyed a general sense of gentility and morality – there were no seductions, illicit relationships or rapes, and the gritty and dangerous lives of the poor did not feature.

William St Clair, the literary scholar, started to collect these albums in the 1980s when they sold for very little in second-hand bookshops. His collection of one hundred copies is now in the UCL Library.

The Browning Readers

In the late 19th century, William Rothenstein wanted to pay tribute to his favourite poet, Robert Browning, and he painted three pictures, of which this is one.

William Rothenstein, *The Browning Readers*, 1900

Rothenstein attempted to establish a relationship between the reader, the poet, the artist and the spectator. The serious readers in this picture are his wife Alice, who is seated, and her sister Grace Knewstub. The room is sparsely decorated in the style of the early nineteenth century, unlike the Victorian rooms that were full of chairs, tables, plants and paintings. It is interesting that no titles of any the books are discernible. It is a scene of serious serenity. Alice, relaxing on a cane chair, is concentrating hard by the light of a window and sitting close to a fire which clearly she had no hand in laying or refuelling, so there is someone else who is running the house. For both of them reading is a leisure pursuit. It is not possible to know which of the Browning poems she is reading, probably not *Porphyria's Lover* or *My Last Duchess*, in which two beautiful women are murdered, although another painting by Rothenstein was of the voluptuous Porphyria. I hope Alice may have been reading one of my favourite Browning poems, *A Toccata of Galuppi's*, which describes the sensual decadence of Venice and ends with a memorable question:

> As for Venice and her people, merely born to bloom and drop,
> Here on earth they bore their fruitage, mirth and folly were the crop:
> What of soul was left, I wonder, when the kissing had to stop?

Edouard John Mentha (1858–1915)

This Swiss artist painted several pictures depicting women working. Here, in this charming picture opposite, a housemaid is in a library which belongs to a scholar of natural history. This was likely to be a personal, rather than an official, library. Clearly the maid with her feather duster dangling behind her, has found dusting the shelves less interesting than a good read.

Women Novelists

In the nineteenth century women novelists added enormously to the culture of our country, including Jane Austen, Mary Shelley, Emily and Charlotte Brontë, George Eliot, Frances Trollope, Elizabeth Gaskell, Edith Nesbit, Frances Hodgson Burnett, and Ouida, and in America Harriet Beecher Stowe and Edith Wharton. Their works circulated widely and millions of copies were sold. In the twentieth and twenty-first centuries there has been an even larger expansion with literary novels to romantic novels. Some of the most famous novelists are Viriginia Woolf, Beryl Bainbridge, Iris Murdoch, Anita Brookner, A.S. Byatt, Angela Carter, Doris Lessing, Catherine Cookson, Jackie Collins, Jilly Cooper and Sally Rooney.

Edouard John Mentha, *Maid Reading in a Library*, 1915

Sally Rooney (1991–)

Sally Rooney published her first novel in her twenties and since then three more. She has a large readership. *Normal People* (2018) sold over one million copies and featured on television. Her latest, *Intermezzo* (2024), tells the complicated relationship of two brothers with an age gap of nine years – one a failing chess prodigy and the other a human rights lawyer self-medicating with alcohol, and their messy love lives as they cope with the death of their father. It became a bestseller, appealing to young readers of both sexes, as it explores the emotions and crises that so many experience in their own lives.

Marylin Monroe (1926–62)

This book is not just about men and boys reading today, for the greater readers of novels are women. It was always the case. I came across a celebrated photograph of Marilyn Monroe (1926–62) reading. She planned her successful film career herself, leaving nothing to chance, even to wearing a memorable swimsuit for this photograph. She always wanted the best: she married the best American football player, the best American playwright, and took as her lover the best American president. In my view, she wanted to be remembered as America's best dressed, not undressed, female – she wanted to leave an impression of culture. This is just what Madame de Pompadour, the mistress of Louis XV, achieved in the eighteenth century in her many portraits. Marilyn does not carry a fan, a purse, a piece of jewellery or hold a lapdog – she holds a book.

There are other photographs of Marilyn Monroe reading books, like Walt Whitman's *Leaves of Grass* and the play, *Death of Salesman*, by her husband Arthur Miller. This famous photograph was taken in 1955 by Eve Arnold, a celebrated photographer who photographed her many times. The book she is reading is the edition of James Joyce's *Ulysses* which was published after the famous censorship trial in 1933. In the sale of Marilyn's library after her death in 1962 it fetched $9,200. Her library also included books by Ernest Hemingway, Ian Fleming, Bernard Shaw, Dorothy Parker and Jack Kerouac.

In the photograph her fingers are inserted towards the end of *Ulysses*, which contains Molly Bloom's forty-page famous monologue in which she expresses pride in her body. The last five lines of her monologue are:

> I put the rose in my hair like the Andalusian girls used or shall
> I wear a red yes and how he kissed me under the Moorish wall
> and I thought well as well him as another and then I asked him

> with my eyes to ask again yes and then he asked me would I say yes to say yes my mountain flower and first I put my arms around him yes and drew him down to me so he could feel my breasts all perfume yes and his heart was going like mad and yes I said yes I will Yes.

Eve Arnold said that she had questioned Marilyn about reading *Ulysses*: 'She kept *Ulysses* in her car and had been reading it for a long time: she said she liked the sound of it and would read it aloud to try and make sense of it but she found it hard going.'

Chapter 6

Why Read Novels?

Books are 'uniquely portable magic'.

STEPHEN KING, THRILLER WRITER

THE FIRST NOVEL I READ WAS *The Count of Monte Cristo* by Alexandre Dumas, as I had seen a black-and-white film with Robert Donat playing Edmond Dantès who had been illegally imprisoned in the Château d'If. After six years in prison, Dantès managed to escape with the help of another prisoner who tells him where he has secreted his fortune. Having secured this, he returns to Paris as the Count of Monte Cristo to destroy the three men who had tried to destroy him – one is driven insane, another shoots himself and the third is ruined and bankrupted. It thrilled me because it is the best justice and revenge story I have ever read. I was lucky that one of my mother's friends had a beautiful copy with a leather spine which she kindly gave to me. I still have it.

It is not surprising this novel was published in Paris in 1838 because the novel as an art form was developed in France and England during the eighteenth century. The first novels often described travels in another country – *Robinson Crusoe* by Daniel Defoe (1719) and *Gulliver's Travels* by Jonathan Swift (1726), but a number were more daring, recounting personal and social relationships involving nubile young women and rakish young men – *Clarissa* by Samuel Richardson (1748) and *Tom Jones* by Henry Fielding (1749).

The novel took off in the nineteenth century with sweeping panoramas of societies and communities with all their social, moral and political challenges and problems. Other genres emerged, including detective stories, political dramas, planetary exploration and family sagas.

Reading so many novels helped me to understand how the world works. It is a very personal act that requires concentration and the dedication of time. I find it is better to try and finish a novel within two or three weeks or else you can lose the thread of it. As Philip Roth has said, 'If you read a novel for more than two weeks, you do not read the novel.'

Sometimes I find a novel does not appeal to me, and after one or two chapters I put it aside for, as Dickens said, 'There are books of which the backs and covers are the best part of it.' If you abandon a book then you are following Chaucer's advice: 'Therefore, who likes not this, let him, turn over page and choose another tale.'

I recently came across a comment by Elif Shafak, one of the most celebrated modern novelists whom Hanif Kureishi has called 'one of the best writers in the world today'. She has written eleven novels in English and Turkish, and has over 1.6 million followers on X. Her most recent book, *There are Rivers in the Sky* (2024), which relates the involvement of two rivers – the Thames and the Tigris – and a boy in the 1840s mudlarking in London and a young girl born on the banks of the Tigris today – is brilliant. This is her answer to the question, 'Why read a novel?'

> I think fiction is the antidote for extremely polarised and fractured times. It is a place we can still hold nuanced conversations, have multiple thoughts at the same time, open up difficult issues, and calmly ruminate. And also do some slow thinking, because we are always rushing into judgements. It is about empathy, trying to put yourself in the shoes of another person, to become that person for a few hours over a few days. I think that is a very good and humbling exercise for the soul.

It is generally recognised that Defoe's *Robinson Crusoe* was the first novel to tell the story of how a man survived after being shipwrecked on an island at the other end of the world for over twenty-eight years, two months and nineteen days. It tells of how he created a shelter for his home, the edible plants he cultivated, the creation of fire for warmth and cooking, how he defended himself with improvised weapons against hostile natives, and how he befriended one to become his assistant and friend, known as 'Man Friday'. In its first year, 2,000 copies were sold for 5 shillings, and it became a steady bestseller. It was the first edition to carry an illustrated picture of its hero. On re-reading it recently, I found it was an easy read because Defoe uses long sentences, some over twenty lines, which helped me with the flow of reading.

Defoe was unusual in that he championed the underdog. Robinson Crusoe was not from the aristocracy or the upper middle class, but from 'the upper station of low life'. Defoe's later novel, *Moll Flanders* (1722), tells of a woman who had to become a thief and a harlot after being seduced and abandoned by her lover; she was married five times, the last to a highwayman and they manage to escape to Virginia and ended happily living on a plantation. In *A Tour Thro' the Whole Island of Great Britain* (1724–6) Defoe supports poor villagers who tear down

Daniel Defoe (1660–1731)

Robinson Crusoe

fences erected by a landlord, Mr Guy, who tries to enclose the common land of the village 'which the poor liked to be as much their property as any rich man's land is his own'.

Samuel Richardson's *Clarissa* was a series of letters written over two years (1747–8) in seven volumes. Henry Fielding's *The History of Tom Jones* (1749), first published in six volumes, won many readers who liked an engaging rascal. It is unsurprising that novel reading was not widespread in the eighteenth century due to its prolixity. Jane Austen enjoyed reading them but realised that their sheer length would not make them bestsellers. She published *Pride and Prejudice* in three volumes in 1813 only after she had 'lopt & crop't so successfully'.

In Samuel Foote's play, *The Author* (1757), one of the characters giving advice to the would-be poet Cape said, 'Although novels are a pretty light summer reading, and do very well in Tunbridge and Bristol, and other watering places: no bad commodity for the West Indies trade neither. Let 'em be novels, Master Cape.' The novel really took-off in the early nineteenth century through the works of three writers of genius – Jane Austen, Walter Scott and Charles Dickens.

Jane Austen (1775–1817)

In 1797 Jane's father, proud of his twenty-one-year-old daughter's literary powers wrote to the publisher Cardell to see whether he would be interested in printing *Pride and Prejudice*. It was rejected by return of post. In 1811, her family printed and published *Sense and Sensibility* and there is no record of a print run, but it was probably quite modest. *Pride and Prejudice*, offered at 18 shillings, was published in 1813, and in the 1830s, after Jane's death, it became one of Bentley's Standard Novels selling 5,000 copies. *Mansfield Park* was published in 1814 and *Emma* in 1815 and offered at 21 shillings, but in 1818 500 copies of *Emma* had to be remaindered at 2 shillings. *Northanger Abbey* and *Persuasion* were published posthumously.

These novels sold modestly during the Victorian period, but it was Henry James at the end of the century who ranked her with Shakespeare. Her sales really took off after the Second World War, motivated by film and TV productions of the novels: she sold in millions, and Jane Austen was included in the school curriculum. In 1994, the renowned literary critic Harold Bloom placed her among the greatest Western writers of all time. Quite a contrast to Scott whose novels today are not much read outside Scotland.

Walter Scott (1771–1832)

Walter Scott published his first novel, *Waverley*, anonymously in 1814 and, as it in its first year sold 4,000 copies, he decided to start a new literary career as a novelist. Until his death in 1832 Scott published a new book every year, including *The Antiquary* (1815), *Old Mortality* (1816), *My Landlord* (1817), *Rob Roy* (1818) which sold 30,000 copies and *Ivanhoe* (1820). By the time of his death he had sold millions of copies and was the most widely read writer in Britain.

This print by Charles Williams (pseudonym 'ARGUS') published in 1825 is a satire on Scott's success. You cannot see the title of the book that the cook is reading, but the spine of the book lying on the table carries the words, *The Heart*

of Midlothian. This means it was not just the middle classes who read Scott, for a working-class cook was so intrigued that she neglected her cooking. Scott had broken new ground.

Charles Dickens (1812–70)

Dickens revolutionised the novel. As a journalist from 1833, he wrote sketches of characters for the press and published most of these in *Sketches by Boz* in 1836. They were issued in twenty paperbacks costing 1 shilling each and they also carried several advertisements to allay the cost of printing. The separate parts were usually printed with a run of 40,000 copies and in the following year he published *The Posthumous Papers of The Pickwick Club* in nineteen to twenty parts. It was not only read in the home, for I did come across a record of twenty men and women gathered in a locksmith's shop to listen to a reading of the newest number of *Pickwick Papers* borrowed from a circulating library at tuppence a day. He was to write sixteen novels and all became bestsellers.

Robert Seymour, *Mr Pickwick addresses the Club*, 1836

My father was responsible for my interest in Dickens. He had left school at the age sixteen when the general school leaving age was twelve, and those extra four years gave him the chance to read many books. I have a copy of the prize he got at his Elementary School in Newport when he was fourteen; a leatherbound copy of Scott's *Kenilworth*. He came to love Dickens and all his novels. He would read aloud to my sister and me the descriptions of some of the characters – Miss Haversham, Scrooge, the Artful Dodger, Micawber, Mrs Gamp, Pecksniff and Podsnap. We got to know them so well that we almost expected them to walk through the door. I have read and re-read all of Dickens' novels several times.

Dickens had a flair for describing his characters in a memorable way. In *Our Mutual Friend* (1865), Alfred Lammle and his wife are unscrupulous social adventurers. In just thirty-eight words he fixes Mr Lammle in your mind's eye:

> A mature young gentleman; with too much nose in his face, too much ginger in his whiskers, too much torso in his waistcoat, too much sparkle in his studs, his eyes, his buttons, his talk, and his teeth.

Skewered forever – as was Pecksniff, the hypocritical architect in *Martin Chuzzlewit* (1844) who was described as being like 'the direction post that is always telling the way to a place and never goes there'.

London was central to Dickens' works. He walked through the deserted streets by night and wrote about their people in the day. His fascination with amateur dramatics made him very perceptive as to how his characters speak. He captured their voices – the social climber Veneering was obsequious; Mr Podsnap a natural bully blustered; Uriah Heep, a creep, cringingly unctuous; Barkis simply honest; and the poetry of Sydney Carton's last words as he stepped up to the guillotine:

> It is a far, far better thing that I do, than I have ever done; it is a far, far better rest that I go to, than I have ever known.

The Popularity of Dickens

Dickens had so many readers in Victorian England because he was upholding their interests and speaking on their behalf against the Establishment. In *Oliver Twist* (1837) he condemned the Poor Law and the use of poor houses where Oliver was born and where he feared that he would become a chimney sweeper. In 1842 an Act was passed making it illegal for children to become chimney sweeps. Dickens did not want people sent to the prisons for debt, there being five in London, and the worst was the Marshalsea. In *Little Dorrit* (1857) he showed how it destroyed the lives of debtors.

Dickens had no time for bishops or the clergy – the Reverend Mr Chadband, a pious humbug in *Bleak House* (1852), had 'too much train oil in him'. In the novel he reproaches all of society for the death in abject poverty of Jo, the crossing sweeper, who had never been to a school or a church, and was always being 'moved along' by the police. He dies while repeating words from the Lord's Prayer, which he had never heard before, but which were being read to him for the first time:

> ... Dead, Your Majesty. Dead, My Lords and Gentlemen. Dead, Your Right Reverends, and Your Wrong Reverends, Reverends of every sort. Dead, Men and Women born with heavenly compassion in your hearts. And dying thus around us every day.

He also castigated school teachers for their bullying and cruelty – Squeers, Gradgrind and Bradley Headstone. Nicholas Nickleby, a teacher for a short time at Squeers' Dotheboys Hall describes how he found the boys;

> Pale and haggard faces, lank and bony figures, children with the countenances of old men, deformities with irons upon their limbs, boys of stunted growth and others whose long meagre legs would hardly bear their stooping bodies, all crowded on the view together; there were the bleared eye, the hare-lip, the crooked foot, and every ugliness or distortion that told of unnatural aversion conceived by parents for their offspring, or of young lives which, from the earliest dawn of infancy, had been one horrible endurance of cruelty and neglect. There were little faces which should have been handsome, darkened with the scowl of sullen dogged suffering; there was childhood with the light of its eye quenched, its beauty gone, and its helplessness alone remaining; there were vicious-faced boys brooding, with leaden eyes, like malefactors in a jail; and there were young creatures on whom the sins of their frail parents had descended, weeping even for the mercenary nurses they had known, and lonesome even in their loneliness.

Neither did Dickens have any time for lawyers, exposing the huge delays of the Lord High Chancellor in the High Court of Chancellery in the never-ending dispute over the will of Jarndyce and Jarndyce in *Bleak House*, which led to impoverishment and even suicide. Mr Tulkinghorn, a sinister lawyer, converted rooms in his house into sets of chambers where lawyers lived like 'maggots in nuts'. He satirised the ambitions of public servants, like the family of the Tite Barnacles in *Little Dorrit*, the civil servants of the day working in the Circumlocution Office, where they spent of most their time promoting their own careers instead of governing well. They were the masters of 'How Not to Do It'.

As Dickens had been a reporter of debates in Parliament, he had no time for MPs or peers:

> Then there is my Lord Boodle, of considerable reputation with his party, who has known what office is and who tells Leicester Dedlock with much gravity after dinner that he really does not see to what the present age is tending. The debate is not what a debate used to be; the House is not what the House used to be; even a Cabinet is not what it formerly was. He perceives with astonishment, that supposing the present government to be overthrown, the limited choice of the Crown in the formation of a new ministry, would be between Lord Coodle and Sir Thomas Doodle supposing it to be impossible for the Duke of Foodle to act with Goodle which may be assumed to be the case in consequence of the breach arising out of that affair with Hoodle. Then giving the Home Department and the leadership of the House of Commons to Joodle with the Exchequer to Koodle, the Colonies to Loodle, and the Foreign Office to Moodle. What are you to do with Noodle? You could offer him the presidency of the Council that is reserved for Poodle. You could put him in Woods and Forests: that is hardly good enough for Qoodle. What follows? The country is shipwrecked, lost, and gone to pieces (as is made manifest to the patriotism of Sir Leicester Dedlock) because you cannot provide for Noodle.

Illustrations in Dickens

Dickens hit upon the idea of making his books more attractive by including illustrations. Few novels printed in the late eighteenth or early nineteenth centuries had illustrations, but each *Pickwick* part had two engravings by a celebrated artist and illustrator. Dickens did not invent the addition of illustrations, for later he recalled that as a boy he had read *The Terrific Register* which had made him 'unspeakably miserable and frightening my very wits out of my mind ... as there was an illustration to every number in which there was always a pool of blood and at least one body. All this for the small charge of a penny weekly.'

In 1843 Dickens decided to publish *A Christmas Carol* by himself, rather than through a publisher, as he thought he could make more money. It did become the most read novel of the nineteenth century, but it did not make him rich, as knowing how important illustrations were in holding the readers' attention, Dickens commissioned four prints from John Leech, the leading illustrator. He also insisted upon yellow endpapers with all the pages having gilt edges, which increased the cost considerably. However, the story was so popular that it started the fashion of Christmas books and Dickens was to write a further four; many other romantic novelists flooded the market.

Apart from writing novels, Dickens found a way to promote them using his theatrical talent by giving public readings. His first was in 1853, from *A Christmas Carol*, at St Martin's Hall on Long Acre, London, to an audience of 2,000, just after the publication of *Bleak House*, in my view his greatest novel. It was also at a time when his life was in turmoil owing to a very public and embarrassingly humiliating separation from his wife, and the beginning of his private affair with Nelly Ternan. A second reading followed in 1857 at Manchester's Free Trade Hall which could take 4,000 people.

The readings brought out Dickens' theatricality and he adored pleasing the huge audiences, some of whom had queued for hours, and even through the night, and they reassured him with their 'roaring sea of responses'. His readings made a lot of money. In 1858 he arranged eighty-five reading tours through England, Scotland and Ireland. In 1862, after speaking in Leamington, Cheltenham, Plymouth, Torquay and Exeter, he boasted to his friend, John Forster, 'Think of the money, £191 a night!' – in today's money £17,600. Dickens was very commercially minded and he knew how much these readings would also increase his sales.

In 1866 Dickens appointed George Dolby, an out-of-work theatre manager, to manage his reading tours and they became close friends. As the actual performances were very demanding, it was Dolby who ensured that Dickens rested during the interval between his two readings with champagne and a dozen oysters. On his tour to America in 1867–8, he gave readings in Boston, New York, Philadelphia and Washington.

When I was a teenager, my father took me to see Emlyn Williams, the famous actor, dressed as Dickens, standing at his desk, reading out dramatic moments from *Oliver Twist*, *David Copperfield*, *Nicolas Nickleby* and *A Christmas Carol*. Most memorably I recall *A Tale of Two Cities* (1859), with the famous opening and the great party held by the hated Marquis St Evrémonde. As the marquis orders his carriage to speed away, it runs over and kills a small boy, and barely stopping he throws out a gold coin, but the coin is thrown back into the carriage by the innkeeper Ernest Defarge. From that moment the marquis is doomed.

W.H. Smith

Later in the century, the expansion of the railways led to W.H. Smith setting up its first stall in Euston Station in 1848 to sell novels and magazines alongside newspapers, including the very popular Yellowbacks, usually thrillers or adventure stories printed with a picture on the front cover. This became known as 'pulp fiction', as it was printed on cheap paper.

Joseph Conrad (1857–1924)

There were other popular novelists who produced brilliant books, including William Makepeace Thackeray with *Vanity Fair*, George Eliot with *Middlemarch* and Anthony Trollope's *Palliser* novels – the best political novels of the century. They were joined at the end of the century by Joseph Conrad who, as a Polish sea captain, had travelled widely, but especially in the East Indies which he wrote about after he had settled in England. His works are very different from other Victorian novels, for he examines the moral and psychological problems which people have to face in a crisis. In *Lord Jim* (1900), his most famous novel, he describes the consequent dismal life of a young captain who, in a great moment of cowardice, abandoned his ship as it was engulfed in a typhoon, thinking it would sink, even though it had a large number of pilgrims on board. It did not sink and he paid the price for his cowardice. I learnt a lot about cowardice from reading this novel.

Conrad's short novella, *Heart of Darkness*, has an interesting history as a book. It appeared in three editions in *The Blackwood Magazine* in 1899 and drew little attention and in a book of three short stories in 1902 entitled *Youth* – again attracting little attention, even though T.S. Eliot used a direct quote in his 1925 poem *The Hollow Men*, 'Mistah Kurtz – he dead.' In 1938 Orson Welles produced a radio programme and wanted to make a film, but that never materialised. The first Penguin paperback edition that I can find appeared in 1973.

As it contained two compelling issues – imperialism and racism – the novel really took-off after the Second World War and today it features in the curriculum of most sixth forms. I was quite surprised at the sheer volume of its readership, for when I searched Abebooks, the largest online retailer of second-hand books, for a copy of *Heart of Darkness*, I came across hundreds of new editions and books about it. Its younger readership boosted when TikTok's BookTok added *Heart of Darkness*.

When Conrad had sailed up the Congo River, he witnessed the cruelty and greed of Belgian colonialism in the acquisition of ivory. His central character sought to meet a man called Kurtz who was living far up the river in a trading post and who had become the unofficial but worshipped leader of many Africans, whom Conrad described as 'cannibals' or 'savages'. Kurtz had written a seventeen-page pamphlet for The International Society for the Suppression of Savage Customs and there was a scrawled note written later on the foot of the last page, 'Exterminate All the Brutes.' Later Conrad says this was written 'before Kurtz's nerves went astray and caused him to preside at certain midnight dances with unspeakable rights' – hinting at cannibalism.

He meets Kurtz in the compound of his house that was surrounded by poles carrying the severed heads of Africans. Kurtz who is dying utters his last words, 'The horror! The horror!' This book has led to many contrary opinions. The prizewinning author from Nigeria, Chinua Achebe, condemned Conrad's depiction of the Africans as 'the dehumanisation of Africa and Africans', but others have admired his portrayal of the pitiless, impenetrable, dark jungle which was 'a treacherous appeal to the lurking death, to the hideous evil and to the profound darkness of its heart'. It became the inspiration for the 1979 American film *Apocalypse Now* but its location was transferred to Vietnam.

Conrad answers the question of 'Why Read?' with this:

> My task which I am trying to achieve, by the power of the written word, is to make you hear, to make you feel – it is above all to make you see – and no more – and it is everything.

Yes, seeing is important and the two books which opened my eyes as a teenager were *A Child of the Jago* and *The Hole in the Wall* written in the 1890s by a much-underrated novelist, Arthur Morrison. They reveal how two young boys lived in the squalid poverty of the East London riverside areas, Wapping and Whitechapel, where the levels of unemployment were so high that many had to engage in criminality to survive. *The Hole in the Wall* is the name of a pub in which Stephen, the orphan, had to live with his grandfather, the publican. The book, which is a thriller, reveals his success in overcoming evil with good.

New Genres of Literature: Science Fiction, Detective Stories and Political Novels

In late Victorian England, there were significant changes in the volume of books that were printed and read which helped to create new areas of literary activity.

Science Fiction

When H.G. Wells published *The Time Machine* (1895), *The War of the Worlds* (1898) and *The First Men in the Moon* (1901), he created science fiction. In 1968 Arthur C. Clarke published *2001: A Space Odyssey* which soon sold over three million copies. Science fiction became very popular, especially with boys, and there was a wide range of graphic comics and novels. My favourite is by John Wyndham, *The Day of The Triffids* (1951), which describes an alien invasion of our planet.

Detective Novels

The first character in a major English novel described as a 'detective' was Inspector Bucket in *Bleak House* (1852). His squat, sturdy figure carrying a stick patiently investigates the mystery of Lady Deadlock and eventually discovers what had happened in her early life. Wilkie Collins wrote the first detective novel, *The Moonstone*, in 1868. His detective was Sergeant Cuff, a lean, grizzled elderly man who always wore black, including his top hat. He led the search to find the thief of the valuable moonstone.

In 1887 Conan Doyle, at the age of twenty-seven, created in *A Study in Scarlet* the most famous detective of all time – Sherlock Holmes – with his deerstalker

The first edition appeared in *Beeton's Christmas Annual* of 1887

Basil Rathbone as Sherlock Holmes

hat, pipe, violin and his occasional use of opium. When a visitor entered his apartment at 221B Baker Street, Holmes by carefully inspecting their clothes and shoes, found out where they came from, how they had travelled and why they were so anxious. Conan Doyle increased the popularity of Holmes with short stories that appeared in two volumes in 1892, *The Adventures of Sherlock Holmes* and *The Return of Sherlock Holmes*. He went on writing short stories up to the 1920s and there was one classic novel, *The Hound of the Baskervilles* (1902). The stories were turned into plays in the 1930s and films in the 1940s. I remember going to see as many of the black and white films as I could with Basil Rathbone playing Sherlock Holmes.

These stories were so successful that they were followed by a wave of many more detectives like Sexton Blake by Hal Meredith (1893), Father Brown by G.K. Chesterton (1911), Lord Peter Whimsey by Dorothy L. Sayers (1923), Bulldog Drummond by Sapper (1929), Albert Campion by Margery Allingham (1929), the novels of Edgar Wallace (1932), Philip Marlowe by Raymond Chandler (1939), Adam Dalgleish by P.D. James (1962), and from the late 1920s the most-widely read were Hercule Poirot and Miss Marple by Agatha Christie, and today Inspector Rebus by Ian Rankin and Mick Herron's down-at-heel detective, Jackson Lamb, in the twelve *Slough House* novels first published in 2016.

A sub-set also developed of spy novels – the first being *The Riddle of the Sands* by Erskine Childers in 1903 and perhaps most successfully with John Le Carré's George Smiley in 1961and James Bond in *Casino Royale* by Ian Fleming in 1953.

It is sometimes said that men do not read many novels, but these thrillers have been read by billions across the world and continue to be some of the most popular detective stories today.

Political Novels

While he was an MP, Benjamin Disraeli wrote two political novels in 1844 and 1845, *Coningsby* and *Sybil*, which highlighted the great divide in British society – 'The Privileged and the People formed two nations'. The Tories took this to heart and in 1867 Disraeli moved the amendments which extended the vote to many working men. A senior civil servant, Anthony Trollope (1815–82) wrote astute novels including the six *Palliser* novels about a family obtaining power and position in the hot house of Westminster. Similarly, there have been many American political novels set in the White House and the West Wing.

The two most famous political novels are by George Orwell (1903–50): *Animal Farm* and *1984*. The first, *Animal Farm* (1945), is a brilliant satire. The farm's pigs, led by Napoleon, take over from the humans, charting how liberal ideology can be converted into collective tyrannical authority. The pigs fall out as they come to realise that 'all animals are equal, but some are more equal than others' and they start to emulate human behaviour. This was brilliantly characterised in cartoons by Ralph Steadman.

The second was *1984* a devastating attack on totalitarianism which Orwell completed as he was dying in 1949. It is a classic description of how a state becomes a dictatorship and Soviet Communism under Stalin was clearly his

Even the pigs get married in Ralph Steadman's cartoon

target. Orwell coined memorable phrases: 'Big Brother' (Stalin, now Putin), 'Double Think', 'Thought Police' and 'Newspeak'. It became very popular in the US, with *Time* magazine naming it as one of the best one hundred English novels. It remains widely read in schools today. Orwell's beautiful mastery of the English language means his books and essays have become the source of many famous quotations.

I have found that politicians generally are not avid readers of novels, but are very heavy readers of newspapers, magazines, and the biographies and memoirs of politicians, including those dead and others still alive. Gone are the days when Harold Macmillan in 1917 read his copy of *Aeschylus* in the original Greek as he lay wounded in a shell hole for twelve hours. Unusually, Rishi Sunak's Cabinet included a talented novelist, Jesse Norman, who published *The Winding Stair* in 2023. This explores the struggle for power between Francis Bacon, the Lord Chancellor, and his rival Edward Coke, the Lord Chief Justice. It may sound uninviting, but it is a brilliant story of political rivalry.

Novels of the Twentieth Century

At the beginning of the twentieth century there were two major writers of modernist novels – James Joyce (1882–1941) and Virginia Wolf (1882–1941). In 1922 James Joyce's novel *Ulysses* was published in Paris, since its explicit sexual content would have led to prosecution in England. Paris was chosen because an enterprising American publisher, Sylvia Beach, opened a bookshop, Shakespeare and Company, selling and publishing avant-garde books which had been banned in other countries for supporting political or social minorities, or promoting sexual freedom. She published *Ulysses* for ten editions and I have a copy of her last edition which had no title or author's name on the binding. Today, *Ulysses* is considered a masterpiece with its stream of consciousness from one day in the life of Leopold Bloom. I found it rather tedious, but I admired the last forty pages which are the unpunctuated reflections of his wife, Molly.

Virginia Woolf lived in Monk's House, a small house in the village of Rodmell, East Sussex. Many years later, when we moved into the next village, I took a lot of friends to visit it. A great number of contemporary leading figures from the literary and academic worlds have passed through the door of Monk's House, though very few would have stayed overnight as they very most she could offer was a small, single bedroom. In the garden, she had built a wooden writing shed that was spacious and light, and she used it for all her works: it was her own *Room of One's Own* (1929). Inspired by the garden she wrote, 'I shall smell a red rose, shall gently surge across the lawn ... light a cigarette, take my writing board on my knee and let myself down like a diver very cautiously into the last sentence I wrote yesterday.' I have read *Mrs Dalloway* (1925) and *To the Lighthouse* (1927), but

I most enjoyed her two series of books of essays and criticisms on other writers, *The Common Reader* (1925 and 1932). Her judgment was sound and her writing divine.

Later in the twentieth century three English novelists became bestsellers, including Somerset Maugham, Evelyn Waugh and Graham Greene.

Somerset Maugham (1874–1965)

A prolific and famous writer in his time, Maugham wrote twenty novels including *Of Human Bondage* and *Cakes and Ale*, twenty plays and 120 short stories which I think are his best. Two, *The Alien Corn* and *Rain*, are dramatic tragedies which have appeared on television.

Evelyn Waugh (1903–66)

I enjoyed Waugh's early novels set in the 1920s and 1930s – *Decline and Fall* (1928), *Vile Bodies* (1930), *Black Mischief* (1932) and *A Handful of Dust* (1934). The last title comes from T.S. Eliot's *The Wasteland* (1922) and, like him, Waugh believed the First World War had undermined 'the standards of civilisation' and 'the network of a traditional culture'. He recorded 'the immense panorama of futility and anarchy that was contemporary history'. These books are witty, a sort of comic absurdity full of charlatans, rogues, failed teachers, cads, cadgers and aimable nitwits

Graham Greene (1904–1991)

Graham Greene's novels take the reader on journeys through Cuba, Africa, Liberia, Mexico, Haiti and Vietnam, and all the temptations and experiences of today's life. He described himself as an agnostic Catholic and four of his masterpieces were just that – *Brighton Rock* (evil youth), *The Power and the Glory* (a drunken priest), *The End of the Affair* (marital infidelity) and *The Heart of the Matter* (treachery) which was also the theme of his most famous short story, *The Third Man*, subsequently made into an immensely popular film with Orson Welles. In the preface to *The Power and the Glory*, which features a 'whisky priest' – a phrase he invented – he quotes a passage from *Bishop Blougram's Apology* by Robert Browning:

> Our interest's on the dangerous edges of things.
> The honest thief, the tender murderer,
> The superstitious atheists, demirep
> That loves and saves her soul in new French books –
> We watch while these in equilibrium keep
> The giddy line midway: one step aside ...

Greene's books are full of such characters with an ambiguous mixture of good and evil, where goodness is often flawed and the immoral reveal some goodness. Since he once served in the Secret Service, Greene traces the nebulous border between loyalty and disloyalty.

There are many other widely read novelists – Salman Rushdie, Hilary Mantel, Hanif Kureishi, Kazuo Ishiguro, Robert Harris, Sally Rooney and Sunjeev Sahota.

Salman Rushdie (1947–)

Born in Bombay, Salman Rushdie came to England at the age of seven, and went to Rugby School, then King's College, Cambridge. His second novel, *Midnight's Children*, is about the life of a child born on the first day of India's independence. It launched him into fame, winning the Booker Prize in 1981, and it was selected twice as 'the best novel of all winners' to mark the twenty-fifth and fortieth anniversaries of the prize. If that literary fame was not enough, his book *The Satanic Verses* (1988) made him a world figure through its irreverent depiction of the Prophet Mohammed and some of his Koran verses. On 14 February 1989, the Ayatollah Khomeini issued a fatwa ordering Rushdie's execution for blasphemy. This led to him having to live a guarded and secretive life for many years. In August 2022, while preparing to speak at a public meeting in New York, he was stabbed several times in the head and hands which led to him losing his sight in one eye and the use of one hand. He has continued to write and he has written about this quite brilliantly in *Knife* (2024). As a major novelist, his books will continue to be read for years to come.

Hilary Mantel (1952–2022)

In three novels, two of which won the Booker Prize (*Wolf Hall* in 2009 and *Bring Up the Bodies* in 2012), Hilary Mantel recreated the life of Thomas Cromwell, the leading minister in the court of Henry VIII. They were about power, its exercise and its loss, and their empathy made compelling reading and became immensely popular with versions on television, in the theatre and the cinema – they are the very best historical novels.

Hanif Kureishi (1954–)

Rushdie is joined by many Caribbean, Asian and African writers. Hanif Kureishi's *The Buddha of Suburbia* (1990) was a bestseller, widely read in schools, and made into a popular television programme. He also wrote the screenplay of the hit film *My Beautiful Launderette*. In 2022 he suffered a terrible accident that partially paralysed him, but his speech and mind were not affected. He has been able to dictate a book describing how he nearly died, *Shattered: A Memoir* (2024).

Kazuo Ishiguro (1954–)

Ishiguro left Japan as a five-year-old when his father, a research scientist, accepted a new job in Guildford, Surrey. He attended a local primary school and a grammar school in Woking, continuing to speak Japanese to his parents and having a regular supply of comics, magazines and books sent from Japan. Ishiguro's talent as an English author developed when he studied creative writing at the University of East Anglia, where he wrote three short stories about Japan. I was fortunate to publish these stories in a limited edition, Belmont Press in 2000, for which Ishiguro wrote a new introduction about his early life in England. As a novelist, his first two novels were set in Japan, *A Pale View of Hills* (1982) and *An Artist of the Floating World* (1986), and these were followed by other celebrated novels set in England like *Never Let Me Go* (2005) and *Remains of the Day* (1989) which won the Booker Prize. His great talents have been recognised by the award of the Nobel Prize for Literature in 2017 and a knighthood in 2018.

Robert Harris (1957–)

I got to know Robert Harris when he was the political editor of the *Observer*. As I was one of the most liberal Conservative MPs, he invited me to several gossipy lunches. He gave up his successful journalism to write novels. His first, *Fatherland* (1992), about a world in which the Nazis had won the war, was a bestseller. He recreates the past with a brilliant attention to detail. *An Officer and a Spy* (2013) is a gripping read and the best description of the Dreyfus Affair I have ever read.

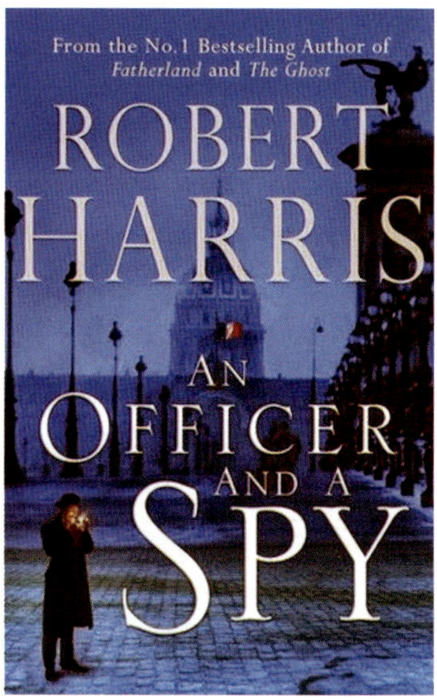

Conclave (2016), now made into a film, tells of a papal election and one of my friends who knows a cardinal said that it is very realistic. His 'Cicero' trilogy tells of the fight for power, the exercise of power and the abuse of power – nothing changes.

All his books are very readable and his latest tells of how Asquith, the Liberal Prime Minister in 1916, wrote love letters during Cabinet meetings dealing with war crises to Venetia Stanley, who may well have been his mistress.

There are other contemporary novelists I enjoy:

Zadie Smith (1975–)

In 2000, at the age of twenty-four, Zadie Smith published her first novel, *White Teeth*. It tells of the friendship between Archie Jones from England and Samad Iqbal from Bangladesh who first met as members of a tank crew in 1945. It follows their lives and marriages to Clara and Alsana, and is a brilliant portrayal how families live together in a multiracial society during the decline of the British Empire. It was a forerunner of novels about societies and cultures coming together in multiculturalism. It is a classic work and one that is so confident its opening paragraph makes a joke about suicide:

> Early in the morning, late in the century, Cricklewood Broadway. On 06.26 hours on 1 January 1975 Alfred Archibald Jones was dressed in corduroy and sat in a fume-filled Cavalier Musketeer Estate, face down on the steering wheel, hoping the judgement would not be too heavy upon him ... this was a decided-upon suicide. In fact, it was a New Year's resolution.

John Le Carré, who made spying an art form, and Jonathan Coe whose novels about the state of England under Margaret Thatcher, *What a Carve Up*, post-Tony Blair, *Middle England*, and post-Liz Truss, *The Proof of My Innocence*, will be read for years to come; and I came across Ali Smith and her brilliant novel *Hotel World* when I chaired the Booker Prize in 2001.

Sunjeev Sahota (1981–)

Sahota's novel *The Spoiled Heart* was published in 2024 and all the characters are working class. It is a political thriller based in Chesterfield about an election for the general secretary of the largest trade union. Just as Dickens made his readers aware of London, so Sahota makes us aware of Chesterfield. The favourite candidate is a middle-aged immigrant who has worked his way up and become a strong socialist for whom the bosses are the enemy. His strapline is 'A Worker for Workers'. He feels no need to appeal to black, brown or white trade unionists. His opponent is a wealthy, middle-class young woman who plays on race as most of the electors are white, and she knows how to hit below the belt. Their final debate is the fairest and best exposure that I have read of the issues of race, colour and faith which face our society today. Unfortunately it did not make the Booker Prize shortlist, probably squeezed out by three American novelists.

Beside Novels

Apart from novels, I have read many other books – histories, memoirs, biographies – and there are three I would like to highlight:

Keith Thomas' *Religion and the Decline of Magic* (1971) is a fascinating description of reading matter before the days of the Enlightenment of the eighteenth century. Thomas explains how 'astrology, witchcraft, magical healing, divination, ancient prophesies, ghosts and fairies are all now rightly distained by intelligent persons. But they were taken seriously by equally intelligent persons in the past and it is the historian's business to explain why this was so.'

The second is A.J.P. Taylor's *First World War, An Illustrated History* published by Penguin in 1963. He was one of my tutors at Magdalen College, Oxford and I learnt a lot by sitting at his feet. Penguin has wonderful pictures with very witty comments. A.J.P. also made me realise that Charles James Fox (1749–1806) was the first Leader of the Opposition.

The third is *The Assassin's Cloak, An Anthology of the World's Greatest Diarists* edited by Irene Taylor and Alan Taylor and published by Canongate Books in 2000. It is a wonderful book of diary excerpts which are frank, full of wit, wisdom and lashes of venom. This is Jean Cocteau's comment on a dinner he had with the Duke and Duchess of Windsor in Paris in 1953:

> Last night I dined at the Anchorenas with the Windsors. After the dinner the Duke had lost his cigarette holder. We were all of us down on all our fours. 'He loses everything,' the Duchess murmured, 'And I am always the one who finds it for him again.' I was thinking: not his crown.

This is George Bernard Shaw in 1929 on T.E. Lawrence:

> We spoke about Lawrence (of Arabia) who is an intimate friend of the Bernard Shaws and his eccentric shyness of publicity. Once Lawrence complained about every move of his being followed by the press. 'Well of course they notice you,' Shaw replied. 'You always hide just in the middle of the limelight.'

Another favourite text of mine is Shakespeare's play *Henry IV* which I first studied at school, in particular Falstaff's speech on honor. In the 2012 BBC adaptation *The Hollow Crown*, John Falstaff is played by Simon Russell Beale.

FALSTAFF: Hal, if thou see me down in the battle and bestride me, so; 'tis a point of friendship.

PRINCE: Nothing but a colossus can do thee that friendship. Say thy prayers, and farewell.

FALSTAFF: I would 'twere bedtime, Hal, and all well.

PRINCE: Why, thou owest God a death. He exits.

FALSTAFF: 'Tis not due yet. I would be loath to pay Him before His day. What need I be so forward with Him that calls not on me? Well, 'tis no matter. Honor pricks me on. Yea, but how if honor prick me off when I come on? How then? Can honor set to a leg? No. Or an arm? No. Or take away the grief of a wound? No. Honor hath no skill in surgery, then? No. What is honor? A word. What is in that word "honor"? What is that "honor"? Air. A trim reckoning. Who hath it? He that died o' Wednesday. Doth he feel it? No. Doth he hear it? No. 'Tis insensible, then? Yea, to the dead. But will it not live with the living? No. Why? Detraction will not suffer it. Therefore, I'll none of it. Honor is a mere scutcheon. And so ends my catechism.

Chapter 7

Why Read Newspapers?

The mighty power of Public Opinion embodied in a Free Press which persuades and checks, and perhaps, even in the last resort, nearly governs the whole.

George Canning, the Foreign Minister, 1822

THE FIRST PIECE OF PAPER THAT REPORTED NEWS about a British current event was a pamphlet published in September 1513 known as *The Trewe Encountre*. It was an eye-witness account of the Battle of Flodden which had occurred on 9 September, listing casualties and those who had distinguished themselves. Such news-sheets appeared in England on a few occasions in the sixteenth century.

At the beginning of the seventeenth century there was a huge appetite for news by merchants, soldiers, landowners, farmers, politicians, literate women and the clergy. They wanted to know what was happening at court, in Parliament and in the City; and also, what plays were being shown in London and if they were worth seeing. Many hurried to the bookshops, the printing presses or to the houses with the post to learn what was novel, interesting, perilous, scandalous or salacious – gossip was a great driver.

News was such an issue that Ben Jonson in 1625 wrote a play, *The Staple of Newes*, satirising a business ('a staple') whose role was to sell news to the public.

> *Newes* was a weekly cheat to draw money in by raiſing this ridiculous *Office* of the *Staple*, where-in the age may ſee her owne folly, or hunger and thirſt after publiſh'd pamplets of *Newes*, ſet out euery Saturday, but made all at home, & no ſyllable of truth in them: then which there cannot be a greater diſeaſe in nature, or a fouler ſcorne put vpon the times. And ſo apprehending it, you ſhall doe the *Author*, and your owne judgement a courteſie, and perceuie the tricke of alluring money to the *Office*, and there cooz'ning the people. If you haue the truth, reſt quiet, and conſider that:

Ficta, voluptatis causa, sint proxima veris.
Fictions meant to please should approximate to the truth

Horace's *Ars Poetica*

Horace is explaining that what is written must keep imagined writing reasonably close to experienced reality. A few lines later, he adds another famous definition: *ut pictura poesis* – a poem is like a picture – so satirical poetry would be ruled out.

Monarchs and governments wanted to ensure that any news questioning or undermining their authority was not going to be circulated widely. Political news was always sensitive and James I (r. 1603–25) set up a censor to approve any publicity and the London Stationers' Company was given a monopoly on the printing and selling of books in England.

The English Civil War (1642–51) saw a great thirst for information about Parliament and the armies in the field which was met by a flood of news pamphlets. At the beginning the parliamentary party had the lead, but in 1643 the Royalists caught up by printing in Oxford the *Mercurius Aulicus* and which later carried several verbatim reports of the trial and execution of Charles I. Oliver Cromwell decided to approve only two periodicals, one to report on Parliament and the other on foreign affairs, as England was then at war with Holland.

After the Restoration in 1660 (the return of the monarchy with Charles II), Parliament was very concerned about the spreading of false news. In 1664, a proclamation was issued by the King for, 'The Suppressing of Seditious and Treasonable Books and Pamphlets which are libels against the Government or against any Public or Private Person whatever to be seized and Makers, Presenters, Sellers, or Publishers of the same to be apprehended and committed to Prison.'

Samuel Butler (1613–80), the seventeenth-century satirical playwright, defined a newsmonger as 'a retailer of rumour who deals in a commodity that will not keep ... true or false is all one to him; for novelty being the grace of both a truth goes stale as soon as a lie'. Desperate to get readers, the *True Protestant Mercury* published in London in 1680 had a heading, 'News, Rare, New, True News, Delicate, Dreadful, Horrible, Bloody News from France and Ireland, you never heard the like before you were born'. Lord Northcliffe, in creating his newspapers at the end of the nineteenth century would have absolutely agreed.

Another source of news were the publications of the Royal Society, which was established in 1663 with the support of Charles II. Their purpose was to stimulate scientific and mathematical experiments, and their work was enhanced by Isaac Newton being the President from 1703 to 1727. They published their findings in the *Philosophical Transactions* of the Royal Society, which was not only read by scholars but all who wanted to find out how science was shaping their world.

One of the Society's members was John Houghton, an apothecary and also a businessman, with a shop close to the Royal Exchange, from where he imported tea, coffee and chocolate. He published weekly *A Collection for the Improvement of Husbandry and Trade 1692–1703*, which provided information for his readers on how they could increase their trade and help them to understand how the Bank of England worked. This was possibly the first sight of a weekly *Economist*.

The source of overseas news came from the Post Office Packet System set up in Tudor times, whereby ships carried not only goods but also information about what was happening overseas, particularly at those times when British forces were engaged in a war. The ships were built to be speedy and were lightly armed. Falmouth became a packet station in 1688 to receive news from France and northern Europe. There were also stations at Dover and Essex which had good road links to London, which proved essential in the early nineteenth century when Napoleon was trying to dominate trade in the English Channel. The service lasted until 1823 when its role was assumed by the Admiralty.

T.G. Dutton, *The New York & London Packet Ship Southampton*, c. 1840

In the seventeenth and eighteenth centuries there were many sources of news usually provided for people who had an interest in knowing what was happening and who paid a subscription for it. From 1758 the *London Exchange*, published by John Casting, reported twice weekly on the price of gold, wheat, rye, barley and oats; the arrival and departure of ships; any issues by the Bank of England and the rates for annuities. A second source were the Bills of Mortality which reported christening and burials in London and Westminster, and later

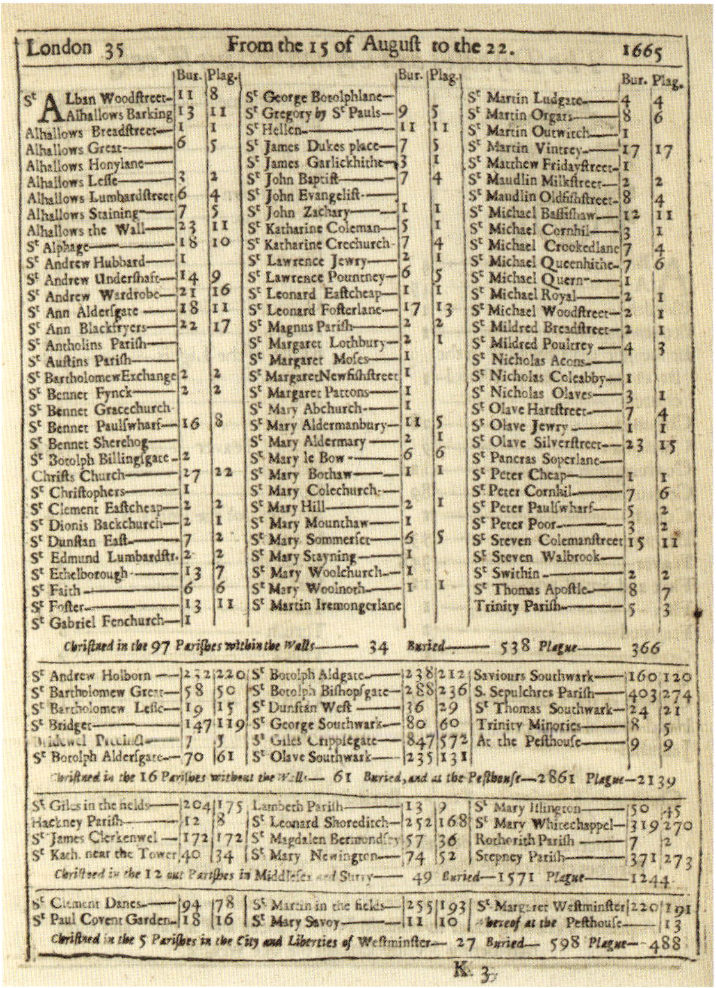

London 35 — From the 15 of Auguſt to the 22. — 1665

	Bur.	Plag.		Bur.	Plag.		Bur.	Plag.
St Alban Woodſtreet	11	8	St George Botolphlane			St Martin Ludgate	4	4
Alhallows Barking	13	11	St Gregory by St Pauls	9	5	St Martin Orgars	8	6
Alhallows Breadſtreet	1	1	St Hellen	11	11	St Martin Outwitch	1	
Alhallows Great	6	5	St James Dukes place	7	5	St Martin Vintrey	17	17
Alhallows Honylane			St James Garlickhithe	3	1	St Matthew Fridayſtreet	1	
Alhallows Leſſe	3	2	St John Baptiſt	7	4	St Maudlin Milkſtreet	2	2
Alhallows Lumbardſtreet	6	4	St John Evangeliſt			St Maudlin Oldfiſhſtreet	8	4
Alhallows Staining	7	5	St John Zachary	1	1	St Michael Baſſiſhaw	12	11
Alhallows the Wall	23	11	St Katharine Coleman	5	1	St Michael Cornhil	3	1
St Alphage	18	10	St Katharine Crechurch	7	4	St Michael Crookedlane	7	4
St Andrew Hubbard	1		St Lawrence Jewry	2	1	St Michael Queenhithe	7	6
St Andrew Underſhaft	14	9	St Lawrence Pountney	6	5	St Michael Quern	1	
St Andrew Wardrobe	21	16	St Leonard Eaſtcheap	1	1	St Michael Royal	2	1
St Ann Alderſgate	18	11	St Leonard Foſterlane	17	13	St Michael Woodſtreet	2	1
St Ann Blackfryers	22	17	St Magnus Pariſh	2	2	St Mildred Breadſtreet	2	1
St Antholins Pariſh			St Margaret Lothbury	2	1	St Mildred Poultrey	4	3
St Auſtins Pariſh			St Margaret Moſes	1		St Nicholas Acons		
St BartholomewExchange	2	2	St MargaretNewfiſhſtreet	1		St Nicholas Coleabby	1	
St Bennet Fynck	2	2	St Margaret Pattons	1		St Nicholas Olaves	3	1
St Bennet Gracechurch			St Mary Abchurch	1		St Olave Hartſtreet	7	4
St Bennet Paulſwharf	16	8	St Mary Aldermanbury	11	5	St Olave Jewry	1	1
St Bennet Sherehog			St Mary Aldermary	2	1	St Olave Silverſtreet	23	15
St Botolph Billingſgate	2		St Mary le Bow	6	6	St Pancras Soperlane		
Chriſts Church	27	22	St Mary Bothaw	1	1	St Peter Cheap	1	1
St Chriſtophers	1		St Mary Colechurch			St Peter Cornhil	7	6
St Clement Eaſtcheap	2	2	St Mary Hill	2	1	St Peter Paulſwharf	5	2
St Dionis Backchurch	2	1	St Mary Mounthaw	1		St Peter Poor	3	2
St Dunſtan Eaſt	7	2	St Mary Sommerſet	6	5	St Steven Colemanſtreet	15	11
St Edmund Lumbardſtr.	2	2	St Mary Stayning	1		St Steven Walbrook		
St Ethelborough	13	7	St Mary Woolchurch	1		St Swithin	2	2
St Faith	6	6	St Mary Woolnoth	1	1	St Thomas Apoſtle	8	7
St Foſter	13	11	St Martin Iremongerlane			Trinity Pariſh	5	3
St Gabriel Fenchurch	1							

Chriſtned in the 97 Pariſhes within the Walls — 34 *Buried* — 538 *Plague* — 366

St Andrew Holborn	232	220	St Botolph Aldgate	238	212	Saviours Southwark	160	120
St Bartholomew Great	58	50	St Botolph Biſhopſgate	288	236	S. Sepulchres Pariſh	403	274
St Bartholomew Leſſe	19	15	St Dunſtan Weſt	36	29	St Thomas Southwark	24	21
St Bridget	147	119	St George Southwark	80	60	Trinity Minories	8	5
Bridewel Precinct	7	5	St Giles Cripplegate	847	572	At the Peſthouſe	9	9
St Botolph Alderſgate	70	61	St Olave Southwark	235	131			

Chriſtned in the 16 Pariſhes without the Walls — 61 *Buried, and at the Peſthouſe* — 2861 *Plague* — 2139

St Giles in the fields	204	175	Lambeth Pariſh	13	9	St Mary Iſlington	50	45
Hackney Pariſh	12	8	St Leonard Shoreditch	252	168	St Mary Whitechappel	319	270
St James Clerkenwel	172	172	St Magdalen Bermondſey	57	36	Rotherith Pariſh	7	2
St Kath. near the Tower	40	34	St Mary Newington	74	52	Stepney Pariſh	371	273

Chriſtned in the 12 out Pariſhes in Middleſex and Surry — 49 *Buried* — 1571 *Plague* — 1244

St Clement Danes	94	78	St Martin in the fields	255	193	St Margaret Weſtminſter	220	191
St Paul Covent Garden	18	16	St Mary Savoy	11	10	*whereof at the* Peſthouſe		13

Chriſtned in the 5 Pariſhes in the City and Liberties of Weſtminſter — 27 *Buried* — 598 *Plague* — 488

K 3

The Bills of Mortality for the week 15–22 August 1665

across the country. These were compiled by parish clerks and their Worshipful Company was given the monopoly of bills which they could then be put up for sale. These carried information that was absolutely vital in a plague year.

Coffee houses had been common in the Muslim world and they spread to Europe in the middle of the seventeenth century, the first opening in Venice in 1647. In 1682, a Greek, Pasqua Roseé, opened a coffee house in St Michael's Alley, Cornhill, in the City of London. Before the days of radio, television and the mobile phone, information about what was happening in the world was sought by agents of government, traders, the armed forces and politicians, and coffee houses became an easy and popular place to meet friends and neighbours who talked and gossiped over whatever interested them. Samuel Pepys obtained 'great pleasure in this place's diversity of company and discourse'. Instead of gin or ale, coffee – which had been introduced by travellers – quickly became popular and Alexander Pope in *The Rape of the Lock* (1712) referred to its importance:

> Coffee which makes the politician wise
> And see through all things with his half-shut eyes.

The owners provided news-sheets for their customers, and politics was popular for the two parties often used coffee houses for their meetings. Their popularity was recognised by a poem of 1672 :

> There's nothing done in all the World,
> From Monarch to the Mouse;
> But every Day or Night 'tis hurl'd
> Into the Coffee House.

Jonathan Swift, on the other hand, warned his readers not to accept 'the echo of a London coffee house for the voice of the kingdom'. Nonetheless, they attracted many gentlemen to relax, chat and read, and what attracted James Boswell was a coffee house that 'was dusky, comfortable and warm'.

A rare image of a seventeenth-century coffee house

Newspapers in coffee houses provided endless comment and debate which no government could police. Today's coffee houses are X, Facebook and Instagram, but social media is without physical contact and that makes it much more dangerous.

The first official newspaper was the *Oxford Gazette*, published on 15 November 1665. Why Oxford? Because the plague had forced the court, Parliament and the judicature to move there from London. The paper was a single sheet printed on both sides and with double columns. It contained besides official notices, court and foreign news, and advertisements.

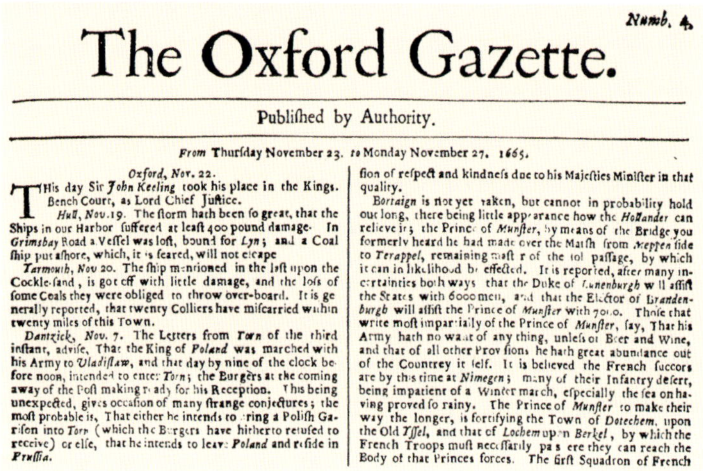

Numb. 4.

The Oxford Gazette.

Publiſhed by Authority.

From Thurſday November 23. *to* Monday November 27. 1665.

Oxford, Nov. 22.

THis day Sir *John Keeling* took his place in the Kings-Bench Court, as Lord Chief Juſtice.

Hull, Nov. 19. The ſtorm hath been ſo great, that the Ships in our Harbor ſuffered at leaſt 400 pound damage. In *Grimsbay* Road a Veſſel was loſt, bound for *Lyn*; and a Coal ſhip put aſhore, which, it is feared, will not eſcape.

Yarmouth, Nov 20. The ſhip mentioned in the laſt upon the Cockle-ſand, is got off with little damage, and the loſs of ſome Coals they were obliged to throw over-board. It is generally reported, that twenty Colliers have miſcarried within twenty miles of this Town.

Dantzick, Nov. 7. The Letters from *Torn* of the third inſtant, adviſe, That the King of *Poland* was marched with his Army to *Uladiſlaw*, and that day by nine of the clock before noon, intended to enter *Torn*; the Burgers at the coming away of the Poſt making ready for his Reception. This being unexpected, gives occaſion of many ſtrange conjectures; the moſt probable is, That either he intends to bring a Poliſh Gariſon into *Torn* (which the Burgers have hitherto refuſed to receive) or elſe, that he intends to leave *Poland* and reſide in *Pruſſia*.

ſion of reſpect and kindneſs due to his Majeſties Miniſter in that quality.

Bortaign is not yet taken, but cannot in probability hold out long, there being little appearance how the *Hollander* can relieve it; the Prince of *Munſter*, by means of the Bridge you formerly heard he had made over the Marſh from *Meppen* ſide to *Terappel*, remaining maſter of the only paſſage, by which it can in likelihood be effected. It is reported, after many incertainties both ways that the Duke of *Lunenburgh* will aſſiſt the States with 6000 men, and that the Elector of *Brandenburgh* will aſſiſt the Prince of *Munſter* with 7000. Thoſe that write moſt impartially of the Prince of *Munſter*, ſay, That his Army hath no want of any thing, unleſs of Beer and Wine, and that of all other Proviſions he hath great abundance out of the Countrey it ſelf. It is believed the French ſuccors are by this time at *Nimegen*; many of their Infantry deſert, being impatient of a Winter march, eſpecially the ſeaſon having proved ſo rainy. The Prince of *Munſter* to make their way the longer, is fortifying the Town of *Dotechem*, upon the Old *Yſſel*, and that of *Lochem* upon *Berkel*, by which the French Troops muſt neceſſarily paſs ere they can reach the Body of that Princes forces. The firſt Squadron of French

The Readers

An early reader was Samuel Pepys who bought on 1 August 1667 the *London Gazette* (as most people had now returned to London from Oxford) and he thought it to be 'a very pretty, full of newes, and no folly in it'. The paper came out three days a week.

At the beginning of the eighteenth century several papers joined the *London Gazette*, including the *Post Boy*, the *Post Man* and the *Flying Post*, with several coming out twice weekly. Newspapers were not just for London, as the Dover and Colchester roads had a 'Post' every other day.

The content of the *Gazette* was controlled by the Secretary of State, Viscount Bolingbroke, who vetted the news provided by the Post Office, which was the clearing house for news. In return, the Post Office was provided with free copies of the *Gazette*, which it could sell. This was the way that readers received the official government line, and so from the very start secrecy and public information were closely intertwined.

In 1695, as MPs could not agree on how to handle the news, the government decided to abolish the London Stationers' Company and its monopoly for printing and bookselling – this spelt the end of press licensing laws. No other country introduced such a radical move because it released in England – where there was a spread of literacy – a huge expansion of free speech and free printing. Another effect was that publishers had to find additional ways of funding their printing costs and their investment in paper, and this led them to increase the number of advertisements, which saw the birth of the advertising industry. In 1769, after newspapers had been established in North America, the *New York Gazette* called advertisements 'the life of a paper'.

Political Newspapers

In 1702 the first daily newspaper, the *Daily Courant*, was published and designed so as 'to give all the material news as soon as every post arrived'.

In Oliver Goldsmith's novel *The Vicar of Wakefield* (1766), the vicar finds himself questioned by the convenor of a radical meeting in a grand house:

> He asked if I had seen the last *Monitor* to which replying in the negative, 'What not the *Auditor*?' I suppose he cried. 'Neither Sir' I returned. 'That's very strange. Now I read all the politics that come out – the *Daily*, the *Public*, the *Ledger*, the *Chronicle*, the *London Evening*, The *Whitehall Evening*, the 17 magazines and the two reviews and, although they hate each other, I love them all. Liberty, Sir, is the Briton's boast and by all my coalmines in Cornwall I reverence its guardians.'

The *Monitor* was published from 1755–65, financed by the Beckford family who were very strong supporters of William Pitt the Elder. It was renowned for its aggressive style which provoked hostile reviews on its articles:

> They are like meddling sermons preached by a phlegmatic preacher, plain, heavy, and soporiferous, they co-operate with the narcotic steams of coffee towards an afternoon's nap: they furnish the city-clubs with political chit-chat and serve to light pipes in the evening and may be comfortably applied to another domestic purpose in the morning.

Over the next few years many other newspapers were published, some lasting a few weeks, others a few months, but more had staying power. Eventually evening and Sunday papers appeared as well. The price of a paper at the beginning of the century was about thruppence and by the end of the century it had risen to sixpence. *The Daily Advertiser* started in 1730 and had increased its print run to 4,500 copies by 1803. Some were so successful that they were bought by other newspapers, so from the very beginning newspapers could make people rich.

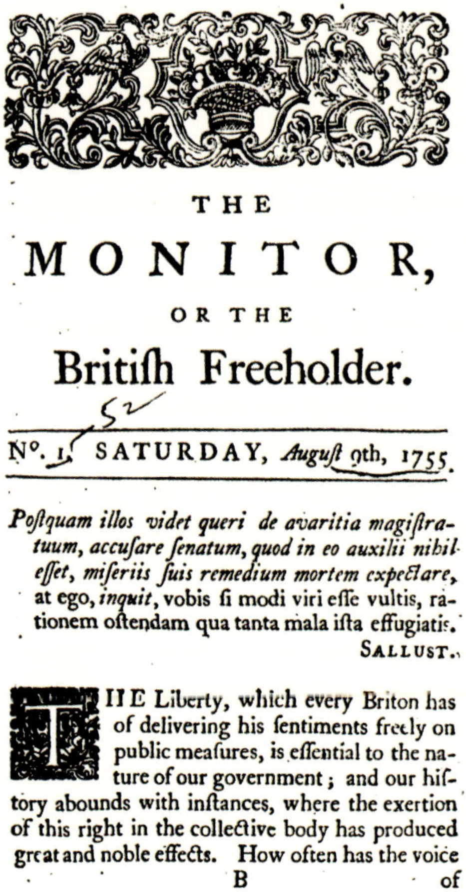

THE

MONITOR,

OR THE

Britiſh Freeholder.

N°. 1. SATURDAY, *Auguſt* 9th, 1755.

Poſtquam illos videt queri de avaritia magiſtratuum, accuſare ſenatum, quod in eo auxilii nihil eſſet, miſeriis ſuis remedium mortem expectare, at ego, *inquit*, vobis ſi modi viri eſſe vultis, rationem oſtendam qua tanta mala iſta effugiatis.

SALLUST.

THE Liberty, which every Briton has of delivering his ſentiments freely on public meaſures, is eſſential to the nature of our government; and our hiſtory abounds with inſtances, where the exertion of this right in the collective body has produced great and noble effects. How often has the voice

B of

Cover page of the first issue of the *Monitor*, 1755

The Growth of Newspapers

In 1709 there were said to be fifty-five regular newspapers. William St Clair has identified their astonishing rapid growth:

Year	Number of copies sold annually
1753	7.5 million
1760	9.5 million
1790	14 million
1793	67 million

In 1790 there were sixty published titles and the fashion for reading newspapers continued strongly into the nineteenth century when the number in 1831 had risen to 148. London, of course, dominated with *The Times*, *Sunday Times* and the *Morning Post*, but it was the large number of local newspapers that steadily built up the national readership. There were also many illegal newspapers published by presses that did not pay the stamp duty of 4 pence per paper. It was a flourishing business and in the decade from 1820 to 1830, 500 printers were prosecuted for non-payment.

Magazines

In 1710 Richard Steele, the Editor of the *London Gazette*, earning a salary of £300 (today's value £39,000) began publishing the *Tatler*, together with his friend Joseph Addison. In 1711 this was replaced by the *Spectator* which, for a time, came out daily and was non-political. It carried articles of general interest, social matters and literary reviews. It soon became a favourite of young women. To show how important the circulation was, Addison said that although the *Spectator* published 3,000 copies a day, it was actually read by twenty times that number by readers in the coffee houses.

The two political parties had their own newspapers – the Tories' being the *Examiner*, which carried on a fierce political war with the *Whig Examiner*. Bolingbroke, the Secretary of State and leader of the Tories, wrote articles for the Tory paper, just as Conservative prime ministers do today.

Jonathan Swift contributed biting articles to the *London Gazette* under the pseudonym Isaac Bickerstaff, so that his victims could not identify their attacker. In 1722 Swift wrote to his friend, Stella, 'These devils of Grub Street that write The Flying Post and Medley will not be quiet. They are always mauling the Lord Treasurer and me. We had the dog under persecution, but Bolingbroke is not active; but I hope to swing him.'

In 1731 the *Gentleman's Magazine* was first published and it was to become the bestseller for the rest of the century – it continued until 1907. It contained essays on social matters, political gossip, book reviews, observations on the weather, occasionally some poems and a few political cartoons reflecting upon the actions of George III.

Dr Samuel Johnson (1709–84)

In the eighteenth century many newspapers were also read by people at home. On 1 January 1757 Robert Dodsley, a poet, bookseller, and friend of Samuel Johnson, launched the *London Chronicle* or *Universal Evening Post* which appeared on three evenings, and it survived from then until 1800. He persuaded Samuel Johnson to write the introductory article for 1 guinea, in which he set out the highest standards for journalists in the hope that the *London Chronicle* would be better. He also warned against false news:

> The Paper which we now invite the Publick to add to the Papers with which it is already rather wearied than satisfied, consists of many Parts; some of which it has in common with other periodical Sheets and peculiar to itself.
>
> The first Demand, made by the Reader on a Journal, is, that he should find an Accurate account of Foreign Transactions and domestick Incidents. This is always expected; but this is rarely performed. Of those Writers who have taken upon themselves the Task of Intelligence, some have given, and others have sold their Abilities, whether small or great, the one or other

Joshua Reynolds, *Dr Samuel Johnson*, 1775

> of the Parties that divide us; and without a Wish for Truth or Thought of Decency, Without Care of any other reputation than that of a stubborn Adherence to their Abettors, carry on the same Tenor of Representation through all the Vicissitudes of Right and Wrong, neither depressed by Detection, nor abashed by Confutation; proud of the hourly Encrease of Infamy, and ready to boast of all the Contumelies that Falsehood and Slander may bring upon them, as new Proofs of their Zeal and Fidelity ... some improvements however we hope to make.

Newspapers In North America

Benjamin Franklin (1706–90) had been apprenticed in the press of James Franklin in Boston, but after quarrelling with his brother he went to Philadelphia, and at the age of eighteen he came to England. He spent nineteen months in England working as an apprentice at the press of John Watts, the most important printer of the eighteenth century. On returning to America in 1728, he partnered with Hugh Meredith, a Welshman, to start a new printing business, and soon they set up a printed newspaper called the *Pennsylvania Gazette*. They went on to establish a network of printing presses from the Carolinas to New England, creating the first newspaper chain. By 1748, Franklin was making a profit of $1,000 a year and in 1753 eight of the fifteen English-language newspapers were published by him. He did not write about political matters for the *Gazette*, preferring to review books and comment on cultural issues. As a young man, he had drafted an epitaph for himself where he described himself simply as: 'B Franklin, Printer.'

During the War of Independence (1775–83), newspapers flourished, for people wanted to know the results of the battles, who had won and who had been killed. As a result, Franklin became more involved in national politics and was one of the five members who drew up the American Declaration of Independence. They decided to make the existence of this document better known by publishing it in the *Philadelphia Evening Post* so that other papers would notice it and publish it more widely.

In 1783 there were thirty-five newspapers in North America, but this rose to 230 by 1800. John Adams, who was the successor to George Washington as the President of the United States, was sent to London where he stayed for three years as the First American Ambassador and he recognised the significance and influence of the London newspapers: 'The London press is an engine by which everything is scattered all over the world.'

Caribbean Weekly News-sheets, 1780s

The printing of news-sheets had spread by the 1780s to parts of the British Empire. In 2022 the bookseller, Quaritch, offered for sale fifty-six issues of the *Royal Gazette* that had been published in Jamaica between January and

SUPPLEMENT
TO THE
ROYAL GAZETTE.

Miss WAINWRIGHT,

CHAPTER of ACCIDENTS.

ANATOMIST,

SHAM DOCTOR.

Gazette to Scotch Gratis.

J. S. COCHRAN,

DAVID DUNCOMB.

Wanted to Hire,

ABLE NEGROES.

GENERAL POST OFFICE

COMET,

Pensacola, Saint Augustine, Georgia, and South Carolina.

RUN AWAY

PAT. AFIRE.

FOR SALE,

TO BE SOLD

For Charter,

MARTHA,

Cuningham & Ballantyne

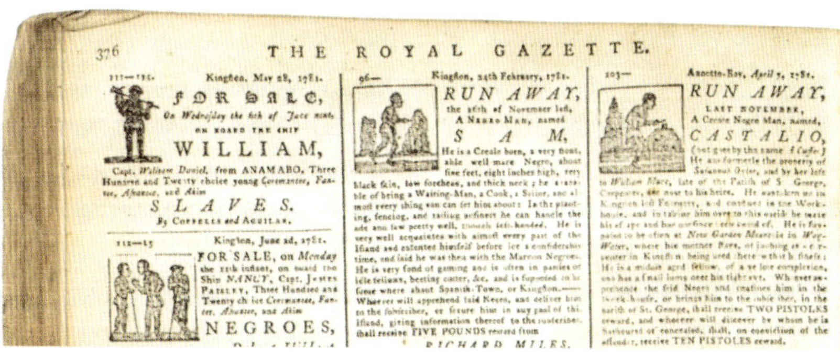
376 THE ROYAL GAZETTE.

Kingston, May 28, 1781.

FOR SALE,

On Wednesday the 6th of June next,

ON BOARD THE SHIP

WILLIAM,

Capt. William Daniel, from ANAMABO, Three Hundred and Twenty choice young Coromantee, Fantee, Ashantee, and Akim

SLAVES.

By Coppells and Aguilar.

Kingston, June 2d, 1781.

FOR SALE, on Monday

NEGROES,

Kingston, 24th February, 1781.

RUN AWAY,

the 26th of November last, A NEGRO MAN, named

SAM,

He is a Creole born, a very stout, able well made Negro, about five feet, eight inches high, very black skin, low forehead, and thick neck

FIVE POUNDS

RICHARD MILES.

Annotto-Bay, April 7, 1781.

RUN AWAY,

LAST NOVEMBER,

A Creole Negro Man, named,

CASTALIO,

TWO PISTOLES

TEN PISTOLES reward.

These advertisements show the true horror of slavery that maintained the Jamaican economy. Runaway slaves were hunted and one called William was up for sale.

December 1781. The Scottish born printer William Ackerman had started the *Jamaican Mercury* and *Kingston Weekly Advertiser*, which he later changed to the *Royal Gazette*.

The contents included ship arrivals, notifications of debts, imported goods and a full page given over to wanted notices for runaway slaves. There was also news about the American War of Independence and it recorded Cornwallis's surrender at York Town in 1781.

The news-sheet also gave an insight into the social life of the colony by advertising the dates for three Shakespeare's plays, including *Richard III* and *Measure for Measure*, and there were advertisements for a dancing school and a flute lesson. News was also included about a Scottish libertine gentlemen's club called Beggars Benison whose symbol was a winged phallus, which was accompanied by an advertisement for 'Velnos' Vegetable Syrup ... An Approved Specific for the cure of venereal and scorbutic complaints'.

Thomas Rowlandson, *Velnos' Vegetable Syrup being sold in London*, 1789

The Fourth Estate

By the beginning of the nineteenth century journalists looked upon themselves as the representatives of the 'Fourth Estate', a phrase which had first appeared in 1787. There is no doubt that they had become a force in the wider debates in the country. In 1820 one of the six Acts to control free speech was to increase the Stamp Duty to 4 pence, but this did not prevent the rise in popularity of Sunday newspapers – 110,000 copies were sold in one weekend in 1829.

Charles Dickens, 1836

A clerk from a counting house leaves at 5:30pm to have his dinner. He

> orders a small plate of roast beef, with greens, and half-a-pint of porter. He has a small plate to-day, because greens are a penny more than potatoes, and he had 'two breads' yesterday, with the additional enormity of 'a cheese' the day before.
>
> He takes up a newspaper, provided by the innkeeper 'after the next gentleman. If he can get it while he is at dinner, he eats with much greater zest; balancing it against the water-bottle, and eating a bit of beef, and reading a line or two, alternately.'

As observed by Charles Dickens in *Sketches by Boz*, 1836.

Reading In Mid-Victorian London

Dickens often described how important newspapers were for the working class. In his Christmas Story *The Chimes* (1844), the sixty-year-old Toby Veck is a postman carrying letters for sixpence or 1 shilling across London, and he was proud that he did it faster than other postmen by trotting, which earned him the soubriquet Trotty Veck. He lived close to poverty, but he must have had some schooling, possibly in a Ragged School which a philanthropist would have funded to teach the poor to read. Occasionally he bought a newspaper to find out how other people were coping with their lives.

Toby enjoyed the news just as much as the gentlefolk:

> It was some short time before the foolish little old fellow could compose himself to mend the fire, and draw his chair to the warm hearth. But when he had done so, and had trimmed the light, he took his newspaper from his pocket, and began to read. Carelessly at first, and skimming up and down the columns ... he came to an account (and it was not the first he had ever read) of a woman who had laid her desperate hands not only on her own life but on that of her young child. A crime so terrible, and so revolting to his soul ... that he let the journal drop, and fell back in his chair, appalled.
>
> 'Why! Lord!' said Toby. 'The Papers is full of obserwations as it is; and so's the Parliament. Here's last week's paper, now;' taking a very dirty one from his pocket, and holding it from him at arm's length; 'full of obserwations! Full of obserwations! I like to know the news as well as any man,' said Toby, slowly; folding it a little smaller, and putting it in his pocket again; 'but it almost goes against the grain with me to read a paper now. It frightens me, almost. I don't know what we poor people are coming to. Lord send we may be coming to something better in the New Year nigh upon us!'

In *Great Expectations* (1860) Pip is taken by Wemmick, the clerk to the Old Bailey lawyer Mr Jaggers, to his home in south London where he meets Wemmick's father, known as the 'Aged Parent', and whose remaining enjoyment was to read news aloud:

> Wemmick explained to me, while his Aged Parent got his spectacles out, that this was according to custom and that it gave the old gentleman infinite satisfaction to read the news aloud. 'I won't offer an apology,' said Wemmick, 'for he isn't capable of many pleasures – are you Aged P?'
>
> 'Alright, John, alright,' returned the old man seeing himself spoken to.
>
> 'Only tip him a nod every now and then when he looks off his paper,' said Wemmick, 'and he'll be happy as a king. We are all attention, Aged One.'

The invention of the steam press in the early nineteenth century was rapidly taken up by newspaper printers as the old hand presses could produce just 200 copies an hour. By 1850 *The Times* in London printed 10,000 copies an hour. The spread of the railways across Britain in the 1840s allowed London publishers to send newspapers and magazines to the northern cities, and W.H. Smith saw the opportunity to increase its sales by setting up stalls on the station concourses to provide travellers with magazines and books.

The Elderly, 1880s

It was G.K. Chesterton (1874–1936) who observed that elderly people read newspapers while younger students read old documents. That view was shared by Charles Dickens in his chapter on London Recreations in *Sketches by Boz*, 1836, where he tells of an elderly couple, who had been retired for over twenty years, and lived in a modest house in the Kilburn Road with a very small garden. The old man had only two recreations – tending his garden and the newspaper 'which he peruses every day from beginning to end, generally reading the most interesting pieces of intelligence to his wife during breakfast'. This was certainly true for me in my eighties. During the Covid-19 pandemic, I re-read many of my favourite authors – Defoe, Dickens, Goldsmith, Greene, Rushdie, Ishiguro and Robert Harris. Every day my wife and I get *The Times*, *Financial Times* and the *Daily Mail*, and at the weekend the *Telegraph* and the *Guardian*. For us, it is like meeting old friends.

This Victorian painting shows that old men did not read newspapers just at breakfast!

Edward Frederick Brewtnall (1846–1902), *A Summer Afternoon*, 1879

Alfred Harmsworth, Lord Northcliffe (1865–1922)

Alfred Harmsworth left school at sixteen to become a freelance journalist and soon afterwards created a weekly magazine, *Answers to Correspondents*, to answer questions which he composed, including, for example, 'Can monkeys smoke?', 'How to cure freckles?', and 'The destiny of lost baggage?' Together with *Comic Cuts*, he sold two million copies a week. He and his brother Harold bought a 'sleeping' *Evening News* and in May 1896 launched the *Daily Mail* with the slogan, 'A Penny Newspaper for Half a Penny' – Alfred was a genius with headlines. Three hundred thousand copies were sold on its first day, and by 1902 it reached a million – the largest in the world with its strong coverage of sport, women's issues and competitions. In 1911 Alfred offered a reward of £1,000 (ten times the average wage) in a competition to find the best bunch of sweet peas – there were 38,000 submissions. By 1911 Harmsworth Publishing controlled the *Mirror*, *Observer* and *Times*, as well as the *Daily Mail*, and during the First World War it published 40 per cent of the morning papers and 45 per cent of the evening press. In 1905 Alfred was raised to the peerage as Lord Northcliffe, and his brother Harold followed in 1914, becoming Lord Rothermere. The views they promoted were chauvinistic, jingoistic and a persistent hostility to anything German. Northcliffe was one of the over-mighty press barons but looked upon himself as a public educator, reaching out beyond the elites to ordinary working people. He made journalism a profession.

This poem appeared in the *New Yorker* in January 1946 and was republished recently:

The Seven Ages of a Newspaper Subscriber

From infancy, from childhood's earliest caper,
He loved the daily paper.

Propped on his grubby elbows, lying prone,
He took, at first, the Comics for his own.
Then, as he altered stature and his voice,
Sports were his single choice.

For a brief time, at twenty, Thought became
A desultory flame,
So with a critic eye he would peruse
The better Book Reviews.

Behold the bridegroom, then—the dazzled suitor
Turned grim commuter,
Learning without direction
To fold his paper to the Housing Section.

Forty enlarged his waistline with his wage.
The Business Page
Engrossed his mind. He liked to ponder well
The charted rise of Steel or Tel & Tel.

Choleric, pompous, and too often vext,
The fifties claimed him next.
The Editorials, then, were what he scanned.
(Even, at times, he took his pen in hand.)

But witness how the human viewpoint varies:
Of late he reads the day's Obituaries.

PHYLLIS MCGINLEY (1905–78)

A Good Answer to Why Read a Newspaper

Up to this century newspapers were read for news, but today most young people get their news from their mobile phones, wristwatches and computers. That has led to the closure of many newspapers. The best have survived by employing journalists not just to report what has happened, but to comment and subject it to a critical examination of its veracity and an appreciation of its consequences.

Chapter 8

Why Read Religious Books?

> A good book is the precious life blood of a master spirit, embalmed and treasured up on purpose to a life below life.
>
> JOHN MILTON, *AREOPAGITICA*, 1644

FROM THE VERY BEGINNING, THE STRENGTH, survival and spread of major religious faiths depended upon a book. For Christians, the Bible; for Jews, the Talmud and the Torah; for Muslims the Koran; for Sikhs, the Guru Granth Sahib; and for Hindus, the Mahab Harata and the Ramayana.

As for Christianity, in the fourth and fifth centuries monasteries were established and needed books, not just for the daily liturgy, but also to implement the rules of their monks. Chapter 38 of St Benedict's Rule directed the reading out aloud of biblical passages as the monks ate their meals. Chapter 40 obliged the monks to study texts for a directed number of hours each day in the monastery library. The Doctors of Faith, saintly theologians like Ambrose, Anselm, Jerome and Gregory, were writing texts covering Christian beliefs and practices to encourage and spread Christianity.

The first translation of the Old Testament from Hebrew to Greek occurred in the first century BCE and it was undertaken by Jews to help other Jews who no longer understood Hebrew. It is probable that this translation was prompted by King Ptolemy II, as he had a passion to collect the greatest books in the world for his famous library in Alexandria.

St Jerome (c. 342–420 CE)

Born in Slovenia, Jerome travelled to Rome to study the Hebrew Bible which was thought to be a copy of the one that had been written by St Matthew, and he translated part of it into Greek. He also translated many other biblical texts into Latin from Hebrew, Aramaic and Greek. His Latin text formed the Vulgate, which superseded all the previous Latin translations, and it was accepted by the Council of Trent in 1546 as the most authoritative. Jerome had spent some of

his life as a hermit living in the desert and there was a rumour that he had tamed a lion by removing a thorn from its paw. That is why Albrecht Dürer in 1519 included a lion in his print, above.

St Augustine (354–430 CE)

The most widely read Christian evangelist was St Augustine who, when he recounted his reason for his damascene conversion, recalled it was principally due to him opening a particular passage in the Bible. Resting under a fig tree, he had heard a child nearby singing, 'Pick it up and read it, Pick it up, read it' – in Latin *Tolle, lege*. He picked up the Bible, opening it at random, and read from

Chapter 13 of St Paul's Epistle to the Romans, verses 13-14:

> Not in rioting and drunkenness, not in chambering and wantonness, not in strife and envying; but put ye on the Lord Jesus Christ, and make not provision for the flesh, in concupiscence.

St Augustine's teachings on Predestination and Original Sin were due to him reading from a book.

Monasteries were the only institutions capable of the producing a book and so they established a *scriptorium* where monks and trained scribes copied out texts by inscribing them with quills on parchment.

Scribe monks at work in 1283

The Venerable Bede (c. 672–735 CE)

The first significant book in England was written by the Venerable Bede in 731, *Historia ecclesiastica gentis Anglorum* (Ecclesiastical History of the English People). Many copies were made by scribes on vellum and parchment, and some copies still exist. It covers the period from Julius Caesar's invasion in 55 CE, but its most important section dates from the arrival of another Augustine in 597 CE.

When I went up to Oxford in 1955, all students were required to show that they could read Latin and French, and were tested by an exam called Prelims at the end of the second term. In my year, two failed to pass and were sent down.

Our two set texts were Bede's *Historia* and a book on the provinces of France by the French historian, Jules Michelet, *Histoire de France*. I remember attending lectures on both these books, but this entry requirement was abandoned by Oxford in the 1960s.

The Lindisfarne Gospels, (c. 715–20 CE)

This beautiful book was written and decorated in the Abbey of Lindisfarne, an island off the northeast English coast. It is the text of the four Gospels written in Latin. However, in the tenth century it was translated into Old English, which was written between the lines of manuscript. This makes it the first translation into English of the New Testament. It features decorated initials and ornamental patterns similar to the Celtic knotwork of the *Book of Kells*.

The monks of Lindisfarne wanted to celebrate their first bishop, Cuthbert. A note added in the tenth century asserted 'That Eadfrith, the Bishop from 698–721 actually wrote the English texts himself using the insular script on vellum.' A goldsmith, Billfrith the Anchorite, made a fine leather and jewelled binding case to protect the Gospels in the eighth century, but the casing disappeared following raids by the Vikings.

Protestantism

Martin Luther's anger at the selling by the Dominican monk Johann Tetzel of papal indulgences for the remission of sins had built up over years but became a public outrage when on All Saints' Day, 31 October 1517, he nailed his ninety-five *Theses* on the church door of the Castle Church of Wittenberg and, suitably for a scholastic debate, he wrote them in Latin.

What had started as an attack upon the power, wealth and corruption of the papacy became a movement that made the Bible the sole source of religious authority and also available to ordinary people in their own language. The papacy realised the potential danger and Pope Leo X dismissed Luther as 'a drunken German who will change his mind when sober'. On 1 June 1520 the Pope excommunicated Luther with the Papal Bull, *Exsurge Domine*. Luther waited six months to make his dramatic response, when in December he joined some students burning books by scholastic authors and threw a copy of Rome's ecclesiastical laws onto the flames.

By throwing the Bull onto the fire, Luther used the very weapon of the Church – for his own works had been burnt by the Papal Nuncio. It was a defiant act. Like Samson, he wanted to uphold God by bringing the temples down. It was to change the course of history.

A page from the Lindisfarne Gospels

His success in establishing Protestantism was due to the printing press. Between 1520 and 1530, 620 pamphlets were printed and Luther's own writings constituted a third of all German books printed in the first four decades of the sixteenth century. In 1520 he published *To the Christian Nobility of the German Nation*, which was an appeal to the Holy Roman Emperor and other nobles to read his attack upon the supremacy of the spiritual power of the Pope over a monarch's temporal power. Four thousand copies were sold within a few days and thirteen further editions were printed in two years. At the Diet of Worms in 1521, ordered by the Holy Roman Emperor Charles V, Luther uttered his famous declaration, 'Hier stehe ich. Ich can nicht anders. Gott helfe mir' (Here I stand. I can do nothing else. God help me). Charles V issued an edict condemning Luther a 'notorious heretic' and ordered Catholics to burn his books.

Between 1517 and 1521 Luther had printed thirty sermons and other works in some 370 editions. These were burnt in St Paul's Churchyard in London in 1521 where the fire was watched by Cardinal Wolsey and the papal ambassador. Luther had already been working with a Wittenberg printer, Johann Grunenberg, which meant that each edition could be as large as 1,000 copies – showing the speed and flexibility of the Gutenberg press – and it led to over 300,000 copies in German, not Latin, being circulated in Europe. Not even the great power of the emperor could stifle the power of the press.

This was followed in 1522 by Luther's translation of the New Testament into German. It was a breakthrough which was read by hundreds of thousands, and it also encouraged other reformers, like England's William Tyndale, to produce their own vernacular translations. The literate German language of today derives from the Middle German dialect used by Luther.

The Path to the English Bible

There was a translation in the late fourteenth century by John Wycliffe (*c.* 1320–84), but the Church considered it to be heretical and forty-four years after his death, his bones were dug up and burnt. However, a small number of manuscripts of his Bible have survived – he had justified the English version by saying, 'It helpeth Christian men to study the Gospel in that tongue which they know best – Christ's sentence.'

Tyndale's Bible, 1526

> To cause a boy that driveth the plough
> to know more of the Scripture than thou doest.

William Tyndale was a theologian, a Catholic priest and a leading scholar, fluent in several languages, including Greek, Latin, Hebrew and German. In 1522, when he acquired a copy of Martin Luther's New Testament in German, he was inspired to begin his English translation. He sought the approval of the Bishop of London, Cuthbert Tunstall, for an English version of the Bible, but he was told it would be heretical. So in 1524 he moved to Northern Europe, living a nomadic life trying to keep ahead of the force of the Catholic Church and the Holy Roman Emperor. He was never to set foot in England again. With astonishing commitment and passion, he set about translating the New Testament and arranged for it to be printed in Worms in 1526; he revised it and published two further editions in 1534 and 1536.

Justification by faith was a concept that was to create a revolution which challenged the central authority of the Church and the power of the clergy. Ordinary people – at least those who could read – could now make up their own minds, or in Tyndale's own words, expressed to a group of priests before he left England, his purpose was to 'cause a boy that driveth the plough to know more of the Scripture than thou doest'.

Tyndale produced one of the major founding works of the English language, for about 85 per cent of the famous King James Bible of 1611 was his. His language was simple and at times monosyllabic, so that simple people could grasp it: 'The word was with God and the Word was God'; 'Under the sun'; 'Let there be light'; 'Pour out one's heart'; 'the apple of his eye'; 'fall flat on his face'; 'eat, drink and be merry'; and 'Our Father which art in Heaven' are memorable phrases that people could remember, repeat and cherish.

Cuthbert Tunstall was so appalled by Tyndale's Bible that he ordered all the copies in London to be bought, and on 26 October 1526 had 6,000 Bibles burnt on the steps of St Paul's. He also redoubled his efforts to destroy as many copies as he could by getting an English merchant in Antwerp, Augustine Packington, to buy copies as they came off the press in the Low Countries. Tyndale rather welcomed this, as he took the money and arranged for even more editions to be published. However, Tunstall's destruction was remarkably effective, since only one copy of Tyndale's Bible has survived, and it is in a library in Stuttgart.

Copies began to circulate in England in the late 1520s, drawing down upon Tyndale the wrath of Henry VIII, 'The Defender of the Faith', Cardinal Wolsey and Thomas More – the great heretic hunter who attacked Tyndale viciously, descending at times to coarse scatology. In the early 1530s, when Henry VIII had decided to break from Rome and had married the Protestant Anne Boleyn, he asked Thomas Cromwell to persuade Tyndale to return to England to reinforce the establishment of the Anglican Church, but Tyndale said he would return only if Henry sanctioned a Bible in English.

The Catholic Church continued to pursue Tyndale and in 1535 he was betrayed to the officers of the Holy Roman Emperor, Charles V, by an Englishman, who had befriended him in Antwerp but who was a passionate Catholic. Eighteen months later on 6 October 1536 Tyndale was burnt at the stake, uttering his last words, 'O Lord, open the King of England's eyes.' This dying wish was fulfilled, for in that very same year Henry VIII agreed to publish a Bible in English. This consisted of 85 per cent Tyndale and 15 per cent of the books of the Old Testament which were not included by translated by another priest, Miles Coverdale. That Bible was known as the 'Coverdale Bible'.

William Tyndale's death at the stake, 6 October 1536

The language of the Court in England was English, but many ordinary people spoke Middle English. The religious reforms that started in 1529 and ended in 1536 with Henry VIII's decrees for every church to have a Bible chained to a pillar and that all prayers were to be in English, were the solid rock upon which the Church of England was built and helped to establish English as the main language for all.

The late seventeenth century was so dominated by Shakespeare, Ben Jonson and the other playwrights that one tends to forget the number of significant books that shaped our history and our language which were published during the short reign of Edward VI and Elizabeth I's long reign. There were two significant books that established the ascendancy of the English language.

The Booke of Common Prayer, 1549

This was the first single manual for worship in English designed both for the priest and those of his congregation who could read. It pulled together many regional differences and other source books from pre-Reformation days, and it included the Collects specially written by Archbishop Cranmer. To secure more annual reading of the Bible, it proscribed that 'It shall be done in ordre without breakyng one pece thereof from another. For this cause be cut of Anthemes, Responds, Invitatories as such thynges as did breake the continual course of the Readying of Scripture.' It was issued and enjoined by the Act of Uniformity in 1549. It has been slightly amended over the years, but it has many words, phrases and prayers that are deeply embedded in the English language. It is still in use nearly five hundred years later.

Foxe's Book of Martyrs, 1563

For years John Foxe (1516–87) had been compiling the records of Christian martyrs from the early days of Christianity right up to the persecution of Protestants in the reign of Bloody Mary (1553–8). In 1563 he published in English his work which ran to 1,741 pages. In his lifetime there were three other editions in 1570, 1576 and 1580, which were generally abridged to two volumes and even to one volume.

It became the bestseller for over 200 years because he included woodblock illustrations of the death of many of the martyrs. In 1571, a Decree of Convocation ordered that copies should be placed in all cathedral churches, and in the homes of archbishops, bishops, archdeacons and resident canons for the use of servants and visitors. Many country churches also provided chained copies which increased the readership enormously, and even those who could not read saw the illustrations which would be explained to them. The book became the bulwark of Protestantism in England and when it first appeared there were still many people who had memories of the martyrs whom Mary Tudor had condemned to be burnt at the stake.

The Holy Bible, 1611, newly translated out of the original tongue

In 1603 when James VI of Scotland became James I of England, five English versions of the Bible existed, but only two had been authorised by the Anglican Church. The first was the Bible, which had been authorised by King Henry VIII in 1539, and the second was the Bishop's Bible in 1568, translated during Elizabeth I's reign but was little read as it was rather obscurely written. The Geneva Bible of 1560 was more popular but was unauthorised and full of anti-royalist notes.

In 1604 the Puritan party petitioned the King to improve upon these Bibles. Six committees in Oxford, Cambridge and Westminster were appointed and worked for six years to complete their translation from Hebrew, Latin and Greek. Apart from the original text in those three languages, they also drew upon the two earlier translations by Tyndale and Coverdale which provide a substantial amount of the final version. They read out the passages aloud and the best were then forwarded to an overseeing committee of six sitting daily for several months in the Stationers' Hall in London. It was published in 1611 and it has become known as the King James Bible. It is extraordinary that a book of such beautiful language should have been decided by committees. Its words have been read out in churches for hundreds of years and it is engraved into our language. Lord Macaulay, the Victorian historian, said of it, 'A book which if everything else in our language should perish would alone suffice to show the whole extent of its beauty and power.'

The Bibles were sold for 10 shillings unbound and 12 shillings bound. It is one of the most read books in the world and billions of copies of this version have been published, making it one of the world's most influential religious texts.

Translating Foreign Texts, 1877

In Victorian England there was a great deal of interest in translating religious texts from other cultures. These included the Koran, the *Analects* of Confucius, the *Ramayana*, the *Bhagavad Gita*, *Shahnameh*, and many of these books became available in libraries and some shops.

Lord Leighton had a Koran reading desk which looks as if it had been made in the eastern Mediterranean. The girl in his *Study at a Reading Desk* (1877) is almost certainly reading a copy of the Koran which was first translated in 1734 by Robert Gale. It was translated again in 1861, *The Koran, Commonly Called the Alcoran of Mohammed* by John Medows Rodwell (1808–1900), an Anglican clergyman and Islamic scholar who was a friend of Charles Darwin. His translation was less combative and had a 'nineteenth century positivistic approach'. It soon went to a second edition and in the 1990s Everyman's Library published it. If the girl in Leighton's *Study* is studying the Koran, it would be Rodwell's translation.

Lord Frederic Leighton, *Study at a Reading Desk*, 1877

Chapter 9

Why Read Poetry?

Poetry, like music, is to be heard.

Basil Bunting

Poetry has always meant a lot to me. My interest started at my Church of England primary school, Holy Trinity in Southport, as we had been evacuated there from the Blitz in London. This was the first time I came across a lot of books and, particularly, poetry. I won a prize and was given a book of verses for children which included Blake's *The Tyger*.

Being the first poem devoted to a single animal, *The Tyger* has inspired other poets like Ted Hughes who strikingly defines in *The Jaguar* the special features of a wild cat whose 'stride is wildnernesses of freedom'. Blake would have enjoyed that image. Hughes also wrote, 'Blake saw his Tyger in a vision and tried to make sense of it by controlling it, yoking it with the lamb and the God of Job.' It was not until I was much older, that I realised that the question which Blake poses is a theological time-bomb:

> Did he who made the Lamb make Thee?

My sister had a poetry book called *Turn Again Lane* which contained poems that were easy to read and remember. I recently managed to track down a copy of this book and it has brought back so many happy memories, as we cling so fiercely to the books of our childhood:

> Turn Again Lane.
> It is there today.
> Where old folk chatter
> And children play.

After two grammar schools, I went to St Paul's School and I was lucky to have two brilliant teachers – P.D. Whitting for History and C.P. Longland for English Literature – and they both infected me with a love for those two subjects. I came across a lot of poets that were new to me – Alexander Pope, Robert Browning and, most memorably Gerard Manley Hopkins. I had never heard of Hopkins, but I came to love his poetry and how with Sprung Rhythm he created wonderful, colourful pictures:

Pied Beauty

Glory be to God for dappled things –
For skies of coupled-colour as a brinded cow;
For rose-moles all in stipple upon trout that swim;
Fresh-firecoal chestnut-falls; finches' wings;
Landscape plotted and pieced – fold, fallow, and plough;
And all trades, their gear and tackle and trim.

All things counter, original, spare, strange;
Whatever is fickle, freckled (who knows how?)
With swift; slow; sweet; sour; adazzle, dim;
He fathers-forth whose beauty is past change:
Praise Him.

Lovers of music, whether classical, rock, jazz, punk or reggae, love both playing and listening, and for some it is the pathway to the peaceful centre of the soul. Poems lead not only to enjoyment but also to reflection through the musicality of their words. The ideas, sentiments and passion of the poet are more simply, shortly and memorably expressed than several pages of prose. When I find a poet I particularly enjoy, I try to collect all their first editions, as I have with Browning, Hardy, Kipling, Ted Hughes, Seamus Heaney and Louis MacNeice.

As I had collected many satirical poems, I persuaded the publisher Methuen to publish my first anthology of poetry, *I Have No Gun But I Can Spit* (a line from W.H. Auden), which is a collection of satirical poems and lampoons, for over the centuries England has had produced some brilliant satirical poets. My second anthology, published in 1982, was *London Lines*, about the places and faces of London in poetry and song, and it also includes wonderful photographs by David Lister of places and people, as I wanted to engage the attention of the reader by seeing as well as reading.

I was fortunate to come to know Matthew Evans, the Chair of Faber & Faber, and we became close friends, and in my view he was by far the best of all London publishers, dealing brilliantly with a huge army of prima donna writers. My first

Faber anthology was *The Faber Book of War Poetry*. As most war anthologies focus on the horrors of war, I tried to broaden out the selection to cover poetry from the women left behind, people who were exceptionally gallant or brave, nurses in the Vietnam War writing about the injuries, those who suffered from military injustice and punishment, the training of recruits, female warriors and the commemoration of the dead.

Dulce et Decorum Est

Bent double, like old beggars under sacks,
Knock-kneed, coughing like hags, we cursed through sludge,
Till on the haunting flares we turned our backs,
And towards our distant rest began to trudge.
Men marched asleep. Many had lost their boots,
But limped on, blood-shod. All went lame; all blind;
Drunk with fatigue; deaf even to the hoots
Of gas-shells dropping softly behind.

Gas! GAS! Quick, boys! – An ecstasy of fumbling
Fitting the clumsy helmets just in time,
But someone still was yelling out and stumbling
And flound'ring like a man in fire or lime. –
Dim through the misty panes and thick green light,
As under a green sea, I saw him drowning.

In all my dreams before my helpless sight,
He plunges at me, guttering, choking, drowning.

WILFRED OWEN

John Singer Sargent, *Gassed*, 1919

In my second Faber anthology, *The Faber Book of Landscape Poetry*, I was able to identify the actual location that inspired each poem. I was helped by Christopher Reid, a fine poet himself and Faber's Poetry Editor. I greatly enjoyed compiling the next, *The Faber Book of English History in Verse*, as I had to write a short explanation of each poem's importance in our history. It was also published in a shorter paperback for children. My fourth literary anthology was entitled *Unauthorised Versions*, containing parodies of famous poems, and Faber managed to print the original poem alongside the parody, making it much more fascinating and amusing to read.

Poetry Today

The Covid-19 pandemic led to a surge in reading poetry. In Scotland, Donna Ashworth, a poet in her forties who had been a singer and pop artist, first posted on Facebook in 2018, but her blog really took-off in 2020, *History Will Remember When The World Stopped*. Her poems are about the personal problems of ordinary people, very often women in their thirties and forties trying to manage their lives, coping with love, children and grief. By 2023, Ashworth had published five poetry books, selling 70,000 copies, and she has a million followers on Facebook and 200,000 on Instagram.

When my wife Mary began to write poetry in the 1980s, I became aware of a large community of poets coming from a wide range of society, heritages and faiths. They often meet together in coffee houses or school halls to read their poems to each other and to discuss them.

They are supported by publishers, often sole individuals, but occasionally a husband-and-wife team, who help to get some of the poems into magazines and the quarterly *Poetry Review*. Several of Mary's poems appeared in this way and as a result she published two books of poems under the name Mary Muir, with the latest appearing in 2023. Her poems are positive and optimistic and this is the last poem in *Ex Situ II*:

NOW

Bin yesterday,
leave loss and love and lines,
the only signifier is today.
Live now, live this day, nowhere else.
Look round you, feel the now,
this heat, this cold,
the sound of children's shouts
this taste of apple skin under your tongue,
the sky beyond the window, leafed in green
and all the words you're thinking now,
sound them out slowly so they run with you
to fall before tomorrow comes.
Today is everything;
hold only now.

I am proud to have the first editions of Mary's two poetry books.

Chapter 10

Poetry of the 16th and 17th Centuries

> The only way to win immortality is to do things worth the writing or write things worth the reading.
>
> George Pettie, 1581, Tudor translator

SHAKESPEARE, JOHNSON, MARLOWE and all the other playwrights so dominate the late sixteenth and seventeenth centuries that the development of the reading of poetry tends to be overlooked.

It was the booksellers and publishers, rather than the poets, who were the key figures compiling poetry collections in order to increase their sales. The first important collection of poems was *Songes and Sonettes*, 'written by the Ryght Honourable Lords Henry Howard, late Earle of Surrey, and Others', compiled and printed by Richard Tottel in 1557. Apart from publishing his famous *Songes and Sonettes* anthology, which became known as *Tottel's Miscellany*, he edited other books, including one on animal husbandry. His main customers were law students and he found the way for them to become buyers and readers of these other books. Surrey's poems and Thomas Wyatt's satires which had previously been circulated in manuscript to their friends were now saved for posterity.

Of the 372 poems in Tottel's *Songes and Sonettes*, over ninety had never appeared anywhere else, apart from manuscripts shown only to a few friends. So, that monopoly of enjoyment was broken and opened up to other readers. Tottel had a winner, for within eight weeks a second edition was published, and it led to eleven editions over thirty years. This was a breakthrough in the reading of poetry. We know that Shakespeare was one of the readers because in *The Merry Wives of Windsor*, Slender, the foolish cousin of Justice Shallow, refers to 'My book of Songs and Sonnets.'

To make the book more readable, Tottel inserted a title for each poem to arrest the attention of the reader, such as *Description of the Restless State of a Lover with a Suit to his Ladie to rue on his dying heart*. Some recorded failure: *A Lover Complaineth Himself Forsaken* and *The Lover Praieth his Service to be accepted and his defaults pardoned.*

These poems were written by men and were read by educated young men. They reflected upon various aspects of erotic desire – proceeding from a meeting, fascination, attraction, a kiss, disappointment or success, love giving way to lust and even a rape.

Tottel appealed to his customers:

> It relleth nowe (gentle reder) that thou thinke it not euill doon, to publifh, to the honor of the Englifhe tong, and for profit of the ftudious of Englifhe elo-quence, thofe workes which the vngentle borders vp of fuch treafure haue heretofore enuied thee. And for this point (good reder) thine own profit and pleafure, in thefe prefently, and in moe hereafter, flial anfwere for my defence.

It was a male dominated process, but there was one miscellany published by a female poet, Isabella Whitney, *A Sweet Nosegay or Pleasant Posye*.

Other publishers followed suit and published what we would call anthologies, though that word was first coined in 1625. *A Smalle Handfull of Fragrant Flowers*, just sixteen pages, was published in 1575, and the author is thought to be Nicholas Breton, a minor pastoral poet, but this has been disputed. In 1578 Richard Jones, a draper but also a bookseller, published *A Gorgious Gallery of Gallant Inventions*. He also made a direct plea to the reader:

> Since I poore booke are put into thy hand
> Although the tome or volume little bee,
> Yet, Reader deare that I be throughly scanned
> With zealous minde, I begg and crave of thee.

I am indebted to a brilliant piece of scholarship by Professor Megan Heffernan of the DePaul University, *Making the Miscellany* (2021). The only poetry book published by Tottel with which I was familiar was *Tottel's Miscellany*, and I have much enjoyed the history and analysis of Heffernan and so many others – I am a late learner.

The Influence of George Gascoigne (1535–77)

George Gascoigne was one of the most colourful of the century's poets. Trained as a lawyer in Gray's Inn, he abandoned the law and became an MP for two years, but failed to be re-selected as he was 'a notorious rufilianne', 'a common rhymer' and a deviser of 'slanderous pasquelles' (lampoons). He served as a soldier for two years, fighting in 1572 in the war of the Netherlands where he was captured, and having squandered must of his inherited wealth he went to prison for his debts. However, he also attended Elizabeth I's court. He was a pioneer in various branches of literature and a prolific writer of plays, poetry, comedies, masques and satires, as well as publishing prose books on hunting and falconry. One of his comedies in English, *Ariosto*, became a source for Shakespeare's *Taming of the Shrew*. In 1573, his *A Hundreth Sundry Flowres bound up in one small Poesie* was regarded by Her Majesty's commissioners as being offensive and two years later he published a revised edition entitled *Poesies of Gascoigne Esquire*, which included most of his own poetry with a few changes for the 'well smelling noses of learned readers'. This was the first time a book had appeared with a single poet's name. In the preface to the 1575 book he added, 'Certayne Notes of instruction on the making of verse or ryme in English', which is the first essay on English versification. His advice to poets was to be more adventurous and more imaginative with some 'aliquid salis – a pinch of salt and wit'. The first and most necessary point of writing a poem is to 'grounde it upon some fine invention ... and increase some good and fine devise showing the quicke capacity of the writer'. His poem – *Despysed Things May Live* shows the quality of his poetry:

> Despysed things may live, although they pyne in payne:
> And things ofte trodden under foote, may once yit rise again.
> The stone that lieth full lowe, may clime at last full hye;
> And stand aloft on stately tow'rs, in sight of every eye.
> The cruell axe which felles the tree that grew full straight;
> Is worne with rust, when it renews, and springeth up on height.

In 1575 Gascoigne assisted in devising masques to be presented before Elizabeth I at Woodstock. In the annual gift of exchanges for her courtiers, he gave her a copy of a play which he had translated into Latin, French and Italian. An engraving, which I suspect he must have commissioned, showed him making the presentation to the Queen.

In 1929 Edward Elgar (1857–1934), as Master of the King's Music, was invited by Walford Davies, the organist at St George's Chapel, Windsor, to write an appropriate work to celebrate King George V's recovery from a serious illness. The literary world was rather surprised when Elgar chose one of Gascoigne's poems, *Good Morrow*.

It was performed in Windsor Castle in December that year – this is two of his five verses:

Good Morrowe

You that have spent the silent night
In sleepe and quiet rest,
And joye to see the cheerfull lyght
That ryseth in the East:
Now cleare your voyce, and chere your hart,
Come helpe me nowe to sing:
Eche willing wight, come beare a part,
To prayse the heavenly King.

The Rainbowe bending in the skye,
Bedeckte with sundrye hewes,
Is like the seate of God on hye,
And seemes to tell these newes:
That as thereby he promisèd,
To drowne the world no more,
So by the bloud which Christ hath shead,
He will our helth restore.

Sir Philip Sidney (1554–86)

In 1591, 108 love sonnets were published in three slim volumes entitled *Astrophel and Stella*, which had been written by Sir Philip Sidney in the 1580s. He was the most celebrated soldier in late Elizabethan England, famous for offering his water bottle to another soldier as he lay dying in battle in 1586. His father-in-law, Elizabeth's spymaster, Francis Walsingham, gave Sidney the most lavish state funeral that had ever been held. Previously only his family and friends knew of his poems which had been circulated in manuscript and copied many times.

The sonnets, although dedicated to his wife, were written to his mistress Lady Penelope Rich, whom he had once hoped to marry. They expressed his devotion to his 'Stella' and the various stages of their erotic association. What made the poems popular was a selection known as the 'Kiss Sonnets', for kissing was to lead to other delights and linked their lovers' souls and bodies together:

O Kisse, which dost those ruddie gemmes impart,
O Gemmes, or frutes of new-found Paradise

Breathing all blisse and sweet'ning to the heart,
Teaching dumbe lips a nobler exercise.

The success of *Astrophel and Stella* created a vogue for other poets to write romantic sonnets. Over twenty were published in the 1590s, but few have survived.

Sidney's popularity ensured a large readership and it transformed the market for poetry. It was something of a surprise that a man who was known for his courage in battle could write such fine romantic poems expressing the deep love that he felt for his mistress.

What this publication showed was that a successful book of poems could be sold with the name of the poet on the cover and that was a breakthrough.

Sir John Suckling (1609–42)

John Suckling was one of the Cavalier poets close to Charles I, like Edmund Waller, Robert Herrick and Richard Lovelace. At the age of eighteen he inherited considerable estates which allowed him to play a much more active part in the politics and active society of the early seventeenth century.

This is his most famous poem, from 1637:

Why so pale and wan fond lover?
    Prithee why so pale?
Will, when looking well can't move her,
    Looking ill prevail?
    Prithee why so pale?

Why so dull and mute young sinner?
    Prithee why so mute?
Will, when speaking well can't win her,
    Saying nothing do't?
    Prithee why so mute?

Quit, quit for shame, this will not move,
    This cannot take her;
If of herself she will not love,
    Nothing can make her;
    The devil take her.

Anthony Van Dyck, *Sir John Suckling*, *c.* 1638

Suckling had also written four plays but they were not popular. In this portrait by Van Dyke he is reading the First Folio of Shakespeare, hoping perhaps that his plays would become as celebrated.

Suckling is best remembered for adding phrases to the English language derived from the game of cribbage which he invented. It is played by two players and each keep their own score by fixing one round peg into a series of holes. Each set of five holes is called a street and there are four streets on each board. The winner is the player who reaches the last street. These well-known phrases come from the game:

level pegging – when each player has the same score
streets ahead – when one player is well ahead
having filled more streets
pegged out – finished, it's all over
left in the lurch – the lurch is the part of the board
behind the start line
bilking – cheating at cribbage
His Nibs – this the name given to the Jack of Diamonds.

Both Jane Austen and Charles Dickens were keen cribbage players. In Dickens' 1841 *Old Curiosity Shop*, Dick Swiveller teaches cribbage to the small, ragged girl known as 'The Marchioness'. Churchill enjoyed playing both cribbage and bezique.

William Shakespeare (1564–1616): Sonnets

The trend for writing romantic sonnets fell out of fashion, apart from one glorious book published on 20 May 1609 with the simple title, *Shakespeare's Sonnets*. The 154 sonnets were mainly written in the 1590s and by that date Shakespeare was sufficiently well-known that his book of poems could bear only his name. The first 126 are addressed to a young man and the remaining twenty-eight to a woman, 'The Dark Lady'. They range much more widely than earlier romantic sonnets, covering passion, loneliness, death, lust, homoeroticism, infidelity and the transience of life. Some of their most memorable phrases have slipped into common usage. A few years after Shakespeare's death a second edition was published in 1640, but this has been condemned as the poems addressed to a man had been changed to address a woman in order to reduce its homoeroticism and to downplay any question of Shakespeare's sexuality.

In one exam I took at school, we were asked to comment upon Sonnet 60 and that soon became my favourite. Its fourteen lines describe what inevitably happens to us all as we pass through life and, when things were not going so well for me, I took some consolation from its line: 'Crooked eclipses 'gainst his glory fight'.

Like as the waves make towards the pebbl'd shore,
So do our minutes hasten to their end;
Each changing place with that which goes before,
In sequent toil all forwards do contend.
Nativity, once in the main of light,
Crawls to maturity, wherewith being crown'd,
Crooked eclipses 'gainst his glory fight,

And Time that gave doth now his gift confound.
Time doth transfix the flourish set on youth
And delves the parallels in beauty's brow,
Feeds on the rarities of nature's truth,
And nothing stands but for his scythe to mow:
And yet to times in hope my verse shall stand,
Praising thy worth, despite his cruel hand.

John Donne (1572–1631)

The publication of the collected poems of John Donne in 1633, two years after his death, was a major step forward in the development of poetry. Donne never allowed his poems to appear in print, and they had circulated in manuscripts among his family, friends and fans. The enterprising publisher John Marriot seized upon the opportunity of publication, as John Donne had been a celebrity, famous for his sermons as Dean of St Paul's Cathedral which had drawn very large congregations. Over 4,000 manuscript copies from over 239 different sources were tracked down by Marriot and the book ran to 400 pages.

In 2023, Katherine Rundell, a fellow of All Souls, Oxford, published *Super-Infinite*, a biography of Donne which won the Ballie Gifford prize for the best non-fiction book of the year. It is a brilliant work and I hope it will attract many more to read Donne's poems which can be blunt, often aggressive, using concise descriptions with new words – for example, 'soldier's bumbast' and 'mountebankes' drugtongue'. There are irregular rhythms and puzzling phrases which need to be read and re-read to unravel and untangle their meaning.

Donne's *Satires*, written as a young man studying law at the Inns of Court, are blunt about how the life of a lawyer is unattractive. It was clear that he did not want to become one:

Continuall claims I have made, injunctions got,
To stay my rival's suit, that he should not
Proceed. Spare me! ...
When sicke with Poëtrie and possest with Muse
Thou wast, and mad, I hop'd; but men which chuse
Law practice for mere gaine bold soules of repute
Worse then imbrothel'd strumpets prostitute ...
His hand still at a bill, now he must talke.
And to every suitor lye in every thing.

Not much seems to have changed!

He has a withering wit, shown in *Satire I*, in which he castigates the plagiarism of a poet who copied the words of another:

But he is worst whom (beggardly) doth chaw
Others' wits' fruits, and in his ravenous maw
Rankly digested, doth those things out spew
As his own things; and they're his own, 'tis true,
For if one eat my meat, though it be known
The meat was mine, th' excrement is his own.

In 1601 Donne married Anne Seymour against the wishes of both his father and his employer, and for a short time he was sent to prison for his disobedience. It says much for Anne's devotion that she went ahead with the wedding knowing the consequences, and it proved a happy marriage in which she bore him twelve children. As a young man he wrote many amorous and sensual poems which seem to indicate he had several affairs. As an older man, he wrote divine poems that reflect a conflict he tried to resolve between carnal longing and spiritual longing. They contain some of the most beautiful love poems in the English language. This is an extract from *Elegy XIX: To His Mistress Going to Bed*.

Come, Madam, come, all rest my powers defy,
Until I labour, I in labour lie.
The foe oft-times having the foe in sight,
Is tir'd with standing though he never fight.
Off with that girdle, like heaven's Zone glistering,
But a far fairer world encompassing.
Unpin that spangled breastplate which you wear,
That th'eyes of busy fools may be stopped there.
Unlace yourself, for that harmonious chime,
Tells me from you, that now it is bed time.
Off with that happy busk, which I envy,
That still can be, and still can stand so nigh.
Your gown going off, such beauteous state reveals,
As when from flowery meads th'hill's shadow steals.
Off with that wiry Coronet and shew
The hairy Diadem which on you doth grow ...
Full nakedness! All joys are due to thee,
As souls unbodied, bodies uncloth'd must be ...

Must see reveal'd. Then since that I may know;
As liberally, as to a Midwife, shew

Thy self: cast all, yea, this white linen hence,
There is no penance due to innocence.
To teach thee, I am naked first; why then
What needst thou have more covering than a man.

Another amorous poem, *The Sunne Rising,* which has appeared in many anthologies chastises the sun for waking up lovers:

Busie olde foole, unruly Sunne;
Why dost thou thus,
Through windowes, and through curtaines call on us?
Must to they motions lovers seasons run?
Sawcy pedantique wretch, goe chide
Late schoole boyes, and sowre prentices,
Goe tell Court-huntsmen, that the King will ride,
Call countrey ands to harvest offices;
Love, all alike, no season knows, nor clyme,
Nor houres, dayes, months, which are the rags of time.

I took one of the phrases in the first verse, 'rags of time', as the title of the Commonplace books I published for my seventy-fifth, eightieth, eighty-fifth and ninetieth birthdays. I included in one, this limerick on John Donne:

That fine English poet John Donne
Was want to admonish the sunne
You busie old foole
Lie low and stay coole
For I am in bed having Funne.

An edition of John Donne's poems appeared in 1684. His reputation really took off the in the twentieth century when his work appealed to post-war Britain. I remember a cousin of mine, who had become an English teacher after he was demobbed from the Second World War, urging me to read the Metaphysical poets, particularly John Donne. Penguin published his poems in the 1950s, along with this comment, 'The number of copies printed of the first issue of this latest selection considerably exceeds the total of all copies of all editions of Donne's poetry printed since his death.'

I was fortunate to buy the 1633 first edition of his poems and luckily the paper has not deteriorated, almost as fresh as on its first publication nearly four centuries ago. On two plain pages at the front of the book, there has been written in a Victorian hand, I think, by two different booksellers 'With the autograph of Joshua Reynolds', clearly hoping to help sell a book which was not doing too well, and the price is marked down to 10 and sixpence. This is now a collector's item and I had to pay a little more than 10 shillings and sixpence for it!

A miniature of John Donne, aged eighteen, while studying at the Inns of Court, a line engraving by William Marshall, 1649, probably based on a lost miniature of 1591 by Nicholas Hilliard

John Milton (1608–74)

Milton was a prolific writer of prose and poetry. His most famous epic poem, *Paradise Lost*, was published in 1667 for which he received £10 and a further £10 after the first impression of 1,300 copies had been sold. This great poem in blank verse ran to over 200 pages in its first edition. It describes the struggle by Satan, who left heaven crying, 'Better to reign in Hell than serve in Heaven', and his acolytes Beelzebub, Moloch, Belial and Mammon to regain control of Heaven. Milton's rallying cry to the faithful is to describe in great detail how terrible Hell is – a prison where sinners were 'chained on a burning lake', tortured by demons, hit by 'wracking whirlwinds', heads and hands were lopped off, and all were 'consumed by an unextinguishable fire'. This punishment was to last for all eternity. No previous writer had ever drawn such a vivid picture and it was widely read in successive centuries, but rather less today.

'And Laughter holding both his sides.'

For the School Certificate that I took at sixteen, we read Milton's brilliant minor poems written in the 1630s, *Il Penseroso, Lycidas, The Masque Comus* and *L'Allegro* with its wonderful description of happiness:

> Haste thee nymph, and bring with thee
> Jest and youthful Jollity,
> Quips and cranks, and wanton wiles,
> Nods, and becks, and wreathed smiles,
> Such as hang on Hebe's cheek,
> And love to live in dimple sleek;
> Sport that wrinkled Care derides,
> And Laughter holding both his sides.
> Come, and trip it as ye go
> On the light fantastic toe,
> And in thy right hand lead with thee,
> The mountain-nymph, sweet Liberty …

Every morning at school we recited the Lord's Prayer in Latin and often sang a hymn with verses taken from another of Milton's poems, *On the Morning of Christ's Nativity*, which are embedded in my memory:

> XIII
> Ring out, ye crystal spheres!
> Once bless our human ears,
> If ye have power to touch our senses so;

And let your silver chime
Move in melodious time;
And let the bass of heaven's deep organ blow;
And with your ninefold harmony
Make up full consort of the angelic symphony.

XV
Yes, Truth and Justice then
Will down return to men,
The enamelled arras of the rainbow wearing;
And Mercy set between,
Throned in celestial sheen,
With radiant feet the tissued clouds down steering;
And Heaven, as at some festival,
Will open wide the gates of her high palace-hall.

Chapter 11

Poetry of the 18th and 19th Centuries

Reading is to the mind what exercise is to the body.

RICHARD STEELE, *THE TATLER*, 1709

ALEXANDER POPE WAS THE MOST PROLIFIC POET of the early eighteenth century, but he is read much less today. However, he does fill several pages of the *Oxford Dictionary of Quotations* with his pithy lines:

> Know then thyself, presume not God to scan,
> The proper study of Mankind is Man.
>
> To err is human, to forgive, divine.
>
> For fools rush in where angels fear to tread.
>
> On her white breast a sparkling cross she wore,
> Which Jews might kiss, and infidels adore.

The last couplet comes from a short booklet which was one of my A-level books, *The Rape of the Lock*, which describes how a young gallant cuts off a ringlet of hair from the most beautiful girl at Queen Anne's Court – a satirical rape.

The two most remembered poems of the eighteenth century are Thomas Gray's *Elegy Written in a Country Churchyard* and William Blake's *Jerusalem*.

Thomas Gray, *Elegy Written in a Country Churchyard*, 1751

The *Elegy* was printed as a small pamphlet of six pages and cost sixpence, and dismisses the memorials of the high and mighty:

> The Boast of Heraldry, the Pomp of Pow'r,
> Are all that Beauty, all that Wealth e'er gave,

Awaits alike th' inevitable hour.
The Paths of Glory lead but to the Grave.

And praises the poor:

Let not Ambition mock their useful toil,
Their homely joys and Destiny obscure
Nor Grandeur hear with a disdainful Smile
The short and simple annals of the Poor.

Far from the madding Crowd's ignoble Strife
Their sober Wishes never learn'd to stray,
Along the cool sequester'd Vale of Life
They kept the noiseless tenor of their way.

Words and phrases have been plucked out of these verses for the titles of books and films.

Gray did not write very much poetry and Dickens commented that by writing this single poem, 'No man has walked into Parnassus with such a slender volume in his hand.' I have a copy of the second edition which was printed in the following year, 1742. In 1854 a copy of the poem in Gray's own hand was sold at a sale for £130 – in today's money £12,000 – but if another copy was found in his own hand in an old trunk in a dusty attic it could now command over £100,000.

William Blake, *Jerusalem, c.* 1808

This was the first and greatest ecological poem which ends with the optimistic vision of a new Jerusalem in England. Michael Foot, a former leader of the Labour Party, once told me that the second verse was an expression of free love.

And did those feet in ancient time
Walk upon England's mountains green?
And was the holy Lamb of God
On England's pleasant pastures seen?

And did the countenance divine
Shine forth upon our clouded hills?
And was Jerusalem builded here
Among those dark Satanic Mills?

Bring me my bow of burning gold!
Bring me my arrows of desire!
Bring me my spear! O clouds, unfold!
Bring me my chariot of fire!

I will not cease from mental fight
Nor shall my sword sleep in my hand
Till we have built Jerusalem
In England's green and pleasant Land.

This poem was set to music by Hubert Parry in 1916 and has become since then an unofficial anthem for England. It has been sung at rugby matches and adopted as the official anthem for the Women's Institute.

Blake wrote a considerable amount of poetry, some obscure and challenging. He also added some very beautiful illustrations to accompany his poetry which he printed in small runs from his own workshop. They did not sell well, and many had to be sold after his death in 1827. Today, they are all very expensive collectors' items. His poems were not widely read in the nineteenth and twentieth centuries, and his first biography was published in 1863. The appreciation of his genius took-off from the mid-twentieth century and it recognised him as a great original artist and poet:

The Garden of Love

I went to the Garden of Love,
And saw what I never had seen:
A Chapel was built in the midst,
Where I used to play on the green.

And the gates of this Chapel were shut,
And 'Thou shalt not' writ over the door;
So I turn'd to the Garden of Love,
That so many sweet flowers bore.

And I saw it was filled with graves,
And tomb-stones where flowers should be:
And Priests in black gowns, were walking their rounds,
And binding with briars, my joys & desires.

The Lyrical Ballads, 1789: 'The still sad music of humanity'

This slender book of poems starts with a long and great poem by Samuel Taylor Coleridge, *The Rime of the Ancient Mariner* (1798), which takes up a third of the book. It ends with Wordsworth's *Lines Composed a Few Miles Above Tintern Abbey* (1798), which proclaims his passionate love of living in the country and being close to nature. This extract was the inspiration of the Romantic Movement which led to Keats, Shelley and Byron:

> For I have learned
> To look on nature, not as in the hour
> Of thoughtless youth; but hearing oftentimes
> The still sad music of humanity,
> Nor harsh nor grating, though of ample power
> To chasten and subdue.—And I have felt
> A presence that disturbs me with the joy
> Of elevated thoughts; a sense sublime
> Of something far more deeply interfused,
> Whose dwelling is the light of setting suns,
> And the round ocean and the living air,
> And the blue sky, and in the mind of man:
> A motion and a spirit, that impels
> All thinking things, all objects of all thought,
> And rolls through all things. Therefore am I still
> A lover of the meadows and the woods
> And mountains; and of all that we behold
> From this green earth.

Nineteenth-Century Poets

William St Clair's research revealed that in the period 1780 to 1830, fifty thousand new books of poetry were published, as well as the reprinting of earlier poets. He also showed that Walter Scott and Lord Byron made fortunes. Scott received £2,000 for *Marmion* and *The Lady of the Lake*, and Byron's publisher Murray paid him £20,000 over nine years, and for some poems he received 500 guineas.

The two major poets of the nineteenth century were Alfred Tennyson and Robert Browning. There were two other influential poets at the turn of the century, Thomas Hardy and Rudyard Kipling. My favourite is Browning. He wrote thirty-eight *Dramatic Monologues*, which are brilliant and imaginative for he brings to life fictional characters who in their own words describe their ideas and their passions. In *The Bishop Orders His Tomb at Saint Praxed's Church* (1845) you can hear the spidery voice of the Bishop dying 'by such slow degrees' and telling his sons, to whom he has given villas, to build for him a great tomb that would be greater than his predecessor Gandolf, with 'peach-blossom marble' and ''ome lump, ah God, of lapis lazuli' and 'let the blue lump poise between my knees/ Like God the Father's globe on both His hands.'

> And then how I shall lie through centuries,
> And hear the blessed mutter of the mass.

In *Bishop Blougram's Apology* (1855), the worldly bishop tries to persuade the literary man, Mr Gigadibs 'Over the glasses' edge when dinner's done' of the advantages of his cynical life:

> All we have gained then by our unbelief
> Is a life of doubt diversified by faith,
> For one of faith diversified by doubt;
> We called the chessboard white,— we call it black.

My favourite is *A Toccata of Galuppi's* (*c.* 1850), where an Englishman, who had never visited Italy, is stimulated by this music to reflect upon Venice.

> As for Venice and its people, merely born to bloom and drop
> Here on earth they bore their fruitage, mirth and folly were the crop
> What of soul was left I wonder, when the kissing had to stop.

Browning's poem *The Lost Leader* (1845) was quoted in the House of Commons in 1957. Harold Macmillan had to resign as Prime Minister following the Profumo Scandal. Nigel Birch MP, a senior ex-Treasury Minister who had resigned with the Chancellor of Exchequer a year earlier as Macmillan would not agree to a cut in expenditure, took his revenge by quoting the following:

> Life's night begins: let him never come back to us!
> There would be doubt, hesitation and pain,
> Forced praise on our part – the glimmer of twilight,
> Never glad confident morning again!

Macmillan had to sit and listen and then slunk out of the Chamber.

If I was asked what is the most memorable line of poetry in the nineteenth century, I would chose that last line of *A Toccata of Galuppi's*:

> What of soul was left I wonder, when the kissing had to stop.

Francis Palgrave (1824–97)

While at Balliol College, Palgrave met Matthew Arnold and also became a close friend of Alfred Tennyson. At the age of twenty-two he joined the Education Department in London, where he stayed for the rest of his working career until 1885 when, for the next decade, he was a professor of poetry at Oxford.

In the 1850s Browning was writing his *Dramatic Monologues* and while these were great, they were very long, and Tennyson was also writing long poems. Palgrave decided to compile an anthology, *The Golden Treasury of the Best Songs and Lyrical Poems in the English Language*, to feature famous shorter poems as they were more accessible and more readable to non-literary readers.

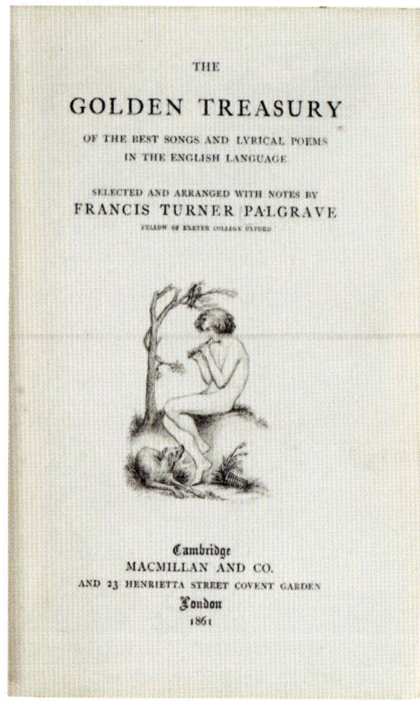

THE
GOLDEN TREASURY
OF THE BEST SONGS AND LYRICAL POEMS
IN THE ENGLISH LANGUAGE
SELECTED AND ARRANGED WITH NOTES BY
FRANCIS TURNER PALGRAVE
FELLOW OF EXETER COLLEGE OXFORD
Cambridge
MACMILLAN AND CO.
AND 23 HENRIETTA STREET COVENT GARDEN
London
1861

He began his anthology in the sixteenth century with several of Shakespeare's sonnets, and songs from the plays, alongside Milton's early poems, but there were no extracts from *Paradise Lost*. Many of the poems he chose were no more than twenty lines – sonnets and poems of three, four or five verses with simple memorable rhymes. He also chose several from the Cavalier Poets – John Suckling, Robert Herrick and Richard Lovelace. The anthology ended with a longer poem, Wordsworth's *Lines Composed a Few Miles Above Tintern Abbey*. Some of the songs and poems chosen were already traditional and popular, such as Henry Carey's *Sally in our Alley*, Robert Burns' *Ode to a Mouse*, William Cowper's *On the Loss of the Royal George*, and Gray's *Elegy Written in a Country Churchyard* and Charles Wolfe's *The Burial of St John Moore at Corunna*.

Palgrave was clever to call it *The Golden Treasury*, as it indicated it contained the best, and helped to make it a bestseller. He ended his dedicating preface with these words:

> If this Collection proves a storehouse of delight to Labour and
> to Poverty, – if it teaches those indifferent to the Poets to love

> them, and those who love them to love them more, the aim and the desire entertained in framing it will be fully accomplished.
>
> F.T.P. May, 1861

His publisher, Macmillan, was at first rather reluctant to print poetry and the first run was only 2,000 copies but it sold so well that by the end of 1861 it had been reprinted four times. The *Treasury* reminded the British public that we had a long, brilliant tradition of writing fine verse, something to remember and of which to be proud. Towards the end of the First World War, T.S. Eliot was teaching an Elizabethan Literature class and his advice to the students was 'Read sonnets in the *Golden Treasury*.'

Thomas Hardy (1840–1928)

Thomas Hardy's last novel, *Jude the Obscure* (1896), was savaged by reviewers, with the *Pall Mall Gazette* dubbing him 'Hardy the Decadent'. The Bishop of Wakefield made it known that he had thrown the book on to the fire and had asked his local library to withdraw it from their shelves. Hardy was so hurt by the criticism that he decided never to write another novel. Since 1890 Hardy had been writing poetry but none had been published, and in 1896, he explained the reason:

> Poetry, perhaps expresses more fully in verse, ideas and emotions which run counter to the inert crystallised opinion – hard as rock – which the vast body of men have vested interests in supporting. To cry out in a passionate poem that (for instance) the supreme mover or movers, the prime force or forces, must be either limited in power, unknowing or cruel – which is obvious enough and has been for centuries – will cause them merely a shake ofama the head; but to put it set in argumentative prose will make them sneer or foam and set all literary contortionists jumping upon me, a harmless agnostic as if I were a clamorous atheist which in their crass illiteracy they seem to think is the same thing ... If Galileo had said in verse that the world moved the Inquisition might have left him alone.

Later he said, 'Better fail in poetry than succeed in prose.' But he did not fail, for T.S. Eliot said of him, 'At times his style touches sublimity without even passing the stage of being good.'

He meant what he said, commenting, I believe, on his own wife's death:

God's Education (1909)

I saw him steal the light away
That haunted in her eye:
It went so gently none could say
More than that it was there one day
And missing by-and-by.

I watched her longer, and he stole
Her lily tincts and rose;
All her young sprightliness of soul
Next fell beneath his cold control,
And disappeared like those.

I asked: 'Why do you serve her so?
Do you, for some glad day,
Hoard these her sweets — ?' He said, 'O no,
They charm not me; I bid Time throw
Them carelessly away.'

Said I: 'We call that cruelty —
We, your poor mortal kind.'
He mused. 'The thought is new to me.
Forsooth, though I men's master be,
Theirs is the teaching mind!'

In Hardy's great novel *Tess of the D'Urbervilles*, his comment on her tragic and wretched life, which ended with her being hanged in Dorchester jail for the murder of a wealthy suitor, was 'The President of the Immortals had finished his sport with Tess.'

Although I read *The Woodlanders* at A-level, I came to prefer Hardy's poetry more than his novels. He had met his first wife in Cornwall, but he never really showed her much love, respect or consideration. It was a distant marriage and she took to living in the attic, while he stayed in the rest of the house. After her death, he felt such remorse that he wrote a series of poems in which he tried to reveal his love for her.

Great Things (1917)

Sweet cyder is a great thing,
A great thing to me,
Spinning down to Weymouth town
By Ridgway thirstily,
And maid and mistress summoning
Who tend the hostelry:
O cyder is a great thing,
A great thing to me!

The dance it is a great thing,
A great thing to me,
With candles lit and partners fit
For night-long revelry.
And going home when day-dawning
Peeps pale upon the lea:
O dancing is a great thing,
A great thing to me!

Love is, yea, a great thing,
A great thing to me,
When, having drawn across the lawn
In darkness silently,
A figure flits like one a-wing
Out from the nearest tree:
O love is, yes, a great thing,
Aye, greatest thing to me!

Will these be always great things
Greatest things to me? ...
Let it befall that one will call
'Soul, I have need of thee':
What then? Joy-jaunts, impassioned flings,
Love, and its ecstasy
Will always have been great things,
Greatest things to me!

Rudyard Kipling (1865–1936)

At the age of sixteen, Rudyard Kipling was sent back from England to India to join his parents and to start as the assistant editor of the *Civil and Military Gazette* in Lahore. As a journalist, he had to write about the news and so he talked to as many different people as possible; not only the members of the India Civil Service, but also to the engineers who were building bridges, canals, stations and Indian streets. He also met many Indians, as he travelled with his personal servant, his groom and his punkah-wallah (the servant who operated the fan). Above all, he enjoyed talking to the soldiers, as there was a large military presence in Lahore, which was on the Grand Trunk Road that led to Afghanistan.

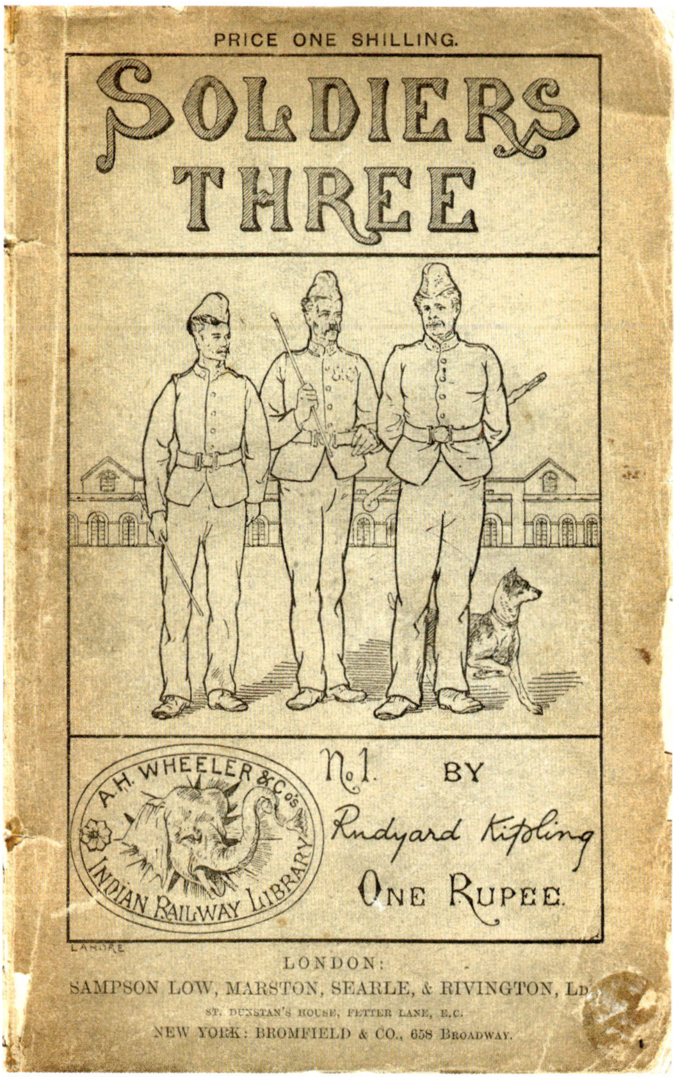

This paperback magazine was sold for 1 rupee in India and 1 shilling in London

The army was the bedrock of the British Empire in India, amounting to 59,000 troops, with 5,000 officers and 114,000 native soldiers. Kipling got to know the Northumberland Fusiliers where he met a Corporal Macnamara, an Irishman, whom he was to immortalise as Private Mulvaney in his short stories, *Soldiers Three*. The two other characters were Learoyd, a Yorkshireman yearning to return to Bradford, and Ortheris a Cockney Londoner whom he recognised as the informant of many of his short stories. He visited the soldiers in their barracks and soon learnt how important beer and going to the local brothels were for them.

In 1895 a quarter of the army were being treated for syphilis and that was even after the army approved some brothels as suitable for English soldiers. These soldiers feature in his first book, *Plain Tales from the Hills*, and he captured their accents and their army slang: 'I'm Privet Mulviney, wid no good overdu' pay a' an' a devouring thirst!'

Kipling was the first poet to wrote about soldiers' lives since Shakespeare, who had included ordinary soldiers in his play, *Henry V*. He did not romanticise them like Macaulay with Horatius defending the bridge, or Chesterton praising Don John of Austria in *Lepanto*. Kipling's soldiers were down to earth.

In the 1890s and the first three decades of the twentieth century, Kipling was by far the most widely read poet at a time. His poem, *If*, was regularly voted as Britain's most popular poem:

> If you can keep your head when all about you
> Are losing theirs and blaming it on you,
> If you can trust yourself when all men doubt you,
> But make allowance for their doubting too;
> If you can wait and not be tired by waiting,
> Or being lied about, don't deal in lies,
> Or being hated, don't give way to hating,
> And yet don't look too good, nor talk too wise:
>
> If you can dream—and not make dreams your master;
> If you can think—and not make thoughts your aim;
> If you can meet with Triumph and Disaster
> And treat those two impostors just the same;
> If you can bear to hear the truth you've spoken
> Twisted by knaves to make a trap for fools,
> Or watch the things you gave your life to, broken,
> And stoop and build 'em up with worn-out tools:

If you can make one heap of all your winnings
    And risk it on one turn of pitch-and-toss,
And lose, and start again at your beginnings
    And never breathe a word about your loss;
If you can force your heart and nerve and sinew
    To serve your turn long after they are gone,
And so hold on when there is nothing in you
    Except the Will which says to them: 'Hold on!'

If you can talk with crowds and keep your virtue,
    Or walk with Kings—nor lose the common touch,
If neither foes nor loving friends can hurt you,
    If all men count with you, but none too much;
If you can fill the unforgiving minute
    With sixty seconds' worth of distance run,
Yours is the Earth and everything that's in it,
    And—which is more—you'll be a Man, my son!

He wrote a group of military poems. These are the first verses from the most popular:

Danny Deever (1890)

'What are the bugles blowin' for?' said Files-on-Parade.
'To turn you out, to turn you out,' the Colour-Sergeant said.
'What makes you look so white, so white?' said Files-on-Parade.
'I'm dreadin' what I've got to watch,' the Colour-Sergeant said.
For they're hangin' Danny Deever, you can hear the Dead March play,
The Regiment's in 'ollow square—they're hangin' him to-day;
They've taken of his buttons off an' cut his stripes away,
An' they're hangin' Danny Deever in the mornin'.

Gentleman Rankers (1892)

We're poor little lambs who've lost our way,
Baa! Baa! Baa!
We're little black sheep who've gone astray,
Baa—aa—aa!
Gentlemen-rankers out on the spree,
Damned from here to Eternity,
God ha' mercy on such as we,
Baa! Yah! Bah!

Screw-Guns (1890)

For you all love the screw-guns — the screw-guns they all love you!
So when we call round with a few guns,
 o' course you will know what to do — hoo! hoo!
Jest send in your Chief an' surrender —
 it's worse if you fights or you runs:
You can go where you please, you can skid up the trees,
 but you don't get away from the guns!

This became the regimental song of the Royal Artillery in which I served for my National Service, and it was often sung at Mess dinners.

Kipling also created a soldier whose name for a time was used to describe all soldiers, 'Tommy Atkins':

We aren't no thin red 'eroes, nor we aren't no blackguards too,
But single men in barricks, most remarkable like you;
An' if sometimes our conduck isn't all your fancy paints,
Why, single men in barricks don't grow into plaster saints;
While it's Tommy this, an' Tommy that, an 'Tommy, fall be'ind,'
But it's 'Please to walk in front, sir,' when there's trouble in the wind
There's trouble in the wind, my boys, there's trouble in the wind,
O it's 'Please to walk in front, sir,' when there's trouble in the wind.

Apart from his poem, *If*, Kipling's poetry is not read widely today for it is very much of the time of late Imperial India. However his short stories have been more critically acclaimed, and Somerset Maugham, a great short story writer himself, said that Kipling was a master who could bear comparison with Guy de Maupassant and Chekhov.

Chapter 12

Poetry of the 20th and 21st Centuries

Only an owl knows the worth of an owl.

TED HUGHES

IN THE TWENTIETH CENTURY the reading of poetry expanded dramatically. The First World War saw the emergence of soldier poets and armchair poets who between them published 2,225 books, but four-fifths of these were written by civilians. Most of the soldier poets came from public or grammar schools and had been brought up on *The Select Epigrams from the Greek Anthology* published by J.W. Mackail in 1890, which extolled dying in battle as a noble, patriotic self-sacrifice: 'being dead they have not died'. While the war waged endlessly on, with mounting daily deaths and hideous injuries, a few poets expressed the horror of lying dead in the mud of the Somme where personal courage did not count much against the machine guns, gas, bombs and tanks.

There were four great soldier poets: Robert Graves, Wilfred Owen, Isaac Rosenberg and Siegfried Sassoon. Rosenberg was the only one from the working class, and I greatly admire his poem, *Louse Hunting* (1916/17). Wilfred Owen has emerged as the most popular and I think the greatest. After suffering from shellshock and while in a hospital in Scotland, Owen met Siegfried Sassoon who encouraged him to write more, but only five of his poems were printed before his death, which sadly occurred just seven days before the 1918 Armistice. His first book of poetry was published in 1920 and a fuller edition appeared in 1931 – both contain his two most famous poems, *Dulce et Decorum Est* and *The Anthem of Doomed Youth*. Owen's poetry of pity and much of Sassoon's of anger were not included in *The Oxford Companion of English Literature* published in 1960, but today their works are firmly embedded in the poetry curriculum of our schools. When, as Education Secretary in 1987 I was visiting a comprehensive school in a less prosperous area of Manchester, I was delighted to see the English class acting out Owen's *Dulce et Decorum Est*, which described a gas attack:

Gas! GAS! Quick, boys!—An ecstasy of fumbling
Fitting the clumsy helmets just in time,
But someone still was yelling out and stumbling
And flound'ring like a man in fire or lime.—
Dim through the misty panes and thick green light,
As under a green sea, I saw him drowning.

Siegfried Sassoon used biting satire to express the folly of war in *The General*:

'Good-morning, good-morning!' the General said
When we met him last week on our way to the line.
Now the soldiers he smiled at are most of 'em dead,
And we're cursing his staff for incompetent swine.
'He's a cheery old card,' grunted Harry to Jack
As they slogged up to Arras with rifle and pack.

But he did for them both by his plan of attack.

W.B. Yeats (1865–1939)

This Irish poet, dramatist and writer inspired the revival of Irish literature and theatre. His poetry revels in spiritualism, the occult, Irish ballads and mythology. He won the Nobel Prize for Literature in 1923. His most famous poem was *The Second Coming* and I have heard his line, 'Things fall apart; the centre cannot hold', quoted by score of politicians explaining their expected early demise.

Turning and turning in the widening gyre
The falcon cannot hear the falconer;
Things fall apart; the centre cannot hold;
Mere anarchy is loosed upon the world,
The blood-dimmed tide is loosed, and everywhere
The ceremony of innocence is drowned;
The best lack all conviction, while the worst
Are full of passionate intensity.

Edward Thomas (1878–1917)

Another poet who was only published posthumously was Edward Thomas in two books following his death in the First World War. He said once that his poetry, 'is the utterance of the human spirit when it is in touch of a world to which the affairs of this world are parochial'. His world was the beauty and peace of the English countryside where he described local and familiar things. In my *Faber Book of Landscape Poetry*, I included eight of Thomas' poems, including the most anthologised poem in the English language, *Adlestrop*. A month before the outbreak of the First World War, Thomas and his wife took a train from London Paddington to stay with Robert Frost at Ledbury. The train made an unexpected stop at a small station, Adlestrop, and that made the village famous for ever. Nothing could be more parochial than a steam train stopping at a Gloucestershire station, on a hot day, when 'no one left and no one came' until 'for that minute a blackbird sang':

Adlestrop

Yes. I remember Adlestrop—
The name, because one afternoon
Of heat the express-train drew up there
Unwontedly. It was late June.

The steam hissed. Someone cleared his throat.
No one left and no one came
On the bare platform. What I saw
Was Adlestrop—only the name

And willows, willow-herb, and grass,
And meadowsweet, and haycocks dry,
No whit less still and lonely fair
Than the high cloudlets in the sky.

And for that minute a blackbird sang
Close by, and round him, mistier,
Farther and farther, all the birds
Of Oxfordshire and Gloucestershire.

T.S. Eliot (1888–1965)

In 1922, T.S. Eliot printed in the literary magazine *Criterion*, of which he was the editor, his poem *The Wasteland*. It depicts the devastation of the world following the end of the First World War, but his poetry is utterly different from what has gone before – a jumbled syntax, typographical variations, and fragments from other writers and other languages. It has been subject to a vast amount of analysis and interpretation, where some criticise it for its obscurity but others recognise it as the pathway to modernism. It certainly needs to be read with notes – this is the concluding passage:

I sat upon the shore
Fishing, with the arid plain behind me
Shall I at least see my lands in order?
London Bridge is falling down falling down falling down
Poi s'ascose nel foco che gli affina
Quando fiam ceu chelidon – O swallow swallow
Le Prince d'Acquitaine de la tour abolie
These fragments I have shored against my ruins
Why then Ile fit you. Hieronymo's mad againe.
Datta. Dayadhvam. Damyata.
Shantih shantih shantih

'Hieronymo's mad againe' refers to Thomas Kidd's *Spanish Tragedy* in which Hieronymo seeks to revenge the murder of his own sons by killing the sons of their murderer before his own eyes. Eliot wants to say that sometimes madness can make murder seem acceptable.

'Datta. Dayadhvam. Damyata' are from Hindu mythology. Give. Sympathise. Control. 'Shantih shantih shantih' has been translated as the 'Peace that passes all understanding.'

This is Wendy Cope's limerick on T.S. Eliot:

No water. Dry rocks and dry throats,
Then thunder, a shower of quotes
From the Sanskrit and Dante,
Da. Damyata. Shantih.
I hope you make sense of the notes.

In the 1950s, as a teenager, I would wake early to join the queue to buy cheap seats in the 'gods' at theatres in London. The queues were often long and some people brought folding chairs. Entertainers appeared, many playing different instruments, and I recall one drawing a violin's bow across a saw, another recited parts from *The Wasteland* – my first introduction to modern poetry.

Three years after its publication, T.S. Eliot was baptised as a Christian and this led to him publishing *The Four Quartets* in the 1940s, which are masterpieces about the passage of time, and they contain the promise of redemption. This is my favourite passage from *Little Gidding*:

What we call the beginning is often the end
And to make an end is to make a beginning.

The end is where we start from. And every phrase
And sentence that is right ...
Every phrase and every sentence is an end and a beginning,
Every poem an epitaph. And any action
Is a step to the block, to the fire, down the sea's throat
Or to an illegible stone: and that is where we start.
We die with the dying:
See, they depart, and we go with them.
We are born with the dead:
See, they return, and bring us with them.
The moment of the rose and the moment of the yew-tree
Are of equal duration. A people without history
Is not redeemed from time, for history is a pattern
Of timeless moments. So, while the light fails
On a winter's afternoon, in a secluded chapel
History is now and England.

W.H. Auden (1907–73)

Auden was the most outstanding poet of the 1920s and 1930s. In 1939 he went to the United States and, sitting in a bar in New York, captured the essence of the 1930s in four words: 'a low dishonest decade'.

In 1935 , his poem *Night Mail* describes a train carrying the post from London to Scotland. Its brilliant rhyming captures what a person travelling on that train would feel and experience. It became enormously popular, and Benjamin Britten wrote music to accompany the poem in a film made by the Post Office. It is a striking example of how a rhythmic poem can become memorable and immensely popular.

This is the night mail crossing the Border,
Bringing the cheque and the postal order,

Letters for the rich, letters for the poor,
The shop at the corner, the girl next door.

Pulling up Beattock, a steady climb:
The gradient's against her, but she's on time.

Past cotton-grass and moorland boulder
Shovelling white steam over her shoulder,

Snorting noisily as she passes
Silent miles of wind-bent grasses.

Birds turn their heads as she approaches,
Stare from bushes at her blank-faced coaches.

Sheep-dogs cannot turn her course;
They slumber on with paws across.

In the farm she passes no one wakes,
But a jug in a bedroom gently shakes.

Dawn freshens, Her climb is done.
Down towards Glasgow she descends ...

In 1936 he wrote *Funeral Blues* following the death of a gay lover which was very personal and deeply moving:

Stop all the clocks, cut off the telephone,
Prevent the dog from barking with a juicy bone,
Silence the pianos and with muffled drum
Bring out the coffin, let the mourners come.

Let aeroplanes circle moaning overhead
Scribbling on the sky the message 'He is Dead'.
Put crepe bows round the white necks of the public doves,
Let the traffic policemen wear black cotton gloves.

He was my North, my South, my East and West,
My working week and my Sunday rest,
My noon, my midnight, my talk, my song;
I thought that love would last forever: I was wrong.

The stars are not wanted now; put out every one,
Pack up the moon and dismantle the sun,
Pour away the ocean and sweep up the wood;
For nothing now can ever come to any good.

Some fifty-eight years later in 1994, the poem was read aloud during the film *Four Weddings and a Funeral*. It became a bestseller with millions of viewings and readings around the world – a memorable masterpiece.

Philip Larkin (1922–85)

Despite publishing only four slim volumes of poetry, Philip Larkin significantly increased the reading of poetry. He is the spokesperson for provincial England – Coventry, Sheffield and Hull – where he served as the Librarian of the University of Hull for thirty years. His poetry often describes movement between places – platforms, stations and trains – and one of his most famous poems, *The Whitsun Weddings* (1964), records a rail journey he made from Hull to London, watching many wedding parties leave and join the train. It is entirely appropriate that his fine standing statute is not in the library but in Hull railway station. He also wrote frankly about his own life:

Annus Mirabilis (June 1967)

Sexual intercourse began
In nineteen sixty-three
(which was rather late for me) –
Between the end of the Chatterley ban
And the Beatles' first LP.

Up to then there'd only been
A sort of bargaining,
A wrangle for the ring,
A shame that started at sixteen
And spread to everything.

Then all at once the quarrel sank:
Everyone felt the same,
And every life became
A brilliant breaking of the bank,
A quite unlosable game.

So life was never better than
In nineteen sixty-three
(Though just too late for me) -
Between the end of the Chatterley ban
And the Beatles' first LP.

Larkin was aware of the brevity of life and some ten years after *Annus Mirabilis* he wrote *Aubade*, a word which usually denotes a song that welcomes the dawn, but this poem is much closer to a threnody of death. It also contains several memorable phrases including, 'Most things may never happen: this one will.'

These are verses one, four and five of five verses.

I work all day, and get half-drunk at night.
Waking at four to soundless dark, I stare.
In time the curtain-edges will grow light.
Till then I see what's really always there:
Unresting death, a whole day nearer now,
Making all thought impossible but how
And where and when I shall myself die.
Arid interrogation: yet the dread
Of dying, and being dead,
Flashes afresh to hold and horrify.

And so it stays just on the edge of vision,
A small unfocused blur, a standing chill
That slows each impulse down to indecision.
Most things may never happen: this one will,
And realisation of it rages out
In furnace-fear when we are caught without
People or drink. Courage is no good:
It means not scaring others. Being brave
Lets no one off the grave.
Death is no different whined at than withstood.

Slowly light strengthens, and the room takes shape.
It stands plain as a wardrobe, what we know,
Have always known, know that we can't escape,
Yet can't accept. One side will have to go.
Meanwhile telephones crouch, getting ready to ring
In locked-up offices, and all the uncaring
Intricate rented world begins to rouse.
The sky is white as clay, with no sun.
Work has to be done.
Postmen like doctors go from house to house.

29 November 1977

Larkin wrote very little afterwards and died eight years later, having become one of the most widely read poets.

Seamus Heaney (1939–2013)

Seamus Heaney was born in Ulster, but in his early thirties he moved to live in the Republic of Ireland. Sometimes he is called an English poet, but he once asserted, 'I carry a green passport.' Being brought up on a farm had a profound effect upon his poetry. *Digging* is one of his first poems where he watches

his father digging with his hands on a spade in a field while he sits inside at a desk with his hands holding a pen. It was one of his favourite poems and often included in his public readings. He translated many Irish poems and also the Old English poem, *Beowulf*, a masterpiece which has been read more than any previous version over the centuries. It has outsold any of the Heaney collections of poems and it is a poetic transformation.

Ted Hughes (1930–98)

I came to know Ted Hughes in the 1980s when I was the Education Secretary and he was judging the *Observer* poetry competition for children. He advised young people to look carefully at an object, like a leaf, a tree or an animal, and then describe it in a poem. Later he published his own book of poems for children. He was passionate about reading poetry aloud, encouraging children to do this and also to learn poetry by heart. He wrote a letter to me expressing, 'When children know poetry by heart, they have the guardian angel installed behind their tongue. They have the reefs of language for life to build and read around, a globe of "precepts" and great sheet anchor in the maelstrom of linguistic turbulence.' At that time, I was fashioning the National Curriculum, and I was able to follow his advice and make the reading and learning of poetry by heart part of English lessons in primary schools. Ted had a remarkable and unique way of remembering written words by a series of images in his mind. To show the method's effectiveness he once recited to me, without the text to hand, the first page of Jonathan Swift's famous pamphlet, *A Modest Proposal For preventing the Children of Poor People From being a Burthen to Their Parents or Country.*

For me, Ted Hughes is one of the greatest poets of the twentieth century. Born in Yorkshire, he lived close to the Pennines and the River Don, and that countryside had an enormous effect upon his poetry: 'the old hairy moors', 'the drumming ploughland', 'clay that clutches my each step', 'hoisting heather and stones to the sky'. Then, the weather – rain, storms, sleet, snow, mists, and all the many animals, sheep, piglets, old sows, frogs, mice, gnats, owls and skylarks. Also brambles, weeds, and the fish – pike, salmon and trout. When Ted moved to North Devon, he took up farming and in Moortown he wrote a poetic diary of the day's work. He bought a bull, but its hooves grew too large and impeded the bull from covering a cow and he wrote a poem showing how dangerous it was to engage in hoof-cutting a bull. His descriptions reveal how man has to relate to nature with all its failings and challenges, showing the dark side where brutality and violence are never far away. Like Browning, he engaged with the 'dangerous edge' of things: it is this which makes his poetry memorable.

Hughes was also a prolific writer for children – *The Iron Man* and *The Iron Woman* are widely read in schools, and *Meet My Folks* and *How the Whale*

PIKE A POEM BY TED HUGHES WOODCUT BY ROBERT BIRMELIN

Pike, three inches long, perfect
Pike in all parts, green tigering the gold.
Killers from the egg: the malevolent aged grin.
They dance on the surface among the flies.

Or move, stunned by their own grandeur,
Over a bed of emerald, silhouette
Of submarine delicacy and horror.
A hundred feet long in their world.

In ponds, under the heat-struck lily pads---
Gloom of their stillness:
Logged on last year's black leaves, watching upwards.
Or hung in an amber cavern of weeds

The jaws' hooked clamp and fangs
Not to be changed at this date;
A life subdued to its instrument;
The gills kneading quietly, and the pectorals.

Three we kept behind glass,
Jungled in weed: three inches, four,
And four and a half: fed fry to them---
Suddenly there were two. Finally one

With a sag belly and the grin it was born with.
And indeed they spare nobody.

Two, six pounds each, over two feet long,
High and dry and dead in the willow-herb---

One jammed past its gills down the other's gullet:
The outside eye stared: as a vice locks,
The same iron in this eye
Though its film shrank in death.

A pond I fished, fifty yards across,
Whose lilies and muscular tench
Had outlasted every visible stone
Of the monastery that planted them---

Stilled legendary depth:
It was as deep as England. It held
Pike too immense to stir, so immense and old
That past nightfall I dared not cast

But silently cast and fished
With the hair frozen on my head
For what might move, for what eye might move.
The still splashes on the dark pond,

Owls hushing the floating woods
Frail on my ear against the dream
Darkness beneath night's darkness had freed,
That rose slowly towards me, watching.

150 COPIES PRINTED BY E. & L. BASKIN & RICHARD WARREN AT THE GEHENNA PRESS NORTHAMPTON MASSACHUSETTS 1959

For Kenneth Baker Greetings from Ted Hughes

Became are wonderful for the nursery. I read *Nessie the Mannerless Monster* to our children many times. Together with Seamus Heaney, he published an anthology for children, *The School Bag*.

Heaney and Hughes were friends and together they published *The Rattle Bag*, a remarkable anthology of poems which they had both read and collected over the years. In the copy Hughes gave to me, he stressed how different it was from Palgrave's *Golden Treasury* by writing, 'The Stone, Bronze and Iron Treasury'. There are no lyric poems from the Cavalier poets and only one poem each from Bryon, Browning and Tennyson, but there are lots from Shakespeare, William Blake, D.H. Lawrence, Thomas Hardy, Wilfred Owen, W.B. Yeats, Gerard Manley Hopkins; and from America, Walt Whitman, Emily Dickinson, Elizabeth Bishop and Wallace Stevens. It is quite brilliant.

In *The Wasteland*, T.S. Eliot transformed poetry of the twentieth century and triggered a revolution. We are lucky in England that at the same time we had poets like Auden, McNeice, Larkin, Hughes and Heaney. Their poetry has swept through the English-speaking world with memorable, compelling poems that became attractive to young people.

Heaney and Hughes were very familiar with each other's poetry and in a letter which Seamus wrote to Carol Hughes after Ted's death in 2008, he paid a generous tribute to Ted's posthumous selected translations which included Heaney's stunning oceanic metaphor:

> The delights are dolphin-like, the mighty talent rising again and showing his bark above the elements – I got the book and swum in and out of the different coves and caves, safe havens (few), and strange strands. A strong sense of being lifted on the tide of it all.

Poets I have also enjoyed are Carol Ann Duffy (1955–) and Benjamin Zephaniah (1958–2023) who alas is dead, but in the poems recorded by him you can hear his voice and catch the beautiful Caribbean rhythms and cadences. I also liked *Poppy* in the debut poems by Joseph Minden which go in and go out of places, and go in and out of history.

Wendy Cope (1945–)

Cope is the poet who makes me smile and laugh out loud. Her first book was published in 1986, *Making Cocoa with Kingsley Amis.* Her poems are about how to cope with the day-to-day problems of life – the title of a later book is *Two Cures of Love*. She is also a brilliant parodist, excelling in the ones on Shakespeare sonnets. I have also included in this book two of her limericks on John Donne and T.S. Eliot.

Men and their Boring Arguments (1988)

One man on his own can be quite good fun
But don't go drinking with two –
They'll probably have an argument
And take no notice of you.

What makes men so tedious
Is the need to show off and compete.
They'll bore you to death for hours and hours
Before they'll admit defeat.
It often happens at dinner-parties
Where brother disputes with brother
And we can't even talk among ourselves
Because we're not next to each other.

Some men like to argue with women –
Don't give them a chance to begin.
You won't be allowed to change the subject
Until you have given in.

A man with the bit between his teeth
Will keep you up half the night
And the only way to get some sleep
Is to say, 'I expect you're right.'

I expect you're right, my dearest love.
I expect you're right, my friend.
These boring arguments make no difference
To anything in the end.

Chapter 13

The Fun of Satirical Poetry

I have no gun but I can spit.

W.H. Auden

THROUGHOUT OUR LONG HISTORY SOME POETS have directed their anger, scorn and wit at our monarchs, politicians, statesmen and anyone in an important position who had been pompous, stupid, vain, vacuous or venal. Satirical poetry was present in Rome 100 BCE:

> The epigrams you write are always bland
> And paler than skin powdered with white lead,
> Without a grain of wit or drop of bile,
> And still, you fool, you want them to be read!
> A face without a dimple has no charm;
> Food is insipid, lacking vinegar's zing,
> Give honey apples and bland figs to toddlers;
> I savour Chian figs which know to sting.
>
> Martial

This type of poetry was not just for enjoyment; it had a purpose which W.H. Auden recognised:

> Satire is angry and optimistic – it believes that once people's attention is drawn to some evil, they will amend their ways.

A second champion of satirical writers was John Milton in *Areopagitica*, who advised them to go for 'the greatest persons':

> For a satire as it was born out of a tragedy, so ought to resemble his parentage, to strike high, and adventure

> dangerously at the most eminent vices among the greatest persons, and not to creep into every blind tap-house, that fears a constable more than a satire.

A third champion is John Dryden, the finest satirist of the late seventeenth century, whose advice was:

> ... the nicest and most delicate touches of Satire consist in fine Raillery ... how easie it is to call Rogue and Villain, and that wittily? But how hard to make a Man appear a Fool, a Blockhead or a Knave, without using any of those opprobrious terms? ... there is still a vast difference betwixt the slovenly Butchering of a Man, and the fineness of a stroak that separates the Head from the Body, and leaves it standing in its place.

No poet would have dared to attack Henry VIII, Mary Tudor or Elizabeth I, but Cardinal Wolsey proved a good target. In the early years of Henry VIII's reign he had enormous power – as a Cardinal, as Archbishop of York and Lord Chancellor of England. He dined off gold plate, had his red hat carried before him and built Hampton Court. He fell from grace when he could not secure a divorce for the King, who had him arrested, but he died before he could be tried.

One piece of doggerel is rumoured to have been written by Henry VIII but there is no direct evidence:

> Begot by butchers but by bishops bred.
> How high his Highness holds his haughty head.

John Skelton in his 1522 poem, *Why come ye nat to Courte?* attacked Wolsey's ascendancy.

> To tell the truth plainly,
> He is so ambitious,
> So shameless, and so vicious,
> And so superstitious, And so much oblivious
> From whence that he came ...
>
> Such is a king's power,
> To make within an hour,
> And work such a miracle,
> That shall be a spectacle

Of renown and worldly fame:
In likewise now the same
Cardinal is promoted,
Yet with lewd conditions quoted,
As hereafter ben noted,
Presumption and vainglory,
Envy, wrath, and lechery,
Covetise and gluttony,
Slothful to do good,
Now frantic, now stark wood ...

Set up a wretch on high
In a throne triumphantly,
Make him a great estate,
And he will play checkmate
With royal majesty ...

Any satirist who attacked Charles I would have soon been condemned by the Court of Star Chamber either to be branded, pilloried or ear-cropped. Cromwell, too, brooked no criticism. However, with the restoration of Charles II, satire flourished, and the leading satirist was John Dryden (1631–1700). His poem *Absalom and Achitophel* was published in 1681 at the beginning of the Exclusion Crisis (1679–81) which challenged the right of Charles' Catholic brother, James, to be his heir. Absalom was the Duke of Monmouth, Charles II's illegitimate son, and Achitophel was Anthony Ashley Cooper, the Earl of Shaftesbury, the leading critic of the King, who had earlier been one of his ministers, being the first 'A' in the 'Cabal' of five on whom Charles II depended (the other four being Clifford, Buckingham, Arlington and Lauderdale). He became the first unofficial leader of the Opposition and was accused of High Treason and went abroad to avoid arrest and execution.

Of these the false Achitophel was first,
A name to all succeeding ages curst.
For close designs, and crooked counsels fit;
Sagacious, bold, and turbulent of wit.
Restless, unfix'd in principles and place;
In pow'r unpleas'd, impatient of disgrace.
A fiery soul, which working out its way,
Fretted the pigmy body to decay,
And oe'r-inform'd the tenement of clay.
A daring pilot in extremity;

Pleas'd with the danger, when the waves went high
He sought the storms; but for a calm unfit,
Would steer too nigh the sands, to boast his wit.
Great wits are sure to madness near alli'd,
And thin partitions do their bounds divide;

FROM *ABSALOM AND ACHITOPHEL*

George Villiers, 2nd Duke of Buckingham (1628–87)

This is another attack on one of Charles II's ministers, being the 'B' in the Cabal of five. He was a libertine and went through a large fortune, spending £30,000 on his robes for Charles II's coronation. He soon fell out with the King and by 1670 a group of friends ran his estate and paid him an allowance.

Some of their chiefs were princes of the land:
In the first rank of these did Zimri stand:
A man so various, that he seem'd to be
Not one, but all Mankind's Epitome.
Stiff in opinions, always in the wrong;
Was everything by starts, and nothing long:
But in the course of one revolving moon,
Was chemist, fiddler, statesman, and buffoon:
Then all for women, painting, rhyming, drinking;
Besides ten thousand freaks that died in thinking.
Blest madman, who could every hour employ,
With something new to wish, or to enjoy!
Railing and praising were his usual themes;
And both (to show his judgment) in extremes ...

Both James Callaghan and Margaret Thatcher quoted from the four lines I have underlined in the run-up to the General Election in 1979.

Charles II (1630–85)

John Wilmot, 2nd Earl of Rochester (1647–80) was another renowned libertine and an occasional companion of Charles II. This poem was published after Wilmot's death.

There reigns, and long may he reign and thrive,
The easiest prince and best bred man alive:
Him no ambition moves to seek renown,

Like the French fool to wander up and down,
Starving his subjects, hazarding his crown.
Nor are his high desires above his strength,
His scepter and his p--- are of a length,
And she that plays with one may sway the other,
And make him little wiser than his brother.
I hate all monarchs and the thrones they sit on,
From the Hector of France to the Cully of Britain.
Poor Prince, thy p--- like the buffoons at court,
It governs thee, because it makes thee sport;
Tho' safety, law, religion, life lay on't,
'Twill break through all to its way to c---.
Restless he rolls about from whore to whore,
A merry Monarch, scandalous and poor.

Joseph Addison (1672–1719)

... Peace to all such! but were there one whose fires
True genius kindles, and fair fame inspires,
Blest with each talent and each art to please,
And born to write, converse, and live with ease:
Should such a man, too fond to rule alone,
Bear, like the Turk, no brother near the throne,
View him with scornful, yet with jealous eyes,
And hate for arts that caus'd himself to rise;
Damn with faint praise, assent with civil leer,
And without sneering, teach the rest to sneer;
Willing to wound, and yet afraid to strike,
Just hint a fault, and hesitate dislike ...
Alike reserv'd to blame, or to commend,
A tim'rous foe, and a suspicious friend;

ALEXANDER POPE,
FROM *THE EPISTLE TO DR ARBUTHNOT*, 1734

This is 'the most studied and delicate piece of invective in the language'. It is certainly the most quoted. Pope's attack probably arose from Addison's view that the best translation of the *Iliad* was by Thomas Tickell and this view was expressed just before Pope was to publish his own. Addison had generally encouraged Pope's critics and although they had been friends, Pope had become conscious of 'a deceptive friendship.' Never has malice been so economical.

George III (1738–1820)

George III was very proud of managing the Windsor farms himself, which provoked satire in both verse and cartoons where he acquired the nickname, 'Farmer George'.

Peter Pindar, the satiric versifier, picked upon the King's visit in May 1787 to Whitbread's London brewery to poke fun at his repetitive staccato way of speaking and his muddle over hay, grain, hops and malt.

'Birthday Ode' (an extract), 1787

To Whitbread now deign'd Majesty to say,
'Whitbread, are all your horses fond of hay?'
'Yes, please your Majesty,' in humble notes,
The Brewer answer'd: 'also, Sir, of Oats:
Another thing my Horses too maintains,
And that, an't please your Majesty, are Grains.'

'Grains, grains,' said Majesty, 'to fill their crops?
Grains, grains?—that comes from hops; yes, hops, hops, hops?'

Here was the King, like Hounds sometimes, at fault.
'Sire,' cry'd the humble Brewer, 'give me leave
Your sacred Majesty to undeceive:
Grains, Sire, are never made from Hops, but Malt.'

'True,' said the cautious Monarch, with a smile:
From malt, malt, malt—I meant malt all the while.' -
'Yes,' with the sweetest bow, rejoin'd the Brewer,
'An't please your Majesty, you did, I'm sure.' -
'Yes,' answer'd Majesty, with quick reply,
'I did, I did, I did, I, I, I, I.'

The cartoon, opposite, from 1794, was even more explicit:

George, Prince of Wales (1762–1830)

From the age of eighteen, the future George IV had fallen in with a group of profligate young rakes who spent their time drinking and whoring. This satirical poem, *The Devil Divorced*, appeared when he was twenty-one – anyone could fill in the blanks:

First on my list a man of rank appears,
Far versed in wickedness above his years.
The ---------- of ------------, if I can ought foretell,
Will most assuredly come down to hell.
Whenever vice or lewdness lead the way,
With what officious zeal doth he obey!
Him no ambition moves to seek renown;

To be esteemed the *greatest buck* in town
Appears to be his wish and sole delight.
Full many times at twelve o'clock at night
I've known him drunk, with half a dozen more,
Kick up a row, break lamps, perhaps a door,
And to conclude the night, to bilk his w-----e.

There is little caricature in this explicit act of royal fornication dated 1 April 1786. The garter of Maria Fitzherbert, the Prince of Wales's mistress, reads 'mal y pense' and George's 'soit'. No previous cartoon had been so explicit and I know of no such cartoon involving a senior member of the royal family that has appeared since. This is George's unique record.

The Duke of Wellington (1769–1852)

You are 'the Best of Cut-throats', do not start—
The phrase is Shakespeare's, and not missapplied;
War's a brain-spattering, windpipe-slitting art,
Unless her cause by right be sanctified;
If you have acted once a generous part,
The world, not the world's master, will decide,
And I shall be delighted to learn who,
Save you and yours, have gained by Waterloo? ...

LORD BYRON, FROM *DON JUAN*, CANTO NINE

William Wordsworth (1770–1850)

This is Robert Browning's scathing denunciation of Wordsworth's desertion of the liberal cause. The underlined part of this poem was quoted to great dramatic effect by Nigel Birch in 1963 in the House of Commons debate on the Profumo Affair. He was taking revenge on Harold Macmillan for the way he had received the resignation of himself, the Chancellor of the Exchequer and Enoch Powell in 1957. Macmillan referred to this as 'a little local difficulty' and went on an overseas tour. When Macmillan's back was against the wall over Profumo, with these words Birch called for a new leader and Macmillan slunk out of the House.

The Lost Leader, 1845

Just for a handful of silver he left us,
Just for a riband to stick in his coat—
Found the one gift of which fortune bereft us,
Lost all the others she lets us devote;
They, with the gold to give, doled him out silver,
So much was theirs who so little allowed:
How all our copper had gone for his service!
Rags—were they purple, his heart had been proud!
We that had loved him so, followed him, honoured him,
Lived in his mild and magnificent eye,
Learned his great language, caught his clear accents,
Made him our pattern to live and to die!
Shakespeare was of us, Milton was for us,
Burns, Shelley, were with us,—they watch from their graves!
He alone breaks from the van and the freemen,
He alone sinks to the rear and the slaves!

We shall march prospering,—not through his presence;
Songs may inspirit us,—not from his lyre;
Deeds will be done,—while he boasts his quiescence,
Still bidding crouch whom the rest bade aspire:
Blot out his name, then, record one lost soul more,
One task more declined, one more footpath untrod,
One more triumph for devils and sorrow for angels,
One wrong more to man, one more insult to God!
Life's night begins: let him never come back to us!
There would be doubt, hesitation and pain,
Forced praise on our part—the glimmer of twilight,
Never glad confident morning again!

Best fight on well, for we taught him—strike gallantly,
Menace our heart ere we pierce through his own;
Then let him receive the new knowledge and wait us,
Pardoned in heaven, the first by the throne!

Robert Browning, 1845

King George V (1865–1936)

Max Beerbohm revived satire in the late nineteenth century. In the poem, *Ballade Tragique à Double Refrain* (1912), a Lord-in-Waiting and a Lady-in-Waiting are at Windsor Castle:

SCENE: A Room in Windsor Castle
TIME: The Present
Enter a Lady-in-Waiting and a Lord-in-Waiting

SHE: Slow pass the hours—ah, passing, slow!
My doom is worse than anything
Conceived by Edgar Allan Poe:
The Queen is duller than the King.

HE: Lady, your mind is wandering;
You babble what you do not mean.
Remember, to your heartening,
The King is duller than the Queen.

SHE: No, most emphatically No!
To one firm-rooted fact I cling
In my now chronic vertigo:
The Queen is duller than the King.

HE: Lady, you lie. Last evening
I found him with a Rural Dean,
Talking of district-visiting ...
The King is duller than the Queen.

Max Beerbohm, *A Sailor King (George V)*, 1914. It is cartoons like this that are said to have delayed Max's knighthood for twenty-seven years.

A Land Fit for Heroes, 1920

These words below, by G.K. Chesterton (1874–1936), are a refutation of the only too prevalent slander that parliamentary leaders are indifferent to the strict fulfilment of their promises and the preservation of their reputation for veracity.

They said (when they had dined at Ciro's)
The land would soon be fit for heroes;
And now they've managed to ensure it,
For only heroes could endure it.

'Chuck it, Smith!' – F.E. Smith (1872–1930)

This is one of the best putdowns of a leading politician. The target, F.E. Smith, could not be grander – Solicitor General, Attorney General and Lord High Chancellor. He was renowned for his boisterous oratory, but he too incurred the wrath of G.K. Chesterton:

Antichrist, or the Reunion of Christendom: An Ode

'A Bill which has shocked the conscience of every Christian community in Europe.' – Mr. F. E. Smith, on the Welsh Disestablishment Bill 1920.

Are they clinging to their crosses,
F. E. Smith,
Where the Breton boat-fleet tosses,
Are they, Smith?
Do they, fasting, trembling, bleeding,
Wait the news from this our city?
Groaning 'That's the Second Reading!'
Hissing 'There is still Committee!'
If the voice of Cecil falters,
If McKenna's point has pith,
Do they tremble for their altars?
Do they, Smith?

Russian peasants round their pope
Huddled, Smith,
Hear about it all, I hope,
Don't they, Smith?
In the mountain hamlets clothing
Peaks beyond Caucasian pales,
Where Establishment means nothing
And they never heard of Wales,
Do they read it all in Hansard –
With a crib to read it with –
'Welsh Tithes: Dr. Clifford answered.'
Really, Smith?

It would greatly, I must own,
Soothe me, Smith!
If you left this theme alone,
Holy Smith!

For your legal cause or civil
You fight well and get your fee;
For your God or dream or devil
You will answer, not to me.
Talk about the pews and steeples
And the cash that goes therewith!
But the souls of Christian peoples ...
Chuck it, Smith!

The Labour Government, 1947

For over thirty years Sagittarius wrote satirical political poems for *The New Statesman*, reflecting on the political news of the moment. Sagittarius was the nom-de-plume of Olga Katzin Miller (1896–1987). Her knowledge of poetry, both English and European, was immense and I enjoyed talking to her. She had a wonderful sense of humour.

Labour had a huge victory in the 1945 General Election, returning 393 Socialists to 213 Conservatives. Less than half of the Labour MPs were from the working class, and Sagittarius could not resist commenting upon the fact that the Cabinet was full of ministers who had been to Oxford and Cambridge. The one working class minister was Ernest Bevin, who became one of the best Foreign Secretaries of the twentieth century.

Two years of Parliamentary civility
Abate the class, if not the Party, feud;
No Labour Member lacks responsibility,
Although his social background may be rude,
While several have a title to gentility
Such as the Tory ranks might not exclude,
And manual labourers, if fairly prominent,
On the Front Bench at least are not predominant.

Both birth and intellect are there displayed;
The Premier is impeccably Oxonian,
A younger son conducts the Board of Trade,
The Chancellor's a perfect old Etonian,
The Foreign Secretary, though self-made,
Is quite magnificently Palmerstonian;
If such as these are Labour mediocrities,
Where is the Tory Cicero, or Socrates?

In 1963 Miller published an anthology entitled *The Perpetual Pessimist* in which she drew upon her wide knowledge of world history and found a quotation for each day of the year – it is a calendar of gloom, an almanack of woe. Similar to a much earlier work published in 1621, *The Anatomy of Melancholy* by Robert Burton, it is a reflection upon man's inhumanity – both were bestsellers.

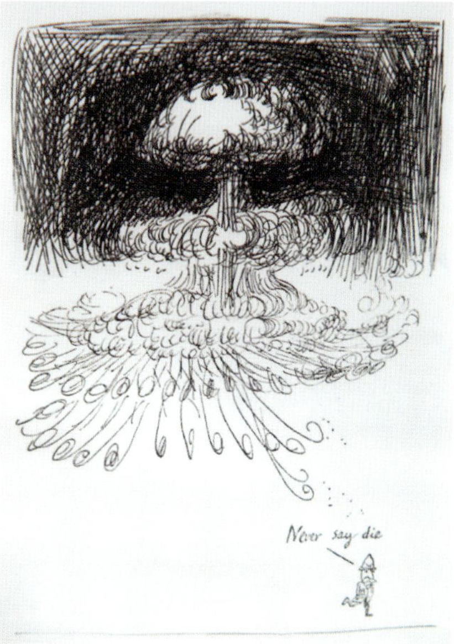

For 13 July, Miller quoted J.C. Squire (1884–1958) to show that poets have a role in lifting the gloom:

> The fat men go about the streets,
> The politicians play their game;
> The prudent bishops sound retreats
> And think the martyrs much to blame;
> Honour and love are halt and lame,
> And greed and power are deified.
> The wild are harnessed to the tame;
> For this the poets lived and died.

Her entry for August 6 marked the first nuclear bomb explosion in Hiroshima, Japan – 250,000 killed.

Epitaph for George Bernard Shaw (1856–1950)

> I strove with all, for all were worth my strife.
> Nature I loathed, and, next to nature, Art.
> I chilled both feet on the thin ice of Life.
> It broke, and I emit one final fart.

MAX BEERBOHM, 1950

This is a satirical take on an 1849 poem by Walter Savage Landor entitled *Dying Speech of an Old Philosopher*.

Enoch Powell (1912–98)

Down with Fanatics

If I had my way with violent men
I'd simmer them in oil,
I'd fill a pot with bitumen
And bring them to the boil.
I execrate the terrorist
And those who harbour him,
And if I weren't a moralist
I'd tear them limb from limb.

Fanatics are an evil breed
Whom decent men should shun;
I'd like to flog them till they bleed,
Yes, every mother's son,
I'd like to tie them to a board
And let them taste the cat,
While giving praise, oh thank the Lord,
That I am not like that.

For we should love the human kind,
As Jesus taught us to,
And those who don't should be struck blind
And beaten black and blue;
I'd like to roast them in a grill
And listen to them shriek,
Then break them on the wheel until
They turned the other cheek.

Roger Woddis (1917–93)

Roger Woddis was a gifted left-wing poet who published a series of coruscating poems and parodies for *The New Statesman* and other magazines. It was a delight to read his wit.

I would like to close with the choice that W.B. Yeats wrote for the 1924 general election, but applicable to them all:

On a General Election

The battle's set twix't Envy, Greed and Pride:
Come Conscience do your duty: choose your side.

Chapter 14

Libraries

> Some books are to be tasted, others to be swallowed, and some few to be chewed and digested.
>
> Francis Bacon

Libraries first appeared in the Near East. By 300 BCE there were fifty of them in cities and towns like Nineveh and Babylon in Mesopotamia. A library allowed a book to survive beyond one generation – posterity was the beneficiary. The Ptolemy kings of Egypt from the third to first centuries BCE wanted to create in Alexandria a library of the greatest books in the world. They were bibliophiles, passionate purchasers of books in all languages, and they appointed Callimachus, a poet born in Libya, as the Chief Librarian. He created the first catalogue by recording all the papyrus rolls, with their authors and details of their lives, and divided the books into categories like history, geography, mathematics and philosophy. Also, being a poet, he divided them into plays, prose and verse. Only seven plays by Sophocles and Aeschylus have survived today, but Callimachus listed one hundred by Sophocles and seventy-three by Aeschylus. At its height, the library included over 400,000 rolls.

Books were so important to the Egyptians that when Mark Antony went to Egypt to seek the favours of Queen Cleopatra in 37 BCE, he flattered her with hundreds of papyrus rolls instead of fine jewels or clothes, as she was an avid reader. When Julius Caesar entered Alexandria, he launched an incendiary attack upon the Egyptian fleet in the harbour – disastrously, its flames spread to the library destroying 40,000 rolls. Plutarch, describing the battle one hundred years later, said the fire spread to the great library and reduced it to rubble, but doubts have been raised and perhaps he was only referring to some warehouses that had been storing recently arrived rolls.

The Roman invasion saw the end of the golden age of the library, which had also been a great community of scholars, as it was never one of Rome's priorities. As the Roman occupation came to an end, Alexandria became for many years a centre of civil disturbances which destroyed buildings, including part of the

Long Room, Trinity College Library, Dublin, built 1712–32

Selling *Encylopedia Britannia* in 1947. Printed editions ceased in 2012.

Tianjin Binhai Library, China, built 2015–17

WIKIPEDIA

Wikipedia 2001

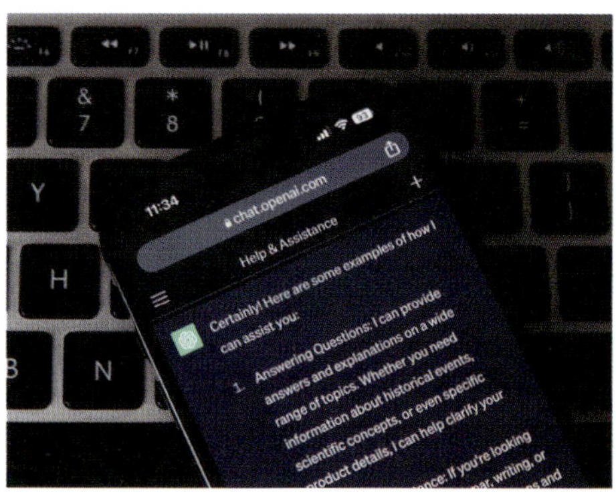

A.I. 2023 and ChatGPT

An artist's impression of the Alexandrian Library

library. In 642 CE Muslims conquered Alexandria and the commander sent a letter to Caliph Omar I, asking what he should do with the books. The reply was, 'With regards to the books you mention, here is my answer. If the books contain the same doctrine as the Qur'an, they are useless, because they merely repeat; if they are not in agreement with the doctrine of the Qur'an there is no reason to conserve them.' So ended the great library of Alexandria – the books and rolls of papyrus were given to the bathhouses as fuel, with their fires burning for months.

Later Development of Libraries

On his death in 1447, Humphrey of Lancaster, Duke of Gloucester, made a generous gift of 281 books to the University of Oxford. In the sixteenth and seventeenth centuries libraries were principally for scholars, like the one founded in 1653 by Humphrey Chetham in Manchester which is still in use today. When Thomas Bodley opened his great library in Oxford in 1602, Francis Bacon welcomed it, 'He built an ark to save learning from a deluge.' It was followed by the Codrington Library at All Souls in 1712, and the Radcliffe Camera in 1749 to house the scientific collection.

The first circulating library was founded in 1726 by Allan Ramsay, a wigmaker and a poet, in his shop in Edinburgh. He charged two pennies a night to borrow a book and his most popular titles were obscene books and plays. Puritans preached against these, as they were subversive to Christian faith, and in Richard Sheridan's play, *The Rivals*, Sir Anthony Absolute fumed that 'a circulating library in a town is an evergreen tree of diabolical knowledge! It blossoms through the year! – and depend upon it, Mrs Malaprop, that they who are so fond of handling the leaves will long for the fruit at last'. In 1770 the Minerva Press opened, and on moving to Leadenhall Street, London, in 1790 it offered 10,000 volumes covering history, philosophy, travel and poetry for a guinea a year.

Alongside circulating libraries, a number of villages set up a library usually supported by the local church and often the books were stored in the vestry. These libraries were the major recipients of texts from the Religious Tract Society created in 1798 to distribute religious texts on a significant scale. This led to one Buckinghamshire clergyman pleading for more copies of *Pilgrim's Progress* and *Robinson Crusoe*, but going on to say, 'Shakespeare will be lost upon them.'

In 1841, with Thomas Carlyle as one of its strongest supporters, the London Library was launched with 500 members and 3,000 books. In 1849, the Clerk of the Library told the House of Commons Libraries Committee that his library consisted of 19,500 books and had twenty-five readers a day, but the books were not for the poor: 'They never considered buying books useful to that class.'

In 1849 William Ewart MP (1798–1869) tabled the Public Libraries Bill in the House of Commons to allow Councils to increase local rates by no more than one halfpenny per £1 for the foundation of a free library and to cover its building and staff, but not for the buying of books. The Bill's proponents claimed that libraries would make the news available to poorer people who could be persuaded not to support the revolutions which extended all over Europe in 1848. The Bill had a very difficult passage through Parliament, as its opponents argued that it encroached upon the liberties of the people, and that libraries and education should not be the concern of government as it was a form of taxation. Such laissez-faire arguments have not disappeared completely even today, as some people think the arts should not receive any taxpayer support. Colonel Charles de Laet Waldo Sibthorp was an Ultra-Conservative MP who said, 'However excellent food for the mind might be, food for the body is most wanted for the people. I did not like reading at all and I hated it when at Oxford.'

The Bill passed with a majority of only seventeen. Manchester and Liverpool were the first to open free libraries in 1852, followed by Birmingham in 1861 and Leeds in 1879, but there was no great surge of library building. Some depended upon philanthropic support, and in 1876 the Mayor of Wigan, who was also a cotton mill owner, provided the land to build a magnificent library designed by Alfred Waterhouse, and a local doctor, Joseph Winnard, gave a substantial sum to purchase books. By 1896 only 334 councils had a free library, including only two parishes in London.

Charles Edward Mudie (1818–90) had a small shop in central London selling newspapers, magazines and stationery. He added books and started to lend them out at one penny for each night. By 1842 he had over 25,000 subscribers and built a large classical-style building with a dome in New Oxford Street, similar to the British Museum, to house them, alongside his shops in Kensington High Street and Queen Victoria Street. By 1871 he had over one million books and in the year of his death he had 7.5 million. His staple was the three decker novels of a famous author to which he added less well-known writers such as Charles Lever, Bulwer-Lytton and Ainsworth. Mudie also offered a wide range of other literature – histories, biographies (such as on David Livingstone), travel books, poetry and Charles Darwin's radical writings. He bought in bulk the first editions of novels and today collectors of Victorian first editions will often find that the top cover of many bear the traces of a Mudie's Library label.

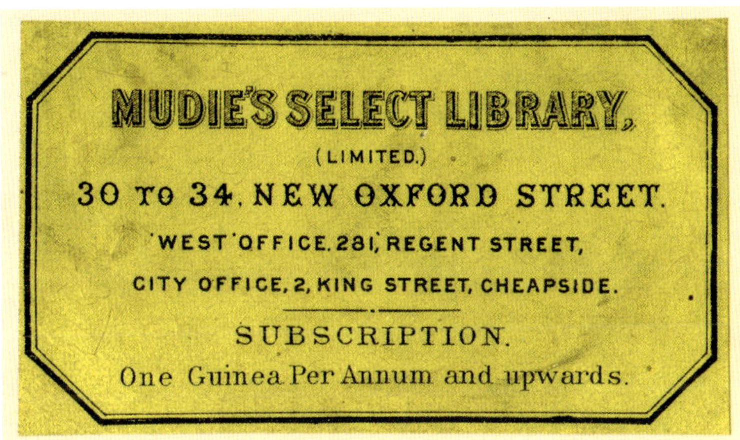

Mudie's Library appealed to the ordinary reader who, for one guinea a year, could borrow as many books as they wished, but not more than one a day. This was at a time when a working-class weekly wage could be as low as a guinea and a half. From 1862 he published a monthly register of new books and their summaries, and also shipped large quantities of books in tin trunks to the Empire. His contribution to the book trade has been overlooked and forgotten, but I believe he did more than any other Victorian to increase the number of readers in Victorian England. At last, Mudie is getting recognition, for in his book *The Book-Makers*, Professor Adam Smyth has recognised him as one of the eighteen figures who have made a significant contribution to the book trade.

Some schools also had libraries and in 1852 Charles Dickens, on visiting one in Manchester, welcomed the school library as 'a great free school bent on carrying instruction to the poorest hearts'.

Carnegie Libraries

Andrew Carnegie (1835–1919) was born in a weaver's cottage in Dunfermline, Scotland. His family migrated to the USA in 1848. He built up America's largest steel company and became a great philanthropist. He decided to finance the building of libraries in places with which he was familiar, often in partnership with the local authority, and the first was opened in Dunfermline in 1883. In all, he supported 2,500 libraries across the English-speaking world, but not all welcomed his generosity, for when in 1904 he gave £40,000 to establish a library in Islington, London, local ratepayers protested against it but fortunately they did not prevail.

Andrew Carnegie laying the foundation stone of the Waterford City Library, 1903

Most town boroughs of a certain size built libraries in the nineteenth and twentieth centuries. One of their purposes was to provide national and local newspapers for their residents to read, as well as to provide books for lending, but this became less important following the breakthrough of cheap paperback novels in the 1940s. Today most people get their immediate news through radio, television or online, so the original purposes of libraries have withered away, and over 800 libraries have been closed in England.

In 1997 Ted Hughes wrote a poem about the library closures at the invitation of Matthew Evans, then the Arts Minister in the House of Lords and a former Chairman of Faber & Faber publishing house. One of the verses said:

Where any nation starts awake
Books are the memory. And it's plain
Decay of libraries is like
Alzheimer's in the nation's brain.

And in my own day in my own land
I have heard the fiery whisper: 'We are here
To destroy the Book
To destroy the rooted stock of the Book and
The Book's perennial vintage, destroy it
Not with a hammer not with a sickle
And not exactly according to Mao who also
Drained the skull of adult and adolescent
To build a shining new society
With the empties----'

The Jewish Underground Library

When the Nazis occupied Warsaw in September 1939, they closed all the Jewish lending libraries and forbade Jews from using public libraries. One of the Jewish librarians, Basia Berman, set about collecting many Yiddish and Polish books

Book sale in the Łódź Ghetto, 1940

and made them available to homeless children through an underground library. A publisher, Lejb Szur, even before the war had rescued between 10,000 and 20,000 books which were added to Basia's collection. To make the library more appealing, and to hide it from the Nazis, she decorated the library rooms with toys and children's picture books. In lending the children two books – one in Polish and the second in Yiddish – she helped them to read Yiddish for the first time. In her memoir she wrote, 'The book became a vital need, almost like bread.' Some children took the books with them to the death camps.

The Nazis created a Jewish Ghetto and, in the summer of 1940 started to send the Jews to the extermination camps. Basia and her husband managed to escape and worked with the Jewish underground to help rescue as many as they could. The Jewish historian, Emily Putzke, who researched the story has written, 'Books were a source of life and sustenance for the human spirit, a way to preserve one's humanity amid a dehumanising reality.'

Libricide

Libraries have often been the victims of war and some were deliberately destroyed by an invading army to erase the records of the country they had conquered. During both world wars the Louvain Library in Belgium was destroyed, and in Sarajevo in 1992 Serbian criminals on the night of 25 and 26 August set fire to the National and University Library of Bosnia and Herzegovina. Over two

The library of Holland House was hit during the Blitz on 23 October 1940

million books, periodicals and documents vanished in the flames which lasted for three days. The Bosnian Serb Leader, Radovan Karadžić, was convicted later as a war criminal and will spend the rest of his life in prison.

George Orwell wrote that 'the most characteristic activity of the Nazis was burning books'. Hitler recognised the power of knowledge that books contained, for they could encourage resistance and assert the freedom of the press. That is why Goebbels, in May 1933, had a great book burning in Berlin and followed this in other German cities. He also created a list of literary figures in England who would be killed after the Nazi invasion: Virginia Woolf, E.M. Forster, H.G. Wells, J.B. Priestley, Aldous Huxley, Bertrand Russell and Noël Coward.

In 1942 Goebbels ordered the closing of all commercial circulating libraries in Germany, as some of their books could undermine the Nazi regime. In comparison, circulating libraries in Britain – for example in Boots and W.H. Smith – thrived in British high streets until the 1960s.

Dictionaries

In 1755, after working on the project for nine years, Samuel Johnson published his *Dictionary of the English Language* in two large volumes covering 42,773 words. The volumes were large and heavy, 50 cm tall and 10 cm wide, and they have to be read on a table. *The Dictionary* is one of the great achievements of the English language and I am lucky to have acquired a first edition. I enjoy opening the volumes at a random page and scanning down the list of words, some of which have dropped out of use, and finding how Johnson meticulously recorded their provenance, the time they were first used and quotations of their use which Johnson provided from his own extensive reading.

In 1857 Frederick Furnivall persuaded the Oxford University Press (OUP) to create a modern dictionary to be known as the *Oxford English Dictionary* (OED). He was followed by Albert Murray (1837–1915), the President of the Philological Society and the headteacher of Mill Hill School, who in 1878 was tasked by the OUP to complete the compilation. Both Furnivall and Murray asked a wide range of people to send to them a single word in an envelope, written on a slip of paper 6 x 4 in, that included its provenance, its meaning, the date it was first used and a quotation in which it had been used. Hundreds of thousands of slips were sent in, not just from literary scholars but from a wide range of passionate readers.

In 2015 a lexicographer Sarah Ogilvie, spent a few days before leaving for a teaching job in America rummaging through the cellars of the OUP, and found a book in a dusty box which was the list of the names and addresses for all the

3,000 people who had sent slips to Albert Murray. She researched as many of these people as possible and recorded the lives of many of them, whether rich or poor, proud or humble, scholar or self-taught, and even lunatics, murderers and pornographers. The results were published in *The Dictionary People* (2023), a brilliant and illuminating history of how the OED was created and with fascinating insights into the social history of late Victorian England. A sheer delight to read.

Thomas Austin from Hitchen, Hertfordshire, who spent periods in an asylum, sent in the largest number of slips: 165,661. He had four children living on the edge of poverty and fell out with Murray when he asked for payment. There were 487 female contributors, many like the spinsters Jemima and Elizabeth Brown who cared for their elderly father in Cirencester and between them submitted 15,000 slips. Elizabeth was an astronomer who had travelled to Russia with her own telescope to watch an eclipse. Another, Jeanette Humphrey, who was writing a book on cooking, sent in 18,700 slips, including three new words or phrases: 'mint sauce', 'piccalilli', and 'short-crust pastry'.

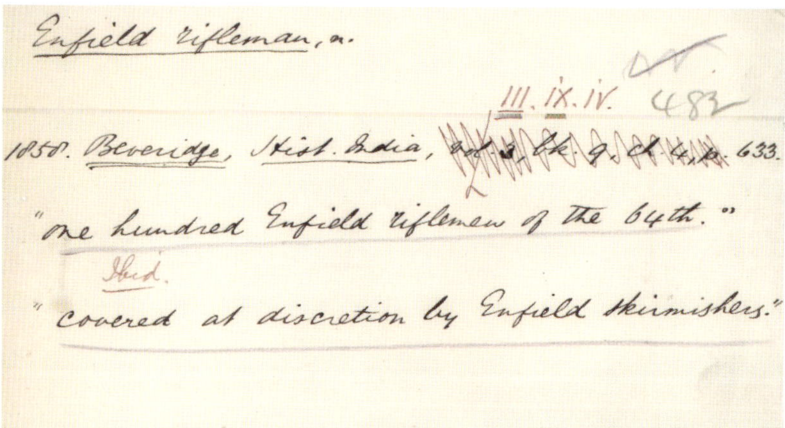
Enfield rifleman, n.
III. IX. IV.
1858. Beveridge, Hist. India, 633.
"one hundred Enfield riflemen of the 64th."
Ibid.
"covered at discretion by Enfield skirmishers."

One of the slips sent from Thomas Austin to Albert Murray

Other contributors included vicars, suffragettes and vegetarians, one of whom contributed 'nutcake'. Doctors contributed and one sent 150 slips relating only to the diseases of the prostrate. Lovers of tennis, which had become popular in late Victorian England, added 'love' in the 1880s, 'centre court' in 1843 and 'ace' in 1854. Weather watchers in their own back gardens added 'raincoat' in 1830, 'rained-in' in 1857 and 'lightning strike' in 1876. The leading Victorian pornographer Henry Spencer Ashbee, a self-made prosperous industrialist who had amassed a library of 1,600 erotica that was almost turned down by the British Museum, though they burnt some of the items, added frequently used swear words and sexual terms.

Albert Murray in his *scriptorium*

Several lunatics sent in slips, including John Dormer, who had frequent spells in Croydon Mental Hospital, and submitted over 150,000 slips adding 'cockatoo', 'hanky-panky' and 'pagoda'. William Minor, committed to Broadmoor Asylum for shooting and stabbing a stranger, sent in 62,720 slips with words from books he had read in his cell – including 'bamboo', 'banana', 'barbecue', 'merino' and 'orology' (the study of mountains). Murray visited him at the asylum.

Murray had an iron hut built in the back garden of his Oxford home which became his *scriptorium*. He enrolled his wife and some of their eleven children into analysing the slips. He himself was responsible for half of the English words which amounted to 171,116 – four times the number in Johnson's *Dictionary*. In 1915 he decided he had to retire, and the last word he worked upon was appropriately 'twilight'.

In 1928 the *OED* was published in ten volumes with 15,500 pages and 1,827,300 quotations. Prime Minister Stanley Baldwin attended the grand launch dinner which included some of the volunteers, but alas no women, as the venue, The Goldsmith's Hall, did not allow females.

Chapter 15

Bookshops, Browsing and Collecting

> Like a dope fiend who cannot move from place to place without taking with him a plentiful supply of his deadly balm, I never venture far without a sufficiency of reading matter.
>
> W. Somerset Maugham, 1932

Bookshops

In 1990 Peter Blayney, a bibliographer, published a paper entitled, 'The Bookshops in Paul's Cross Churchyard'. Through the most extensive and scrupulous research of the many leases issued to shops and businesses in that part of London from 1500 to the Great Fire of 1666 – which destroyed not only St Paul's Cathedral but many of the buildings around it – Blayney revealed how it was the centre of the book trade in London with many shops and publishing houses.

The churchyard of the cathedral, which was surrounded by a wall, was a great meeting place for the hundreds and thousands of Londoners who flocked there to hear the sermons from St Paul's Cross pulpit. The buildings around the courtyard were three- and four-storeys high and included houses and shops, with homes above. There were drapers, haberdashers, embroiderers, trunk-makers, vintners, paper-sellers, a barber, a printing works and a small corner shop that 'selles pinnes, pointes, and walking staves'. Some of the shops sold books as well as paper, pens and ink. There were several publishing houses who were members of the Stationers' Company, a guild founded in 1403 to 'set and improve the regulations of all published works'.

The individual shops had signs or banners hung outside with names that included the Queen's Arms, Green Dragon, Rose, Black Bear, Brazen Serpent and White House, and these passed from one generation to a new leaseholder who usually kept the name. From the leases, Blayney was able to trace the families that lived in these houses for 166 years. Some names cropped up again and again – Cawood, Coston, Broome, Mosley and Norton. Members of the Norton family are recorded in the reigns of both Henry VIII and Charles I. When a bookseller died, quite often his widow continued to run the shop. When in 1603 Caldoch died at the Green Dragon, his widow April kept the lease, marrying again to a Bing who died the following year, but she continued the shop as Widow Bing for several years. Humphrey Mosley used the sign of the Prince's Arm from 1637 until his death, and his widow Anne continued from 1661 up to the Great Fire.

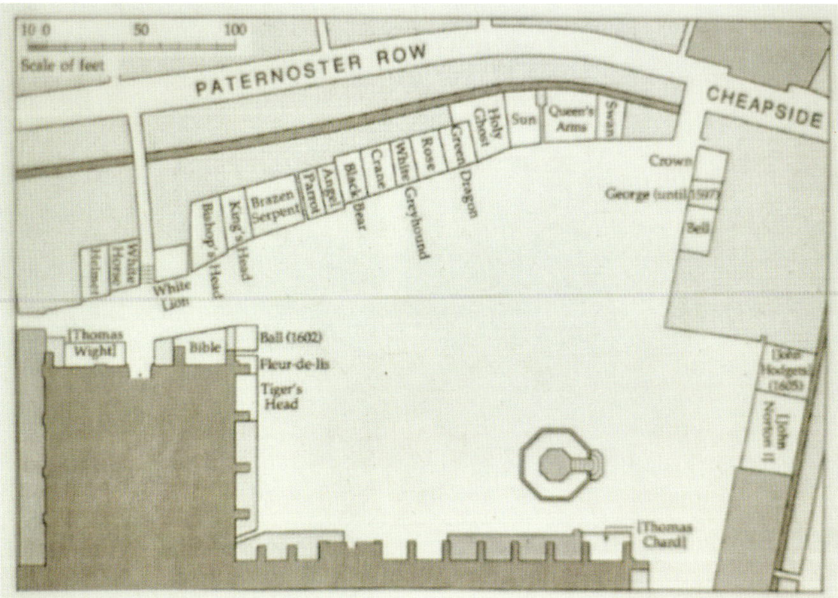

1600 – the shaded area next to the signed shops was also full of shops, and the bays of the cathedral were stuffed tight with small shops

When the Stationers published a book, they would give as their imprint their address in the churchyard, for it had become the centre of the London book trade – a very busy, flourishing area, for book publishing and printing were very profitable. It was common for apprentices to be appointed and often they would have been given a room, probably shared with others, within the three- or four-storey buildings, effectively living above the shop.

Edward Blount was a publisher at The Black Bear and in November 1623 he would have received the first copies of Shakespeare's Folio as he had been one of its main financial supporters who had come together to fund it.

Twentieth-Century Bookshops

In the 1940s Charing Cross Road in London was still full of bookshops and Foyles occupied two of the larger buildings at the top end. I loved just strolling down the long road and dropping into some of them. When I was about fourteen, I came across a book in Foyles which I had never heard of before called *Brewer's Dictionary of Phrase and Fable*, a treasure house of information. Opening the page starting 'Ci', I found fascinating facts about Circe, Circle of Ulloa, circumbendibus, Circumlocution Office, cists, Cistercians, citizens, city of brotherly love and city of destruction. It cost me 7 shillings and sixpence, which meant that I did not have enough for my bus fare back to Twickenham, so I had to walk half the way. The book was well worth it!

Bookshop in Charing Cross Road, London, 1926

When I go into a second-hand bookshop, it is with a smile because it is full of affordable books, and I love meandering slowly along the shelves of novels, poetry, history, gardening, philosophy, war, biographies and sport. Often, I have no idea of what book I want to buy, but by browsing I see so many books that are different, and some I have never heard of, and it is what catches my eye that I will buy. It will be a random encounter. I always felt it was a duty that I had to buy at least one book from every second-hand bookshop that I visited.

Browsing the Shelves

In Samuel Johnson's *Dictionary* of 1759, the word 'browse' was defined as 'to eat branches and shrubs' / 'sheep browsing in ivy', and although there were masses of bookshops in London at that time, the first modern use of the word 'browse' was made in 1863 with 'a person who browses' among books.

In my youth every town had at least two or three second-hand bookshops, and when I was a government minister in the 1980s I used SKOOB, a simple guide to local bookshops, to find out where the good second-hand bookshops were in the towns I was visiting so that I could drop in and spend a few minutes or so browsing. It is sad that so many of these shops have disappeared.

The internet and Amazon have destroyed the simple pleasure of browsing, as they just want to sell you a book at the lowest price with almost immediate delivery. You cannot browse on a screen; a simple pleasure that has almost disappeared.

Bookshops Today

Although second-hand bookshops have all but disappeared, ordinary bookshops in Britain are flourishing, mainly due to the inspired leadership of one man, James Daunt. He opened his first bookshop at the top of end of Marylebone High Street, almost adjacent to the local Conservative Association's offices where I was the local MP. Daunt's shop was very welcoming, and I dropped into it many times, finding the staff knowledgeable about books and admiring how the latest books were displayed in a beguiling way. It became the place where several new publications held their book launches. This developed into a chain of Daunt Books.

In 2011 a Russian oligarch who liked the Daunt chain bought it, and also paid £53 million for Britain's largest bookseller, Waterstone's, which was being hit by Amazon and its sale of books downloaded onto the Amazon Kindle. He appointed Daunt to pull Waterstone's around. Seven years later in 2018 it was sold on to a private equity firm, Elliott Investment Management, for £200 million – an amazing turnaround. In 2019 the fund decided to build an international network of booksellers led by Barnes & Noble, bought in America for $683 million, whose turnover had been falling for some years. Daunt was appointed as the CEO of this huge joint venture. Since then, Foyles in the Charing Cross Road and Blackwell's online sales have been added, and Waterstones is opening ten new stores every year. It has been said that the profit already has more than doubled.

Book Collecting

Books were the first creations of mankind which were collected and so preserved. I know well the urge to own and collect books – at least those that I enjoyed or inspired me. Book collecting took off in Victorian England. In 1834 Sotheby's auctioned the library of a passionate collector, Richard Heber – the first sale lasted twenty-six days – and a series of later sales released into the collecting world tens of thousands of books. Between the years 1851 and 1883 there were 6,000 auctions where the new public libraries and the great scholarly collections at universities and cathedrals could buy early and rare books. Many of the aristocratic families who had famous inherited libraries of great distinction suffered from the long agricultural depression of the 1870s and 1880s and sold their libraries – for example, the Sunderland Library from Blenheim Palace in 1882, the library of the Earl of Gosford in 1885, and the Earl of Jersey's library from Osterley Park which was sold privately. New buyers emerged from the professional middle class.

Carl Spitzweg, *The Bookworm*, *c.* 1850

In the nineteenth century the most significant booksellers were Bernard Quaritch and John Hatchard, who still operate today. They handled what had become an over-supply of rare books. Bookselling had become more scholarly and the profession of librarians developed, leading to the Library Association in 1887, and also to the career of bibliographers. The Bibliographical Society was created in 1892 and this recognised that more information should be provided about rare books, such as their print editions, the publishing house, the condition of the paper and binding, and the book's provenance. Today, there are regular book sales supported by a growing number of book collectors. AbeBooks, which is a collector's delight, offers a wide range of collectible books, the rarest selling for thousands of pounds.

One of the features which makes a modern book more valuable is the dust jacket. A first edition of F. Scott

Fitzgerald's *The Great Gatsby* without its jacket could sell for between £1,000 and £2,000, but with an immaculate jacket it would fetch more than £100,000. The first publication of famous authors are eagerly sought – for example, Graham Greene's was a collection of poems, *Babbling April*, with a print run of 300 copies which he later tried to suppress, and when he found a copy he would burn it. The first printed pamphlet of Robert Louis Stevenson, written when he was fifteen years old, is called *The Pentland Rising* (1866), probably cost sixpence when published but it now sells for thousands. Kipling's first book of poems, *Barrack-Room Ballads* (1892), printed to look like a government document, commands a very high price. The first edition of *The Wasteland* by T.S. Eliot appeared in the magazine of which he was editor, the *Criterion*, in 1924 and I remember seeing some copies of the magazine selling for £150. Later, I bought one for less than £1,000, but a bookseller in 2023 was offering a copy for £15,000. Books and pamphlets like these will continue to increase in value.

Charles Lamb (1775–1834), Writer, Poet and Book Collector

In *The Last Essays of Elia*, Charles Lamb in 1833 revealed his passion for book collecting. He had a strong interest in trying to buy the large folio copies of early works but having little money he only managed to get copies which were 'bound hard, brown, stained, ragged, broken-backed, dragging their covers, scrappy old volumes in single misery'. He was a bibliomaniac, and he collected where he could, delving into the barrows from which books were often sold. He had set his mind on buying a folio of a Beaumont and Fletcher collected plays, and he waited until 10pm one Friday night before setting out from his house in Islington to the bookseller in Covent Garden. When he got home he immediately started to repair the book before daylight. He amassed a very large library of such books, annotated many of them and lent several to his friend Coleridge, who often added his own comments.

Charles Lamb, after Daniel Maclise, lithograph, published 1873

On his death, the books became highly collectible and in a most interesting piece of research *Book Madness: A Story of Book Collectors in America* (2022), Denise Gigante reveals the very determined way that collectors bought books from either English libraries, private collections or at auctions. The battered spines and the handwritten comments increased their value to passionate collectors enormously in Britain and America.

The Folio Society

The Folio Society was founded in 1947 with the aim of producing classic books with beautiful bindings and illustrations. Their purchasers were members of a club and many of the books have become collectors' items. When Joanna Reynolds became the Chief Executive in 2016, she found sales were falling, and she transformed it by publishing many new and relatively unknown writers whose works focus on science fiction and fantasy – George R.R. Martin's *A Game of Thrones* was a bestseller, alongside *Dune* by Frank Herbert, whose third book in that series, *Children of Dune*, sold 1,000 copies. The Folio's *Howl's Moving Castle* by Diana Wynne Jones has a large community on BookTok. These books are not cheap, often exceeding £80 each, but the Society's customers aged below twenty-five now exceed those aged over sixty-five. Books are much cheaper on Kindle and Amazon, but there is still a mass of readers who prefer to hold a book in their hands.

Epilogue to the Future

THE DEATH OF BOOKS HAS BEEN FORECAST many times over the last 5,000 years. In 2022 Brian Cummings, Professor of English Literature at the University of York, published *Bibliophobia*, which is defined as the fear and hatred of books. It is a brilliant and fascinating book covering seven continents, scores of countries, and many races and religions. It shows how books have survived that fear and hatred, and how they have civilised and continue to civilise mankind. Books are the ark of imagination, and they have a relentless capacity to survive. These are some of Cummings' conclusions:

> A book constitutes the coming into being of writing, so that when revolutions take place in its form (such as new media), a terrible beauty is reborn. Change exposes the sightlines in the theatre of mimesis, making seen the unseen, and making its spectators vulnerable inside the illusion ... What follows is a love letter for books, even as I recount the violence done to them. The book is not dead or dying, not yet, it has finitude written into it, as scroll, codex, or tablet, beginning and ends again. In that sense a book carries our mortality within it. Beginning a book for the first time, or finishing it, is a metaphor for life. Closing the book brings mourning, writing is the trace of morbidity, and reading is a little death. We live inside books, and expire with them, even as they outlive us.

Picture Credits

p. 2 © Eileen Hogan / photo author's own
pp. 13, 27, 28, 36, 37, 40, 46, 54, 56, 58, 62, 64, 66, 80, 81, 82, 84 (bottom), 85, 107, 120 (all), 129, 136 (all), 139, 141, 146, 160, 182, 186, 199, 200, 211, 212, 218, 233, 234, 238 courtesy of the author
pp. 9, 57, 76 from The New York Public Library
p. 11 Metropolitan Museum of Art, Rogers Fund, 1917
p. 16 Lorraine Mitchell/Alamy
p. 19 © Alastair Fyfe
p. 21 Metropolitan Museum of Art, purchase, Raymond and Beverly Sackler Gift, 1988
pp. 22 (top), 23, 33, 59, 88, 90, 93, 95, 97 (top), 99, 115 (all), 132, 143, 149, 155, 168, 173, 223, 225, 228, 237 Wikimedia Commons
p. 22 (bottom) Wikimedia Commons/ Valley2city
p. 24 Wikimedia Commons/British Library
p. 29 © British Library
pp. 30, 142 Library of Congress
p. 31 Getty Research Institute
p. 43 © Manuel Harlan / ArenaPAL
pp. 44, 63, 78, 138, 152, 165 Archive.org
p. 49 Princeton University Art Museum, bequest of Junius S. Morgan, Class of 1888
p. 50 From the playing card collection of Adam West-Watson
p. 60 HathiTrust
p. 65 © Bolton Museum and Art Gallery, Lancashire, UK© Bolton Museum and Art Gallery /Bridgeman Images
p. 74 Wikimedia Commons / © The Trustees of the British Museum
p. 83 Washington State University
p. 84 (top) Army Pictorial center
p. 91 Bibliothèque Nationale de France
p. 92, 231 © Bodleian Libraries, University of Oxford
p. 94 Bayerische Staatsgemäldesammlungen – Alte Pinakothek
p. 96 Metropolitan Museum of Art, Gift of Jill Spalding, 2022
p. 97 (bottom) © Bradford Museums & Galleries /Bridgeman Images
p. 101 © Eve Arnold/Magnum Photos
p. 105 (left) IMAGO/H.Tschanz-Hofmann/ Alamy
p. 105 (right) Beinecke Rare Book and Manuscript Library / Yale University Library
p. 106 Victoria & Albert Museum, London, UK/Bridgeman Images
p. 109 Philip V. Allingham / Victorian Web
pp. 111, 128, 137 Wellcome Collection
p. 112 Yellowback Cover Art/Flickr
p. 116 © Ralph Steadman Archive. All rights reserved 2026/Bridgeman Images
p. 123 ©BBC/Courtesy Everett Collection/ Alamy
p. 127 Yale University Art Gallery
p. 130 Granger/Bridgeman Images
p. 147 Biblioteca Monasterio del Escorial, Madrid, Spain/Bridgeman Images
p. 159 IWM (Art.IWM ART 1460)
p. 222 (top) Wikimedia Commons/Diliff
p 222 (centre left) Retro AdArchives/Alamy
p. 222 (centre right) Unsplash/Nolan Monaghan
p. 222 (bottom left) Wikimedia Foundation
p. 222 (bottom right) Wikimedia Commons/ Jernej Furman
p. 226 Flickr/National Library of Ireland on The Commons
p. 227 Bridgeman Images
p. 230 oed.com

Index

F

G

H

I

J

K

Published in 2026 by Unicorn
an imprint of Unicorn Publishing Group
Charleston Studio
Meadow Business Centre
Lewes BN8 5RW

www.unicornpublishing.org

Thanks are due to the following for inclusion of their poetry:
Extracts from 'Men and their Boring Arguments', 'Waste Land Limericks' and 'Young Love' from *Collected Poems* by Wendy Cope, used with kind permission of Faber and Faber Ltd. 'Pike' from *Collected Poems* by Ted Hughes, used with kind permission of Faber and Faber Ltd. Extract from 'Digging' from *The Poems of Seamus Heaney*, used with kind permission of Faber and Faber Ltd. Extract from 'Aubade' from *The Complete Poems* by Philip Larkin, used with kind permission of Faber and Faber Ltd. Extract from 'Hear it Again' © The Estate of Ted Hughes, 1997. Reprinted by permission of Faber and Faber Ltd. Extract from 'The Waste Land' from *Collected Poems 1909–1962* by T.S. Eliot, used with kind permission of Faber and Faber Ltd.

ISBN 978-1-918271-08-9

10 9 8 7 6 5 4 3 2 1

Designed by Felicity Price-Smith
Printed in Scotland by Bell & Bain Ltd